Family Life Education in India

Family Life Education in India

Perspectives, Challenges, and Applications

Edited by

Aparajita Chowdhury

David K. Carson

Cecyle K. Carson

RAWAT PUBLICATIONS

Jaipur • New Delhi • Bangalore • Mumbai

ISBN 81-7033-996-0

Published by
Prem Rawat for **Rawat Publications**
Satyam Apts., Sector 3, Jawahar Nagar, Jaipur 302 004 (India)
Phone: 0141 265 1748 / 7006 Fax: 0141 265 1748
E-mail: info@rawatbooks.com
Website: www.rawatbooks.com

New Delhi Office
4858/24, Ansari Road, Daryaganj, New Delhi 110 002
Phone: 011-23263290

Also at Bangalore and Mumbai

Typeset by Rawat Computers, Jaipur
Printed at Chaman Enterprises, New Delhi

To my parents and family who have educated and trained me for what I am today

—Aparajita Chowdhury

To the loving memory of my father, Jack L. Carson, and mother, Helen V. Bauer Carson. Forever in my heart and mind...

—David K. Carson

To my wonderful mother, Eunice I. Hougland whom I love deeply and who continues to be an inspiration in my life. You're the best!

—Cecyle K. Carson

Contents

Preface

Family Life Education (FLE) as an academic discipline and professional field is new to Indian society. It has tremendous potential to educate and assist people in leading a rewarding and growth-promoting life, as well as in preventing a host of social ills and mental health problems. This edited book examines the need for FLE in contemporary Indian family life. It traces the evolution and development of FLE as an integrated academic discipline and provides widespread coverage of a number of key family themes and issues aimed at creating stable, healthy and happy families. Each chapter in the book emphasizes the practical application and practices in the multiple areas of FLE. Its purpose is to help professionals and concerned citizens in their understanding of contemporary Indian families, especially with regard to such areas as marriage and mate selection, maintaining harmony in the family, parent-child/adolescent and extended family relationships, interface of women and work, family stresses, and the need for appropriate and effective education and prevention programs in both rural and urban areas. Further, some chapters include a discussion of the numerous factors placing Indian families at risk today, and both common and more serious marital and family difficulties. The potential benefits of FLE to Indian society are also discussed. This is especially important in this radically diverse and rapidly changing nation. The concluding chapters include a discussion of target groups and settings for FLE training programs. Also presented is a justification for and outline of a training-the-trainer approach to FLE (including a lay-training component) so that families in this country of over one billion people will have a greater opportunity to cultivate a happier and more fulfilling life.

There is currently no research-oriented, theory-based book on FLE in India, which is scholarly and yet readable, and also applied in its mission and focus. This book fills a crucial void in the academic literature. However, and perhaps more importantly, it provides parents and working professionals with numerous practical ideas for supporting and strengthening marriages and families – from the mate selection stage and continuing throughout the family life cycle. The authors discuss various ways in which professionals from a number of professions and academic disciplines can work together in preventing problems and assisting families in all segments of Indian society.

India is a rapidly developing country, which, in the next 25 years, will be the most populated nation on earth. As the world's largest democracy, it includes within its borders ancient and diverse cultures, languages, and religions. Despite unparalleled modernization and mobilization in recent decades, millions of Indian families, both rural and urban, have remained undeniably close and resilient. Family has always been at the foundation of Indian society, and contemporary Indian people continue to take pride in the centrality of marriage and family life. Children and adolescents are given a special place in the family and community – interdependency, support, and nurturing across the generations are uniquely valued in the Indian family system. Parents and extended family members continue to be the primary socializers of children in ways that are no longer evident in many regions of the world, and parents and adult children tend to maintain close ties even when great geographical distances separate them.

At the same time, today's Indian families are encountering complex and disturbing problems. The majority (roughly 80 per cent) of Indians, who live in villages and rural areas, are still poor, lacking in social resources and supports, and generally isolated from the mainstream. Urban dwellers are also experiencing a multitude of difficulties, which are challenging for traditional family structures and relationships, and putting marriages and families at risk. These problems, both urban and rural, include a prevalence of poverty and disease; overcrowding; water and air pollution; migration of individuals and families from rural to urban areas due to a lack of viable employment and vocational opportunities; a gradual weakening of age-old traditions including transformations in religion, caste, and other social institutions; natural disasters that make transportation, communication and modernization difficult; ethnic conflicts and ongoing political instability; increased crime, social violence and terrorism; inadequate housing and sanitation; poor nutrition and health care; illiteracy and low quality (and sometimes non-existent) education for children; minimal enforcement of child abuse and child labor laws; and especially in rural areas, the continual promotion of early marriages and large families, which facilitates more than impedes the cycle of poverty.

Other changes are having far-reaching implications in Indian family, social, cultural, economic and political life. These include the widespread growth of education (especially women's education), the impact of the mass media and modern communications, Westernization (i.e., gradual adaptation of values and lifestyles of western nations), industrialization and modernization, and economic liberalization. In the age of electronic media, including televisions and computers even in remote areas, the Indian family is being exposed to ideas, ideals, and values swept across from distant societies. More recent crises in families encompass many of the same kinds of problems that have plagued countries in the West at least since the 1960s. These include, for example, marital strain and dissolution, parent-child conflicts, various forms of family violence, substance abuse, juvenile delinquency, school dropout or low school attainment among the lower class, and excessive pressures in many middle and upper class families for adolescents and young adults to achieve academically. Given these conditions and difficulties, the future and well-being of the Indian family is uncertain.

Indian families face a wide variety of everyday problems, including stresses and strains of rearing children, conflicts with in-laws, difficulties associated with various chronic illnesses, and developmental delays and disabilities of children or other family members.

The majorities of urban dwellers today, and even many rural citizens, prefer to live in small nuclear family units. At the same time, they want to maintain close relations with their extended family and have them available during times of crisis. This practice has created role strain, ambiguity, and conflict between family members (such as authority over children between mothers and their mother-in-laws), as well as confusing expectations for children. Moreover, unlike the scenario in the traditional joint family system, elderly members today not only have few roles to play in child socialization, but in educated families they are less likely to live with their adult children and grandchildren due to increased mobility. In many families the result is an absence of clear and consistent role models for the child beyond his or her own parents. In addition, partly due to safety reasons, parents are becoming more restrictive of their children in having free time to interact with peers, either at school or in the neighborhood. This not only reduces children's social network but also tends to instill feelings of fear and distrust. The mass media (especially the electronic media) also aggravates the situation by creating unrealistic aspirations in children and parents, including a "you can or should have it all" mindset.

Exposure to western thinking (European and American) has brought about changes in attitudes towards traditional methods of disciplining, toilet training, feeding, and other childrearing practices. However, because traditional attitudes have not been completely abandoned, many parents alternate between permissive and strict (authoritarian) childrearing, thus creating anxiety and confusion in children and making them more vulnerable to behavioral or emotional disorders. Marital difficulties, coupled with inadequate or conflict-oriented co-parenting practices, are also becoming more prevalent as women are breaking out of traditional roles, becoming educated in greater numbers, and advocating for equal rights, both at home and in the workplace. With so many women employed outside the home today, some Indian researchers contend that children's needs are not being met, and that there is little time for parents to listen to and converse with their children. Studies of female-headed households have shown that these women face numerous problems. Some researchers assert that this increase in single-parent families has contributed to a greater percentage of children and adolescents experiencing serious difficulties. This may be more common in middle and lower class families, where alternative childcare provisions are often not available. In sum, increased role strain, marital difficulties, parent-child conflicts, feelings of guilt, and status confusion are commonly observed among working women, even though there are some economic and self-esteem related advantages. Since more women in India are joining the labor force without proper support and assistance, often in the face of extended family and community opposition, an increase in family difficulties is to be expected.

Also contributing to family problems is a school curriculum and environment that often does not meet children's needs – be they academic or personal. It is not uncommon for teachers to use strict and sometimes physical punishment to maintain order, with which today's Indian youth are not always in agreement. Perhaps most notable in educated families are the extreme pressures for children to achieve academically so they can gain entrance into the prestigious colleges and universities (often with little free time with peers or family play time). This pressure tends to increase the vulnerability of older children and adolescents to various personal and relational difficulties. Thus, on the basis of these fundamental issues, this book has a three-dimensional rationale that includes:

(1) understanding contemporary family and social problems;
(2) dealing with and preventing family and social problems; and
(3) developing potentials within the individual to face the challenges in life.

As part of a comprehensive mental health effort in India, the FLE on the community level holds great promise as a keeper and restorer of the family unit. However, as has been mentioned, the idea of FLE is relatively new in India, and with few exceptions it has not been integrated with current mental health and social welfare programs. Yet, the notion that couples and families need ongoing support and useful information about family life appears to be in the early stages of acceptance in professional circles. This country seems ripe for a preventive approach to marital and family difficulties.

In sum, this book explores the range of marital and family difficulties in light of the undercurrent of social and economic changes in India today, and examines how an FLE movement might take root in the context of the current mental health system and social service practice. The authors discuss the content, scope and potential benefits of FLE training and services in meeting the tremendous needs of married couples and families in India today. Included is an integration of all of the authors' practical experiences in working with couples and families, as well as lessons learned from research conducted on Indian couples and families. The editors sincerely hope that this book will fill an important gap in the Indian family science literature, and serve as a catalyst for needed changes in social policy and community development programs.

List of Contributors

Aparajita Chowdhury, Department of Home Science, Berhampur University, Berhampur, Orissa.

Arundhati Rath, Department of Home Science, Berhampur University, Berhampur, Orissa.

Binayak Patnaik, Lingaraj Law College, Berhampur, Orissa.

Cecyle K. Carson, Department of Communicative Disorders, University of Central Florida, USA.

David K. Carson, Department of Counselor Education, University of Central Florida, USA.

Dibya Prava Pradhan, College of Home Science, Orissa Agricultural University, Bhubaneswar, Orissa.

G. Baradha, Department of Human Development and Family Studies, Avinashilingam Deemed University, Coimbatore, Tamil Nadu.

Minoti Phukan, Department of Human Development and Family Studies, Assam Agricultural University, Jorhat, Assam.

N. Jaya, Dean, Faculty of Home Science, Avinashilingam Deemed University, Coimbatore, Tamil Nadu.

Rita Choudhury, Dhenkanal Mahila Mahavidyalaya, Dhenkanal, Orissa.

Smita Sinha, Department of Linguistics, Berhampur University, Berhampur, Orissa.

Yamuna T.V., Counselor, Parenting and Interpersonal Relations, Coimbatore, Tamil Nadu.

1

Family Life Education in the Indian Socio-Cultural Context

Aparajita Chowdhury

Family Life Education (FLE) has to do with "education for healthy and happy family living". It prepares individuals and families for the roles and responsibilities of family living within the existing socio-cultural and economic context of the society. The concept of FLE in the present form is not very old; rather new to our society. It has made its entry into the field of education, as the need to strengthen the family has never been so urgent as families of today. Indian families are in transition and are being greatly affected by stress and uncertainties of social, political and economic upheavals. FLE thus can play a significant role in enabling the family members and family as a whole to be better informed and equipped on how they can be more effective in handling internal problems and confronting external demands and changes. This chapter discusses extensively about the meaning, needs, subject matter, principles and target individuals for FLE in India. As part of comprehensive mental health efforts in India, FLE as an academic discipline holds great promise as a keeper and restorer of the family unit.

Family is our refuge and our springboard. Nourished by it we can advance to new horizons. In every conceivable manner, the family is a link to our past and bridge to our future (Curran, 1983). Anandalakshmi (1984) indicated that affiliation to the family is a sentiment that pervades almost all social interactions. It is, however, well known that the course of family life is not always smooth. In fact, every family can expect to experience the inevitable stresses, strains, and tough times that are part of the journey. With these challenges comes the potential for danger as well as opportunity for the family. Danger lies in the possibility that a family may be overwhelmed and lack the support and resources needed to deal effectively with stressful life changes. Conversely, opportunity is embedded in the potential for growth and positive changes that promote resilience and healthy outcomes for family members (Pedro-Carroll, 2001).

The family in India occupies a central position in the life of its people and is one of the basic units of the Indian society. Contemporary Indian people continue to take pride in the centrality of marriage and family life. According to Karve (1953), the Indian family organization is one of the three most essential aspects for understanding any cultural phenomenon in India, with the other two being configurations of linguistic region and institution of caste. According to Bharat (1997), the "Indian family system is characterized by certain identifiable features. The first and foremost feature is that it consists of a definite system of role-relationships and sentiments that bind its members together. The members share feelings of family solidarity or 'familisim' and strive to uphold family dignity and status in the society. A high premium is placed on family unity and cohesiveness which are necessary for family stability and survival".

However, the fast pace and all-embracing socio-political and economic changes in India in recent years are having a significant impact on individuals and families (Sinha, 1988). In the age of electronic media, including television and computers in remote areas, the Indian family is being exposed to ideas, ideals and lifestyles that are challenging the structure and stability of the contemporary family unit. Today's Indian families are encountering complex and disturbing problems that include rampant poverty, disease, overcrowding, water and air pollution, migration of families and individuals, lack of viable employment and vocational opportunities, and a gradual weakening of age-old traditions and erosion of values among the individuals. More recent challenges that Indian families are encountering include: marital strains and dissolution; parent-child conflict; various forms of violence both inside and outside family; substance abuse; juvenile delinquency; school dropout or low school attainment; and excessive pressures in many middle and upper class families on children, adolescents and young adults to achieve academically (Chowdhury, 1999; Das, 1999; Nanda and Dash, 1996; Sarkar, 1988). Given these conditions and difficulties, the well-being of Indian family is uncertain. Moreover, family members are not well-prepared or equipped to face the competitive and challenging world of today. Either they are lacking correct information or receiving misinformation from dubious sources that are doing more harm than good. The result is ignorance coupled with doubts, fears and superstitions, and an 'attitude' towards sex, which is apprehensive, excessively liberal, or hypocritical. In the present-day Indian society, young people are exposed to an entirely new pattern of living and a new set of mores, values and standards that are being widely accepted but which stand in contrast to those which were promoted by their parents and grandparents.

The ambiguous values children and adolescents observe today in India, coupled with the absence of positive role models and the increasing gaps between aspirations and possible achievement, have led to a greater sense of alienation and identity diffusion (Singh and Singh, 1996). Parents too appear ill-prepared to cope with rapid social change, having grown up in hierarchically structured and interlinked social groups and collectives that included the extended family and kinship network, as well as caste groups that provided stability and solidarity (Sinha, 1984). The conflict between parents' desire to help their children cope with the competitive demands of the market economy, and their own need to find safety of tradition, expresses itself in the 'cold feet syndrome' when things go wrong in the family (Saraswathi and Pai, 1997). Parents who seem 'modern' in their childrearing practices get anxious when their children or adolescents breach established social codes. Intergenerational conflicts related to marriage, career choice, or separate living arrangements result in the tendency to fall back on tradition. The key concern today is the stress created by the changing composition and dynamics of the family given the differential expectations, values, competencies, and coping styles between parents and children (Verma and Saraswathi, 2002).

There is therefore a tremendous need for education of youth with regard to the knowledge, attitude and skills required for successful family living. Having a better understanding of themselves and others, as well as a clearer concept of their own roles as husband and wives, parents, and responsible members of the society, will help young people today develop their own codes of behavior and of ethics instead of blindly submitting to the codes of behavior currently being promoted as trendy or fashionable. However, Indian families need to be better equipped to deal with the multitude of internal challenges and external demands of contemporary life.

What is Family Life Education?

The purpose of Family Life Education (FLE) is to change or modify the behavior of individuals through the absorption of new information, as well as practice new skills of relating and communicating more lovingly and effectively. FLE has the potential to help families develop healthy attitudes, values and beliefs so that family members can both enjoy one another more and become productive citizens in the greater society.

Moreover, education becomes a means for human resource development by sharpening awareness and by motivating individuals to grow. It can empower families to face the challenges of modern life. Thus, FLE is geared towards training and conditioning the human mind so that individuals can function effectively in contemporary society, and can also learn how to help others do the same. In sum, FLE can be operationally stated as the "education for a healthy, wealthy, and happy family life". Wealth is not necessarily defined in material or monetary ways, but rather in a manner that helps families discover and utilize their already existing strengths and 'riches'. FLE is intended to help individuals and families learn about human growth, development and behavior throughout the life cycle, as well as behaviors and skills that promote healthy communication and caring relationships. FLE prepares individuals and families for the roles and responsibilities of family living within the existing socio-cultural and economic context of the society. It also enables people to be responsible, caring, and conscientious and teaches individuals how to reach their maximum potential for the better life. In addition, FLE is important for all those who recognize the family's role in ameliorating problems in the community through proper socialization of children and youth. It is a vast untapped arena within Indian education in general that includes such subject matter areas as the following: the family as a system (i.e., the whole of the family being greater than the sum of its parts); healthy family roles, functions, and boundaries (including between and within the extended family system); family problems such as various types of abuse and neglect; effective approaches to childrearing and discipline; marriage preparation, education, and enrichment throughout the life cycle; communication skills training; gender issues involved in Indian family life; balancing work and family; the impact of technology on family life; understanding older adults, the aging process, and the family's responsibility; learning about family counseling; and when it might be needed and helpful;

developing a better understanding of family laws and legislations; strengthening families through a family resiliency approach; and identifying the settings for training opportunities for FLE in India.

The overall goal of FLE then is to build new strengths in families through empowering individual family members and the family as a whole. The concept of FLE in India is really very new. In India, a few social welfare agencies (e.g., the Family Planning Association of India, which is a voluntary body dedicated to the promotion of family planning) have been conducting FLE programs in a piecemeal manner. This organization is devoted to promoting the knowledge of family planning as a basic 'human right', as well as promoting population policies which can bring about a balanced development of the resources of the country as a means of enhancing the quality of life. Though some sporadic efforts have been made in India by various other organizations and academic institutions to impart FLE to needy groups, there are currently few programs that are planned and organized on the basis of scientific research (Sarada, 1999).

On the other hand, FLE has enjoyed a much longer history in the Western world. It began in the United States in the beginning of the 20th century. Both Kerckhoff (1964) and Darling (1987) indicate that in the 1880s there was interest in child development as well as management. One result was the founding of the Child Study Association of America in 1888. Interest in psychoanalysis, child development/psychology, and health was evident in the early 1900s. The formation of the American Home Economics Association (1908), the American Social Hygiene Association (1914), and the National Council on Parent Education (1929) – all represented organized activities intended to meet the needs of children and families. Economic and cultural changes impacted children and families during those times. The United States was moving from an agriculturally-based economy, with an emphasis on self-sufficiency, to one which was heavily grounded in business and industry, and one that was beginning to offer and provide some level of services to individuals and families through community and governmental agencies related to education, health care and social services. In the early days, FLE mainly emphasized 'sex education' and 'marriage preparation'. Around 1934 the emphasis shifted to 'preserving family values' through interdisciplinary research, education, and counseling. Thereafter FLE in the US began to embrace and encompass disciplines and professionals from the fields of health, education, sociology, psychology, anthropology, law, medicine, biology, home economics, theology, child development, and family studies. From these efforts, Western scholars have proposed a number of definitions of FLE. Some of these are outlined below:

- [FLE] ".....is a program of learning experiences planned and guided to develop the potentials of individuals in their present and future roles as family members. Its central concept is that of relationships through which personality develops, about which they gain convictions of self worth" (Smith, 1968).
- [FLE is] ".....any activity by any group aimed at imparting information concerning family relationships and providing the opportunity for people to approach their present and future family relationships with greater understanding" (The Vanier Institute of the Family, 1971).
- According to Herold, Kepf, and de-Carlo (1974), "Family life education is the study of individual roles and interpersonal relationships, family patterns and alternative lifestyles, emotional needs of individuals at all ages, and the physiological, psychological and sociological aspects of sexuality".
- Cromwell and Thomas (1976) indicated that ".....Family life education promotes the development, coordination and integration of family development resources to individual family units in order to improve family life".

- "Family life education...builds on strengths of individuals to extend their knowledge of personality development, interpersonal relations, and the influence of environmental factors on behaviors" (Barozzi and Engel, 1985).
- And finally, Tennant (1989) asserts that ".....Family life education is devoted to enabling adults to increase the effectiveness of their skills in daily living, that is, in relating to others, in coping with life events, and in realizing personal potential".

In sum, FLE involves education and experiences for children, adolescents and adults intended to help them solve problems and conflicts in a constructive way, and to equip them for the challenges ahead as they move through the life span (Sarada, 1999). However, FLE still awaits a precise definition in the Indian context.

Why Family Life Education in India?

As stated earlier, Indian families are today encountering complex and disturbing problems of far-reaching consequences. Given current conditions and the magnitude of difficulties, the future and well-being of Indian families is uncertain. The complexity of today's socio-cultural and economic milieu, the multiplicity of forces working upon the individual, and the widening of intergenerational gaps require an educational approach which helps family members find their role in creating a healthy and happy family life (Sarada, 1999). In contemporary India, FLE usually operates through informal channels of education (such as from grandparents, uncles, aunts, big brothers and sisters, i.e., mostly individuals in the joint family system). However, since the joint family system in India is rapidly changing (e.g., due to increased modernization and mobility of youth), there is a tremendous need for a more formal and comprehensive approach to education for family living. Thus, education for family living is essential in preventing contemporary family problems and lessening factors that put children, adolescents, and young adults at risk.

This type of education not only helps prepare family members to face the challenges of family life but also provides them with useful tools for resolving problems once they have begun.

There are three different, though related, rationales for why family life education in India is needed. These are summarized as follows:

Dealing with Contemporary Family and Social Changes

Indian families are undergoing tremendous changes in terms of ideological, functional, structural, and role relationships. During the past few decades the traditional Indian family has moved towards nucleation to meet the demands of globalization and other related factors. This includes a rapid rise in education, especially women's education, and legislations covering economic, social and political spheres, and pertaining to land, property rights, inheritance rights of women, marriage and divorce. These changes have radically altered land ownership patterns, power dynamics within families and family interactions, and obligations and decision-making in our society. All such factors have brought about an upheaval in Indian family and society at large. Major contemporary family and social alterations include changes in Indian family structure and society.

Changes in Indian Family Structure and Function

The Indian family is often understood to be an ideal homogeneous unit with strong coping mechanisms. However, families in a large and culturally diverse country like India have a great plurality of forms that vary with class, caste, ethnicity, and language, as well as the individual choices permitted within each community and group. Moreover, various research studies have revealed that the family in India is also a source of inequality, exploitation, and violence, and often tends to paint an idealistic picture with regard to nurturance, emotional bonding, and support. The institution of marriage and the event of childbearing are considered essential for successful family life, and yet there are numerous couples living together without being married. In addition, increasing numbers of single-parent families and childless families in India are still not accepted as a 'complete' or 'normal' family by the social majority.

During the last few decades, the Indian family has undergone drastic changes in both structure and function (Choudhury, 1999). This has led to changes in the interrelationships among family members and also in the family's obligation process and decision-making. The childrearing and socialization process has also been altered. Although the traditional joint family system has not been completely replaced by the nuclear family, nucleation, as has been indicated, is rapidly becoming the norm. On the other hand, family members have not yet completely severed the psychological and emotional ties with their families of origin. Hence, changes in the structure of Indian families have thus far been extreme. It is apparent, then, that a new type of family is evolving – a blend of the joint and nuclear family system. According to Bharat (1997), the sentiments of unity, sharing, mutual dependence, conformity to family norms, and sense of responsibility towards kin continue to broadly influence family living in India. Moreover, the influence on the family by television, video culture, and growing consumerism has contributed to a process of value erosion. Sinha (1984, 1988) discussed some of the implications of the changing family scene for the socialization process and mental health of individuals. He maintains that socio-economic changes in Indian society have induced certain changes in family experiences that serve as antecedents to various behavioral and psychological consequences in the individual. Sinha (1988) asserted further that contemporary Indian family as being in a 'transitional' phase where structural changes are not entirely accompanied by psychological changes. People wish to live in small, nuclear family units while continuing to draw strength from the extended family, particularly during times of crisis.

This new family pattern is ambiguous and may be transitional. It is possible that it creates confusion and unrealistic expectancies in children and youth that are likely to have far-reaching repercussions on their development. Analysis undertaken by Conklin (1988) and Ramu (1988) suggested that changes are rapidly occurring in Indian families in terms of their role patterns, ethos, and values. According to these authors, Indian family role patterns are changing towards conjugal family patterns where "the conjugal pair is the critical unit" (Ramu, 1988). In this family pattern the power has shifted from the patriarch or 'Karta' to the main breadwinner. Moreover, elderly persons no longer have any key role to play in child socialization, in that parents are the main socializing agents. External agencies also are taking over the socialization roles in the lives of children. These include, for example, 'Anganwadis' and 'Balwadis' in rural areas, day care centers, preschools, and even siblings and peer groups in both urban and slum areas. Sinha (1988) points out that, as a result, clear-cut and consistent role models are not available to Indian children. In addition, some have argued that nucleation has depleted the emotional environment of individuals and made them more vulnerable (Bharat, 1997). Thus, the Indian family is in a fluid, transitional state and is experiencing confusion and contradictions in roles, relationships, and models for emulation. Such a scenario is likely to have widespread implications for the psychological well-being of individuals.

Changes in Indian Society

Due to the various challenges brought about by these socio-economic changes, there has been a distancing between men's and women's roles, as well as between the rich and the poor. These discrepancies have led to migration and displacement of individuals and families from their roots, traditional sources of livelihood, and community bonds and supports. The poorest of the poor are suffering the most, as evidenced, for example, by landless families, families of marginal farmers, and those considered to be members of the Scheduled Castes (SCs) and Scheduled Tribes (STs). There is no place in the present Indian economy for those whose land is appropriated through market forces or those displaced because of urban (and sometimes rural) development projects. Migration has fundamental implications for women and children. Regardless of whether it is men or women who migrate, the effect is same. Repetitive migration deprives the children of their basic services of education and health. Political violence and environmental disasters (natural or man-made) further endanger family life and increase the number of uprooted and destitute families and individuals in the society.

There are also an increasing number of single-parent families and female-headed households in Indian society. Women, who may be widows, divorcees, separated or deserted, are typically forced to be the sole breadwinners in single-parent families. These women have the main earning responsibility for the family when they are not trained or experienced to work in the modern economy. When they have young children to look after, they are further marginalized and exploited, especially in the unorganized sectors of society. Single-parent families are often among the most destitute. A growing number of street children, children laboring in towns and cities, and children in institutions, generally come from such families. In addition, with so many women employed outside the home today, some Indian researchers contend that children's needs are not being met, and that there is little time for parents to listen to and converse with their children. Studies of female-headed households have shown that these women face numerous challenges. Moreover, the increase in single-parent families has contributed to a greater percentage of children and adolescents experiencing serious difficulties. This may be more common in middle and lower class families, where alternative childcare provisions are often not available or affordable. In sum, increased role strain, marital difficulties, parent-child conflicts, feelings of guilt, and status confusion are commonly observed among working women, even though there are some economic and self-esteem related advantages. The ever-increasing number of women in India, who are joining the labor force without proper support and assistance (from within or outside the family), is creating multiple problems for families and the society at large.

Another problem in contemporary Indian society is that increased longevity has resulted in a mushrooming of the elderly population. However, once considered the repositories of experiential wisdom, the status and role of older adults is rapidly diminishing. Since they are considered non-productive, they are often perceived as a burden on their adult children (Desai, 1994). Problems such as disability, chronic or terminal illness, and substance abuse among the elderly are not just individual or family problems. They have an impact on the entire society. The new economic policy with structural adjustment, coupled with by the Government of India's policy of globalization and liberalization, further aggravate the problems of families, especially those which are "at risk". A great deal of modern development has not led to healthy community development, but in fact has struck at the roots of the community. Thus, the existing security net is rapidly diminishing. Further, the print and electronic media are influencing Indian family life in some negative ways. For instance, the media tends to promote individual aspirations (at the expense of family and community), consumerism, and violence in different forms. It has also contributed to changes in attitudes towards traditional methods of rearing and disciplining the children, and in some ways has helped to undermine the institution of marriage.

Also contributing to family problems is the school curriculum and environment that often does not meet children's needs - be they academic or personal. It is not uncommon for teachers to use strict and sometimes physical as well as psychological punishment to maintain order - practices which today's Indian youth are not always in agreement. Excessive pressure on the part of both parents and teachers tends to increase the vulnerability of older children and adolescents to various personal and relational difficulties. Adding to the problem is a lack of enough viable vocational opportunities after proper education is over, resulting in high unemployment among Indian youth.

FLE can play a role in creating awareness and understanding regarding contemporary changes occurring in both Indian families and society in general. It helps prepare individuals with the kind of understanding and perspective needed to deal with contemporary changes and thus live a richer and fuller life.

Preventing Family and Social Problems

The second rationale behind FLE is to prevent family dysfunction and social problems as much as possible. Considering the rapid social change occurring in Indian family life, a preventive approach is necessary at all stages of life cycle. "The goal of preventive science is to prevent or mediate major human dysfunction" (Coie et. al., 1993). The principle that "preventive is better than cure" is a foundation of family life education in India, since family life is the basis for all human development. Until and unless our family life is strong, healthy and enriched, no amount of human resource development will be successful in India.

Problems faced by Indian families today are varied and versatile. These problems and challenges need to be properly identified and then followed by strategic solutions that target them. These include problems with the dowry system, marital separation and divorce, juvenile delinquency, drug abuse, HIV/AIDS, and domestic violence – to name a few. FLE can help both remediate and prevent these and other social pathologies.

Developing Potentials within the Individual Family Members

Another important rationale behind FLE is that this type of education can help instill the strengths and confidence among family members needed to lead a stable, healthy and happy family life. FLE builds upon the positive aspects of family life and evokes those human capacities, which will enhance and enrich individual and family functioning. Positive thinking, awareness and behavior all need to be developed among family members so that positive human traits like self-confidence and trust can be enhanced.

In India, human resources are far from satisfactory both inside and outside of the family environment. It is disheartening to find gender discrimination within Indian families with regard to individual potential and talents. Girls and women in the family are continuously discriminated against both within and beyond the family context. FLE emphasizes equality and fairness in the immediate and extended family so that everyone benefits and no one is left out or behind (i.e., a 'win-win' situation). For too long in Indian society, men have not been truly free because women have been held down. Education about healthy family life can help everyone know and feel good about their roles and functions while fighting against discriminatory practices.

Subject Matter of Family Life Education

The study and implementation of FLE in India is a recent phenomenon. Hence, what is and is not appropriate and effective in an Indian context has much room for debate. However, at least some of what has been created and used in other regions of the world may be helpful starting points for a discussion of needed subject matter for FLE in India. The 1968 report of the National Commission on Family Life Education (NCFLE) in the United States listed the following broad subject matter areas:

- Interpersonal relationships
- Self-understanding
- Human growth and development
- Preparation for marriage and parenthood
- Childrearing

- Socialization of youth for adult roles
- Decision-making
- Sexuality
- Management of human and material resources
- Personal, family, and community health
- Family-community interaction
- Effect of changes on cultural patterns

In 1984, the National Council on Family Relations (USA) developed a framework for Life Span Family Life Education, which further clarified and broadened the content of FLE. This framework identified seven broad areas, each with key supporting concepts identified as follows:

(i) Human Development

- Dimensions of human development – physical, emotional, cognitive, language, personality, moral, social and sexual.
- Patterns of human development over the life span (conception to death).
- Interaction among dimensions of human development (e.g., emotional and sexual).
- Factors affecting individual differences in development.
- Promoting development in self and others.
- Myths and realities of adulthood and aging.
- Dealing with disabilities.

(ii) Sexuality

- Body privacy and protection against sexual abuse.
- Responsibility for personal health (nutrition, hygiene, exercise).
- Communicating about sexuality (personal values, beliefs).
- Normality of sexual feelings and sexual response in accordance with societal expectations.
- Human reproduction and contraception.
- Choices, consequences and responsibilities of sexual behavior.

(iii) Interpersonal Relationship

- Building self-esteem and self-confidence in self and others.
- Assessing and developing personal abilities and talents (both male and female).
- Establishing personal autonomy.
- Respecting self and others.
- Communicating effectively both inside and outside the family.
- Dealing with general emotions, success as well as failure.
- Developing, maintaining and ending relationship.
- Recognizing factors associated with quality relationships.
- Factors influencing mate selection (social, economic, cultural, personal).
- Understanding the dimension of love and commitment.
- Exploring the responsibilities of marriage and performing it appropriately.
- Changes in the marital relationship over time.
- Creating and maintaining a family of one's own.

(iv) Family Interaction

- Family as sources of protection, guidance, affection, and support.
- Family as possible sources of anger and violence.
- Differences in families (joint or nuclear, economic level, racial, role performance, family values).
- Changing needs and expectations of all family members.
- Rights, responsibilities, and interdependence of family members.
- Family transitions (birth, marriage, death, divorce, separation).
- Individual and family roles.
- Factors affecting marital and family relationships.
- Powers and authority in the family.
- Family rules - overt and covert.
- Sources of stress and coping with stress.

- Intergenerational dynamics throughout the life span.
- Family history, traditions, and celebrations.
- Varying influence on family interaction patterns (ethnic, racial, social).

(v) Family Resources Management

- Developing personal resources.
- Resource consumption and conservation – material and non-material.
- Using resources to meet basic needs of family (food, clothing, shelter).
- Expendability of human energy.
- Balancing family and work roles.
- Developing leisure interests.
- Varying needs of family members for privacy and independence.
- Financial planning.
- Responsibility for decisions.
- Exploring career choices.
- Establishing long and short-term goals.
- Influences on consumer decisions (personal values, costs, media, peers).
- Retirement planning.

(vi) Education about Parenthood

- Understanding marital and parental roles.
- Changing parent-child relationships over the life span.
- Preparation (physical and mental) for birth and parenthood.
- Challenges and rewards of parenthood.
- Childrearing practices, guidance, and parenting strategies.
- Importance of parental communication regarding childrearing practices.
- Parent-child communication.
- Family conflict and conflict resolution.
- Providing a safe environment for children.

- Teaching life skills to children (self-sufficiency, decision-making).
- Problems of family violence, abuse, and neglect.
- Varied parenting situations (single parenting, step parenting, adoption).
- Sources of help for parents (family, neighborhood, community).
- Factors to consider in deciding if and when to become a parent.
- Influences on parent styles (social, economic, ethnic).

(vii) Family and Society

- Understanding laws affecting families and policies.
- Protecting civil rights of all people.
- Family conflict and legal protection of family members.
- The influence of religion on families.
- Understanding and obtaining community support services.
- Role of family in society.
- Individual and family responsibility in the community.
- Utilizing the educational system.
- Family participation in the education of children.
- Education throughout the life span.
- Reciprocal influences of technology and families.
- Interrelationship of families, work, and society.
- Population issues and resource allocation.

The strength of this framework is that it is not a stipulated framework but rather one that is based on Western literature in the field that was developed over a period of time. There may be many other subject matter areas and concepts which need to be included in the Indian socio-cultural context. It is important to consider the diversity and multiplicity of Indian society while dealing with such type of general subject matter. However, these seven major subject matter areas listed above may serve as an excellent starting point for the development of a FLE model (or philosophy) for India, as well as a pragmatic approach for the instigation of FLE programs.

Principles of Family Life Education

FLE is life building and character enhancing. These qualities cannot be acquired through the reading of books, although the written word can serve as a foundation for growth and change. Education needs to be made available to people at all stages of life, and with some specific purposes and goals. Just as individuals never stop learning, families too need to be educated about relationship dynamics and developmental issues throughout the life span. A review of the FLE literature identified several basic principles that family life educators should follow while delivering such services to the target population. These principles appear to be trans-cultural:

1. *It is relevant for anyone throughout the life span*: People of all ages need to learn about themselves and the family as a corporate unit in order to be prepared for the ongoing challenges of family life. Each person needs to perform certain functions and master certain developmental tasks in order to build a strong and healthy family.
2. *Based on the needs of individuals, as well as the family as a whole*: FLE should be geared to the immediate needs of individuals, and be sensitive to the social, economic, educational, and cultural nuances that influence each person's needs and the needs of the entire family.
3. *Multidisciplinary approach and multi-professional in its applications*: FLE is interdisciplinary in its nature and origin. Such disciplines as anthropology, biology, economics, home science, law, medicine, philosophy, physiology, psychology, sociology, social work, and women's studies have contributed to its formation and evolution.
4. *It may be offered in different settings*: Different institutions and agencies may offer FLE, including schools, colleges, universities, religious and community organizations, and

governmental and non-governmental agencies working for the development and welfare of the family and community in general.

5. *Practical educational approach*: The main purpose of FLE is to educate and equip individuals and families to have a more fulfilling life as opposed to repairing broken or dysfunctional families. It is more about empowering the learner to use knowledge in making informed, responsible choices. According to Arcus (1990), FLE is intended to help individuals and families "gain *knowledge* about concepts and principles relevant to family living, explore personal *attitudes and values* and understand and accept the attitudes and values of others, and develop *interpersonal skills* which contribute to family well-being".
6. *Respect for differing family values*: One of the qualities of a strong, stable, and healthy family is the presence of family values. A clear set of family values, along with rules and beliefs, help establish expectations about acceptance and desired behavior in a civilized society. Family values play an important role in helping people deal with social change and gain social control over family members, especially children and youth. Family values are important in the formation of social attitudes, acceptance of value differences, and in the acquisition of critical thinking skills.
7. *Professionally trained and qualified persons should deliver family life education*: In order to fulfill the objectives of FLE, it is essential that educators be knowledgeable about the basics of family life and human development across the life cycle. According to the National Commission of Family Life Education in USA (1968), "competently prepared family life educators are crucial to the successful realization of goals" of FLE.

Target Groups for Family Life Education

The New Economic Policy (NEP), which was implemented by the Government of India in 1991, has brought about a marked change in the values and attitude of people. Emphasis on 'quick money' and short-term benefits has already started to dehumanize Indian society, including family life. As a result of the adverse work conditions (or unemployment) of the poor, the disproportionate burden on working women, and the overall value crisis in Indian society, it is feared that family relationships are in danger of eroding (Carson and Chowdhury, 2000). Mishra (1995: 30) summarizes the current state of affairs with regard to the changing Indian family and its influence on family members as follows:

> Family in India, particularly in the urban educated class, is undergoing transformation. The economic, social and cultural forces and reinforced individualism and changes intrinsic to the traditional family system are leading to structural changes. Family members are questioning the roles, obligations and relationships which have been nourishing the inherently social texture of Indian family. The tension experienced in the course of pursuing personal (individual) goals and familial goals are becoming an important source of stress. This situation calls for a perspective which views individuality and relatedness as mutually constitutive and complementary. Such a solution shall constructively utilize indigenous values in which family happens to be a value in itself rather than mere instrument for personal growth.

Some Indian social scientists and family scholars propose that once the conditions of equality are negotiated and obtained at all levels, mental and relational well-being will be an inevitable outcome for a large portion of the society (e.g., Bharat, 1991; Belle, 1990; Sinha, 1984). However, these changes are slow and often met with great resistance (Baral and Bishoyee, 1999; Sinha, 1988). In order to overcome these obstacles and accelerate the process of change within families, certain preparation and training is essential. FLE is thus important in creating harmony within families among all segments of society. As stated earlier, FLE is for anybody who is concerned about the quality family life. The main target groups for such education can be adolescents, young adults, couples, parents, and elderly people. The relevance of FLE to each of these is discussed as follows:

Adolescents

Adolescence is often described as a phase of life that begins in biology and ends in society. It is a stage of transition from childhood to adulthood. Both physically and psychologically, the individual at this stage is not mature enough to understand a great deal about family life, sexuality, and other related issues. Rather, there is no avenue in Indian society for getting accurate, appropriate, and helpful information regarding family life and related sensitive issues dealing with intimate relationships. During earlier time in India, family members living together in the joint family system provided information to younger members of the family. Today, with increased nucleation and both parents often working outside the family, less time and energy is spent addressing crucial issues of children and adolescents, and discussing these issues with them.

FLE can give adolescents a healthy and clear understanding of personal and sometimes difficult life issues and transitions. For example, during puberty, sexual development is more dramatic, and the need for sex education becomes more obvious. The physical changes during puberty often have implications for the development of identity and self-concept and are accompanied by both positive and negative psychological reactions and adjustments. Some of the negative behaviors of adolescents appear to be associated with the absence of appropriate preparatory education in Indian society. Hence, adolescents today are lacking in proper guidance and direction they need to move into adulthood successfully.

Young Adults

Young adults have gained physical and sexual maturity and begin to take on economic and social responsibilities. However, in India, most young adults start their career and married life without proper preparation and knowledge. Moreover, too many young people in Indian society are failing to develop the competencies and skills needed for success in adulthood. Millions of youth are engaging in behaviors that threaten their physical and psychological health. FLE can help prepare young adults for their career and future family life.

Parents

Parenting is a complex process and is dependent on numerous factors, including family structure, reputation, relationships, life experiences and exposure to parenting skills, temperament of parents and children, the quality of the marital relationship, educational and financial status and opportunities, and many others. Individuals today are becoming parents without adequate knowledge about essential parenting skills, child development, and all other aspects associated with being a parent at the various stages of the family life cycle. Further, there is a severe lack of help and support for parents today that was once widely available to parents in India. In addition, participation of women in the workforce has radically changed the nature and structure of the Indian family system.

The reality in India is that there are no childcare facilities supported by government, and few made available by private citizens. Young parents are facing difficulties in managing both career and family, and this without proper knowledge about how to rear children. Moreover, the gradual loosening of extended family ties, erosion of family values, role differentiation and aspiration, geographical distancing of family generations, and the increased entry of women into labor force, have created a new reality in which parents no longer benefit from traditional family structure in their parenting roles. FLE can play a role in mobilizing communities to support young parents and families, and to "take care of their own".

FLE emphasizes positive parenting. Becoming a parent is easy, but being a good parent is a momentous task. Positive parenting has to do with the loving and supportive care provided by the parents, and supported by the child's teachers and the environment in which he or she grows up. Thus, one of the most important objectives of FLE is teaching new parents, as well as those well within the childrearing stage, positive parental skills needed to successfully rear today's children. In contemporary society, both father and mother must accept the responsibilities of caring for children. Hence, the role of fathers in Indian society needs to be redefined (Chowdhury, 1995). FLE has the potential to sensitize the masses regarding the new dimensions of parenting.

Young Married Couples

Becoming a couple is one of the most complex and difficult transitions of family life. One dramatic marker of the 21st century is the astonishingly fast pace of couples' lives in India. Their expectations of each other, aspirations for life ahead, and attitudes about work and family have been changing drastically without realizing the responsibilities attached to these most important functions of life. When healthy patterns are not established and guidelines not adhered to, relationships become strained and conflict often follows.

As a preventive measure, FLE helps prepare young couples lead a more committed, mature, and fulfilling life. FLE provides couples of all ages with the knowledge and skills they need to cope effectively with the challenges of marriage and parenting. One of the most common problems faced by Indian families today is marital strain and dissolution. Marital difficulties, coupled with inadequate co-parenting practices, are also becoming more prevalent as women are breaking out of traditional roles, becoming educated in greater numbers, and advocating for equal rights both at home and in the workplace (Baral, Das and Dash, 1999; Mohanty, 1999). Concepts such as mutual understanding, time for each other, emotional sharing between the couple, and the need for personal or emotional space are relatively recent in India family life. More than ever, couples today need ongoing education and support.

Elderly People

A 'gray revolution' has become widespread throughout much of the world today due to increased longevity, and care of the elderly has emerged as one of the most challenging and complex problems of society. In India, the numbers of elderly people in the age groups of 60 and above are around 100 million. For centuries the welfare of the elderly in India has been the responsibility of the joint family. With increased occupational mobility and attendant migrations, the joint family structure has undergone inevitable changes and has had a profound effect on the quality of life of the elderly. However, in recent times, older adults have experienced a decrease in status, and their wisdom and knowledge (with rare exceptions) is no longer deemed as important by the majority of society. Traditionally, age had value in itself and was synonymous with wisdom, values, and character. Moreover, older family members played a significant role in the rearing of grandchildren and supporting the marriages of their sons and daughters. Today, in a rapidly mobile society and changing world, many elderly individuals are seen as 'second-class citizens'. Interactions between adult children and their aging parents have become not only less intimate and frequent, but in some cases even exploitative and abusive. One of the disturbing patterns of intergenerational relationships in India today is that of neglect and physical and/or psychological abuse of elder family members. FLE has the potential to aid and assist all members of the family system as they struggle to resolve conflicts and maintain close ties in a world that is in tremendous flux, and where unpredictability and insecurity run rampant.

Conclusion

As part of a comprehensive mental health effort in India, FLE holds great promise as a keeper and restorer of the family unit.

However, the idea of FLE is relatively new in India, and with few exceptions, has not been articulated or actualized in current mental health and social welfare programs. Yet, the notion that couples and families need ongoing support and useful information about family life appears to be in the early stages of acceptance in professional circles. This country appears ripe for a preventive approach to marital and family difficulties. It is essential that with changing family structures and patterns, people in all segments of Indian society need to be adequately prepared, and receive continual support, in order to meet the challenges of modern life.

> "Everyone needs to have a family – whether small or large. Everyone needs a safe heaven of peace and happiness."

References

Anandalakshmi, S. (1984). Cultural themes in the Indian context. Paper presented at the Summer Institute in Child Development, Lady Irwin College, New Delhi.

American Home Economics Association (1988). Certification of home economists: Professional development unit guidelines and certification renewal policies. Washington, DC: Author.

Arcus, M.K. (1990). The nature of family life education: Family life curriculum guidelines. Minneapolis, MN: National Council of Family Relations.

Arcus, M.K., Schvaneveldt, J.D., and Moss, J. (eds.) (1993). *Handbook of Family Life Education,* Vol. I and II, Newbury Park: Sage Publications.

Baral, J.K., and Bishoyee, A.P. (1999). Family in transition: Some theoretical and methodological questions. In J.K. Baral and A. Chowdhury (eds.), *Family in Transition: Power and Development* (pp. 1-15), New Delhi: Northern Book Centre.

Baral, J.K., Das, U., and Dash, S. (1999). Power equation in family. In J.K. Baral and A. Chowdhury (eds.), *Family in Transition: Power and Development* (pp. 57-82), New Delhi: Northern Book Centre.

Barozzi, R.L., and Engel, J.W. (1985). A survey of attitudes about family life education. *Social Casework*, 66, pp. 106-110.

Bharat, S. (1997). Family socialization of the Indian child. *Trends in Social Science Research*, Vol.4, No.1, June, pp. 201-216.

Bharat, S. (1991). Alternate family pattern and policies in India. Paper presented at the workshop on Developing Postgraduate Social Work Curriculum on the Family. Unit for Family Studies, TISS, Mumbai.

Belle, D. (1990). Poverty and women's mental health. *American Psychologist*. 45(3), pp. 385-389.

Carson, D.K., and Chowdhury, A. (2000). Family therapy in India: A new profession in an ancient land? *Contemporary Family Therapy* 22(4), pp. 387-406.

Choudhury, R. (1999). The changing family scenario in Orissa: Its impact on mental health. In J.K. Baral and A. Chowdhury (eds.), *Family in Transition: Power and Democracy*. New Delhi: Northern Book Centre (pp. 21-30).

Chowdhury, A. (1995). "Employed mothers and their families in India". In *Early Child Development and Care*, Vol.113, pp. 65-75.

Chowdhury, A. (1999). The status and perceptions of aged in Orissan families. In J.K. Baral and Aparajita Chowdhury (eds.), *Family in Transition: Power and Democracy*. New Delhi: Northern Book Centre (pp. 47-56).

Coie, J.D., Watt, N.F., West, S.G., Hawkins, J.D., Asarnow, J.R., Markman, H.J. Ramey, S.L., Shew, M.B., and Long, B. (1993). The science of prevention: A conceptual framework and some directions for a national research program. *American Psychologist*, October, pp.1013-1022.

Conklin, G.H. (1988). The influence of economic development on pattern of conjugal power and extended family residence. *Indian Journal of Comparative Family Studies*, 19, pp. 187-206.

Cromwell, R.E., and Thomas, V.L. (1976). Developing resources for family potentials: A family action model. *The Family Coordinator*, 25, pp. 13-20.

Curran, D. (1983). *Traits of Healthy Family*, New York: Ballantine.

Das, R.C. (1999). Marriage in transition: A biosocial approach. In J.K. Baral and Aparajita Chowdhury (eds.), *Family in Transition: Power and Democracy*. New Delhi: Northern Book Centre (pp. 16-20).

Darling, C.A. (1987). Family life education. In M.B. Sussman and S.K. Steinmetz (eds.), *Handbook of Marriage and the Family* (pp. 815-833), New York: Plenum.

Desai, N. (1994). Towards family life enrichment. In N. Desai (ed.), *Enhancing the Role of the Family as an Agency for Social and Economic Development* (pp. 118-127). Bombay: Tata Institute of Social Sciences.

Herold, E.S., Kepf, K.E., and de Carlo, M. (1974). Family life education: Student perspectives. *Canadian Journal of Public Health*, 65, pp.365-368.

Karve, I. (1953). Kinship Organisation in India. Poona: Deccan Post Graduate College and Research Institute.

Kerckhoff, R.K. (1964). Family life education in America. In H.T. Christensen (ed.), *Handbook of Marriage and Family* (pp. 881-911). Chicago: Rand McNally.

Mishra, G. (1995). Reflection on continuity and change in the Indian family system. *Trends in Social Science Research*. 2(1), pp. 27-30.

Mohanty, B. (1999). Dual-earner families: A journey to freedom and equality. In J.K. Baral and A. Chowdhury (eds.), *Family in Transition: Power and Development* (pp. 120-130), New Delhi: Northern Book Centre.

Nanda, G.K., and Dash, A.S. (1996). *Disadvantage Schooling, Competence and Invulnerability*, Bhubaneswar: Panchajanya, C/o URPL House.

National Commission on Family Life Education (1968). Family life education programs: Principles, plans, procedures. *The Family Coordinator*, 17, pp. 211-214.

National Council on Family Relations (1984). Standards and criteria for the certification of family life educator, College/University curriculum guidelines and content guidelines for family life education: A framework for planning programmes over the life span. Minneapolis, MN.

Pedro-Carroll, J. (2001). The promotion of wellness in children and families: Challenges and opportunities. *American Psychologist*, November, pp. 993-1004.

Ramu, G.N. (1988). Marital roles and power: Perceptions and reality in urban settings. *Journal of Comparative Family Studies*, 19, pp. 207-227.

Sarada, D. (1999). *Family Life for Adolescent Girls*. New Delhi: Discovery Publishing House.

Saraswathi, T.S., and S. Pai. (1997). Socialization in the Indian context. In *Asian Perspectives in Psychology*, (eds.) H. Rao and Sinha, pp. 74-92, New Delhi: Sage Methodology Series.

Sarkar, C. (1988). *Juvenile Delinquency in India*. Delhi: Daya Publishing House.

Sinha, D. (1984). Some recent changes in the Indian family and their implications for socialization. *The Indian Journal of Social Work*, 45, pp. 271-286.

Sinha, D. (1988). The family scenario of a developing country and its implications for mental health: The case of India. In P.R. Dasen, J.W. Berry and N. Sartorious (eds.), *Health and Cross-cultural Psychology: Towards Application* (pp. 48-70), Newbury Park: Sage Publications.

Smith, W.M., Jr. (1968). Family life education: Who needs it? *The Family Coordinator*, 17, pp. 55-61.

Singh, L.B., and A.K. Singh. (1996). Alienation: A symptomatic reaction of educated employed youth in India. *International Journal of Psychology*, 31 (2), pp. 101-110.

The Vanier Institute of the Family (1971). Report of family life education survey, Part-2, Family life education in the schools. Ottawa: Author.

Tennant, J. (1989). Family life education: Identity and objection and future directions. *McGill Journal of Education*, 24, pp. 127-142.

Verma, S., and Saraswathi, T.S. (2002). Adolescence in India: Street urchins or Silicon Valley millionaires? In R.B. Brown, R.W. Larson and T.S. Saraswathi (eds.), *The World's Youth: Adolescence in Eight Regions of the Globe*. U.K.: Cambridge University Press, pp. 105-140.

2

Understanding Family Life in India

Rita Choudhury

India is a pluralistic and multi-ethnic society, consisting of extremely complex family systems. Within its diversified boundaries of ethnic origins, religions, languages and cultures, the most distinguished feature of India is its "unity in diversity" characteristic of the family system. The major dimensions of this complex organization are its structure and composition, patterns of role relationships, dynamics of interaction, value systems, and family ethos. This chapter discusses the background of family life in India, contemporary Indian families in terms of changing features, and both structural and functional patterns of family in terms of role relationships. It sheds light on the stressors associated with social change and its consequences for Indian families.

Background of Family Life in India

> "The family is not merely a concept; it is an emotional experience."
>
> —Sinha (1999)

India is a diverse society consisting of extremely complex family systems. The notion of "unity in diversity" has become a part of India's self-identity, and different levels of social evolution are found in contemporary India. There are primitive hunters and food gatherers (tribals), shifting cultivators, nomads of different types (migrants), artisans and craftsmen (rural and urban villages), settled agriculturists, and several urban categories that make up the complex socio-economic strata of the society. Further, there are modern academic, bureaucratic, political, industrial, and scientific elites of the society. Thus, we find the past, present and future all colliding in modern India. India is a composite culture, marked by a stable pattern of pluralism.

It has been generally observed that the family has always been the foundation of Indian society, and contemporary Indian people continue to take pride in the centrality of marriage and family life (Mullati, 1995). India is characterized by a tremendous variety of family forms. These forms can be distinguished along several dimensions, including descent, residence, membership, marriage, structure, and dominance. Further, throughout the ages, family types and characteristics in India have changed simultaneously with global civilization and social evolution.

Today, in most communities in India, family descent is traced through the father's line. One's self-identity in the family and society is recognized by the father's name. This has been referred to as 'patriarchal descent'. Matrilineal descent that is recognized through the mother's line is found among a few tribes, such as the Garo, Khas, and Phar in Northeast India; the Nayar, Mapilla, and Lakshdweep islanders; and among several tribal and non-tribal groups of South India. However, patriarchy is the norm of Indian society. In the patriarchal structure of the family, roles and responsibilities, as well as control and distribution of family resources, are strictly determined by age, gender, and generational status. This provides males not only power and status, but also responsibility for making the major decisions for women and children in the family. Patriarchy generally leads to patriliny and patrilocality. These concepts have to do with the societal expectations that, once married, a woman will change residence and acquiring her new family name along her husband's ancestral line. This is a common practice in India even today. Even, in matrilineal and matrilocal sub-cultures in India, patriarchy seems to be prevalent in the form of power held by the woman's brother(s) and not by the woman herself.

Family types in India may also be classified on the basis of marriage and the number of selected mates. In monogamy, an individual can have only one spouse at a time. This type of family is the most preferred and prevalent form in almost all societies. The degree of family stability that this form of marriage (monogamy) can provide is not possible in any other forms of marriage. However, polygamy (having more than one spouse) is prevalent in many areas of India. Although the polyandrous norm is for husbands to have more than one wife and/or mate, polyandry (when women have more than one husband or mate) and group marriages also exist. Polygamy was widely practiced in India among the tribal Hindus and also some Muslim groups. The Hindu Marriage Act of 1955 perpetuates the adoption of monogamy as a rule among the Hindus, but from the Government of India census data it appears that polygamy is still prevalent on a limited scale. The Scheduled Tribes (STs), which form 8 per cent of the total population of India today, still follow their customary law relating to marriage and family. Thus, polyandry is confined to small pockets of people. In North India, it is practiced by the Khasa (Jaunsaris) of the Uttar Pradesh, and the people of Kinnaur, Lahul and Spiti in Himachal Pradesh. Historically, these people have practiced fraternal or adelphic polyandry. Among them, the eldest brother marries a woman, and the younger brothers simultaneously become her husbands (as with the Draupadi and Pandavas in Mahabharata).

When more than one woman can be married to the brothers, such a situation can be referred to as 'group marriage'. Among the 'Todas' of South India, the husbands of a woman need not be brothers. This is known as non-fraternal polyandry. Thus, among the Todas, social paternity is deemed as more important than biological paternity. Hence, the values and norms related to family in India vary according to religion, caste, social class, geography, and residential patterns – all of which reflect differences in the way families and individuals have responded to change. However, irrespective of the family structure and functioning, most distinguishing family forms in contemporary Indian society are discussed in the paragraphs that follow.

Patriarchal Family System

It has been pointed out by social anthropologists and sociologists that the demographic characteristics and socio-religious beliefs and practices in modern India society are having a profound influence on the nature of the Indian family system, and also reflect the changes taking in it. Further, the bulk of socio-anthropological studies indicate that the Indian family is by and large patriarchal. The 'patriarch' of the Indian family is considered as a protective authority figure, worthy of respect by family members (Kapadia, 1972). Exceptions can be found in the southern states of Kerala and Karnataka, and various tribal societies throughout the country, where families are matriarchal or mother centered (Dube, 1974; Chekki, 1974, Mullati, 1989). However, many of these types of families are gradually moving towards patriarchy. Though some of the traditional nature of patriarchy has been lost to some extent in contemporary Indian families, male dominance and female subservience are common. Here, all adult male members, including husbands, elder brothers, fathers, and grandfathers, not only participate in the decision-making process of the family, but are also responsible for the security, protection, and need fulfillment of all the other members of the family. In contrast, girls, women, and other junior male members obey the decisions and commands of their senior male adults whole-heartedly and without question. However, the patriarchal family is changing slowly towards equalitarian interaction more frequently among the educated, urban middle classes, and even in many rural families. In the southern states that include India's matriarchal families, there is also a gradual change towards a more patriarchal system, although they are still maintaining some matriarchal woman's rights (Sardomani, 1985). Elsewhere, patriarchal families continue to be patrilenial and patrilocal, with lineage based on the father's family.

Since the introduction of the Hindu Code Bill of 1954-56, some changes have continued to occur in the Indian family system. Daughters have shared in the father's property. Law has approved interreligious marriages and equal rights to women with respect to adoption, divorce and remarriage. Yet, the century-old tradition of male dominance continues today throughout most of this industrialized society. Some would argue that this mechanism of obedience and respect towards men provides stability to the individual as well as the family. Moreover, they would add that that this process helps to maintain the noble 'name and fame' of the family and its traditional practices because they are considered one's religious duty as a family member.

Joint Family System

The joint family system is the traditional Indian family form and is still practiced today. In this system, all family members live together under one roof and are related to each other in one way or the other (biological and social). The property – God and the sacred hearth – belongs to the family as a whole, and the entire family rejoices and suffers together. The joint family has a combined kitchen, and the ownership of the sources of production and consumption belongs to the entire family. However, throughout the last few decades of socio-economic and technological advancements, significant changes have occurred in the joint family system. A large extended family may still live together and carry out common ventures in daily life and economic pursuit, but today it is likely to have separate living, cooking, and dining. These families can be observed, for example, in large Indian business communities. Married brothers may have separate dwellings but run a common business and meet regularly for a variety of family rituals and at times of crisis and loss. Hence, a large number of families in India, especially in the urban sector, could be described as functionally joint but with separate residences. According to Ramu (1988), "...it appears that people believe in the joint family ideals and wish to maintain close filial and fraternal solidarity when possible, while in practice chose to live in nuclear households".

Besides the patriarchal and joint family systems, as described above, the ongoing socio-economic and demographic changes in India today, coupled with the technological advancements the recent past, have led to the existence of alternate family forms. These include single-parent families mainly headed by women, female-headed families, migrant families dual earner/career families, childless families, and adoptive families. A brief description of some of these family forms is presented below:

Single Parent Families

Single-parent families are those families in which the children reside with one parent who shoulders the major responsibility for their upbringing. Widowhood has always been the major reason for the creation of single-parent homes in India. Bharat (1986) estimated the incidence of single-parent families from the 1981 Government of India census to be about 8 per cent. These families included those who had dependent children below the age of 19, in which one parent was absent due to death, divorce or separation. It was also observed that over 40 per cent of the single-parent families were established because of the death of a parent, and that more than 70 per cent of single parents were women. Parents in these families experience numerous problems and challenges ranging from resource shortages to a host of discipline problems and parent-child conflicts. Moreover, these families are often stereotyped and ostracized by a portion of Indian society.

Female-headed Families

Because women mainly head single-parent families, they are also referred to as female-headed families. However, the woman may have a migrant husband, or a husband may not be productive and contributing his income to the family. These women have the main earning responsibility for the family. As per the Government of India census data, the incidence is 10 per cent (Chatterjee, 1988; Sivamurthy, 1988), but some micro-level studies indicate that 30 to 35 per cent of such families in rural areas are headed by females. These families face severe conditions of economic deprivation, often a lack of support from extended family members, and alienation from the community. In both rural and urban areas, they are generally the poorest of the poor. A growing number of street and working children in towns and cities, and children in institutions, generally come from such families. Policies are yet to recognize female-headed households as a separate and legitimate entity and make the necessary provisions for them.

Migrant Families

Migrant families in recent decades are a by-product of industrialization and urbanization. They have evolved because of a lack of opportunity, capital, assets, pauperization, prospect for diversification of occupation, and changes in foresting laws, to name a few. The result has been a constant migration of families from rural to rural and rural to urban areas across the country. This migration has fundamental implications for both women and children. Kinship networks tend to be disrupted, and the traditional skills of these families are no longer useful in a modern urban economy. Moreover, migration deprives children of the basic services of education and health. Women have to face the triple burden of income earning, childcare, and other domestic responsibilities under conditions of very poor housing, sanitation, and overall quality of life (National Commission on Self-Employed Women, 1989; Parasuraman, 1986). Political violence and environmental disaster further endanger family life and increase the number of uprooted and destitute families and individuals. The recent example is the 'super cyclone' in the state of Orissa in 1999, where thousands of families experienced death and destruction. A significant number of these losses were children and women.

Present-Day Family in India

Despite the many changes occurring in Indian society today, the Indian family as a whole has found a way to remain strong and resilient. The family in India occupies a central position in the life of the Indian people and is the basic unit of Indian society. According to Karve (1953), the Indian family organization is one of the three most essential aspects for understanding of any cultural phenomenon in India, the other two being configuration of linguistic religion and institution of caste.

The family is considered to be a link between constancy and change. It determines the development of individuals and provides stability of support when problems arise. In addition to the provision all that is needed for basic survival, families serve as a buffer between members and society and help them cope with various types and levels of stress. By providing mutual care, regard and affection, the stability and development of the family is extended and various personal goals are fulfilled. People's identities, self-esteem and ideals about worthiness are often conceived and organized around the notion of family.

The Indian family maintains social bonds and boundaries, facilitates group goals, and enhances cohesiveness among its members. This is achieved through a hierarchically organized authority structure in which individual differences in motivation, aspiration and goals are ignored to a considerable extent, particularly when they appear as threats to individual responsibility in the family. Thus, families are referred to as 'Kutumb' and 'Parivar' and typically consist of individuals from several generations. In Indian philosophy, the family protects the rights and duties of the individual. The concept of *Vasundhaiva Kutumbakam*, which means that the entire world is one large family, is widespread in India, and that which is "Good for All" has been at the core of much Indian philosophy.

However, the present-day scenario of the family in the Indian context is leaning towards instrumentality, individuality, and material gain. Family is considered one avenue for accumulating resources through dowry (bride price) in marriages. There is an increasing emphasis today on personal rights, rather than responsibilities, as a family member. This philosophy and practice disrupts the stability and harmony of families on a widespread scale.

Characteristics of the Contemporary Indian Family

Today's Indian family is characterized by certain identifying features. These are as under:

(1) *Family cohesiveness and solidarity*: The first and foremost feature of Indian families throughout the ages has been a definite system of role relationships and sentiments that have bound its members together. The family is not simply a social unit but connotes a value in itself (Mishra, 1995). All members have different roles, which they learn and identify with through culturally mediated socialization. The members share a feeling of solidarity, and each person strives to uphold the dignity and status of the family. A high premium is placed on family unity and cohesiveness, which are necessary for family stability and survival. Sharing and mutual dependence are encouraged, and safety and security of family members is paramount. Elaborate family practices and rituals foster a feeling of

belongingness and convey the message that family bonds are immutable, lifelong, and dependable.

(2) *Fulfillment of religious obligations*: One of the main purposes of the family is the fulfillment of religious obligations, such as ancestral worship. This occurs primarily through the oldest male child and his passing on of socio-religious traditions to the generation. Therefore, marriage is essential in Indian culture to fulfill certain household and religious duties.

(3) *Age and sex seniority*: The family operates in terms of a well-defined hierarchical system organized around age and sex. Age seniority determines both the mutual and authority status of a person. Much value is attached to age seniority, and due respect is given to older members which extends even to the world outside the family. This value is illustrated, for example, through touching the feet of elders in good/auspicious occasions, talking softly in their presence, and accepting their suggestions without any question. Although slight changes in the behavior of younger family members towards elders have been noticed in the present family system, respect for the aged is a basic and consistent theme found in the Indian family system even today.

(4) *Patriarchy*: Patriarchy is another distinguished feature found in Indian families. Family roles, responsibilities and power (control authority) in the family is strictly determined according to age, gender and generation. The eldest male member of the family (senior father or grandfather) is usually called as 'patriarch' and is the supreme authority in the family. He possesses the right to make vital decisions for the family. Other members of the family, including women, children and other adult male members, are subordinate. In recent times it has been observed that this patriarchal system is changing slowly towards a more equalitarian interaction, especially among the more educated urban middle class; however, also in some rural

areas. Even in the matrilineal and matrilocal cultures of India, patriarchy seems to be prevalent in the form of power held by the older brother and not by the woman herself. This century-old system of patriarchy continues to function in the same traditional fashion even in the 21st century and presents many challenges to the modern family.

(5) *Caste system*: Although the caste system in India is gradually changing, family life is still largely influenced by it. The occupation, religious, and cultural life and practices of the Indian people are greatly influenced by the caste to which they belong. The upper-caste people, such as the Brahmins and Khatriyas, are privileged groups who enjoy all of the privileges of belonging to the upper crust of the society. The Sudras are lower caste and underprivileged, and serve those in the upper castes. In between are several other designated castes who know their place in society and by and large accept it.

(6) *Male-female roles*: Male supremacy is another characteristic of Indian families. Male members of the family, including husband, elder brother, father, and grandfather, occupy positions of great power and authority. Females, on the other hand, are placed in a secondary position with regard to status, power, nutrition, health, and education. Division of family tasks and responsibilities is structured along gender, age, and generation. These men are responsible for the more valued outdoor tasks and women for the less valued domestic work. The aged have primarily the directive, decision-making roles in the family, and women generally take on the responsibilities of physical work. Children normally have lighter or no major responsibilities and tasks to perform within the family.

(7) *Cultural and familial identification*: Given the varied ethnic and cultural diversities found in Indian families, each individual finds his/her identity within the context of the family. They learn the fundamentals of their culture

and society from their family. In his *jati* (group), everyone is primarily defined and known by their family and the reputation of the family.

(8) *Family as a link to the society*: A family in India is not only a reproductive unit and a socializing agency, it also serves as their link to society. Kinship begins within the family and is extended through the family. Kinship ties are generally thought to be the most durable, reliable, worthy, and morally enriched among all social groups. Though such ties have weakened to some extent in modern society, kinship and ethnic communities continue to be important sources of support for the Indian families.

(9) *Prevalence of traditional family practices*: Many families practice related to marriage, birth, death, and widowhood are symbolic indicators of Indian families. Child marriage, *sati* (widow immolation) dowry, celebration of the birth of a male child, female feticide and infanticide, fathers as the natural guardians of families, and women leaving their natal home after marriage, are still in practice today. Other family rituals such as naming rites, hair removal rites, rites at the first feed of solid food to a child, beginning of lessons, and celebration of the onset of puberty among girls, are still observed in Indian families.

(10) *Gender inequality*: Gender inequality is commonly observed in Indian families. Sex discrimination has been the logo of the Indian people for centuries. Though there is provision of gender equality in the Constitution, gender inequality is universal, including within the family and at workplace. The ratio of females to males in India is 933 females to 1,000 males (Census of India, 2001, i.e., not far from equal). A women's contribution to household and family is enormous (in both urban and rural families), and yet women continue to be oppressed both within and beyond the home environment. Her dignity and security are often in peril from birth onward, since males are generally preferred by most parents even today.

(11) *Marriage as sacred ritual*: Marriage is the most important and compulsory life cycle ritual for the establishment of a family in Indian society, irrespective of caste and religion. India has all types of marriages, monogamy and polygamy extending back to the Vedic era (Kapadia, 1972). The major mate selection pattern continues to be managed by elders and parents even among the majority of highly educated urban communities and castes. The establishment of marriage as an institution, from mate selection to engagement and the marriage ceremony, and up to the entry of the bride to the groom's parental home, are all religious ceremonies performed and shared by all family members and relatives, friends neighbors, caste members, and especially in rural areas, the entire village/community. Hence, marriage in the Indian society is not only a ritual, but a social and sacred event for the newly married couple the entire family and community. Such is the notion of marriage among Hindus, Christians, Sikhs, Parsis, and Jains.

(12) *Neglect of the girlchild*: A female in an Indian family is frequently neglected right from conception, especially among poor rural families. Infanticide, early assumption of domestic responsibilities, sibling care, and the discontinuation of education early on, especially in rural areas (estimated to be 70 per cent in some areas) but also in poor urban families, are all indicative of the neglect girlchildren in scores of Indian homes. Also, the high incidence of morbidity and malnutrition (90-93 per cent), accidents, and lack of attention to treatment during illness, all bear testimony to neglect of the girlchild in India (UNICEF India, 1990). Early pregnancy, repeated childbirths, and low access to health services have kept the national mortality and morbidity rates for girls excessively high.

(13) *Dowry and atrocities on women*: Dowry is an integrated custom in Hindu Indian marriages. The practice of the dowry system has prevailed for centuries. In this system,

gifts, both in cash and kind, are given to the newly wedded couple to begin their family life with security in the form of material possessions. Amongst rural and tribal communities it was popular as 'brideprice' (Murmu, 1982; Laxminarayan, 1982). The notion of dowry as 'extraction' from the bride's parents (party) has been a new transformation during the last few decades after independence. Increased incidence of poverty and unemployment, coupled with high aspirations for achievement and a desire for comforts and luxuries received from others, have perpetuated the demand for easy access through dowry. Parental desire for finding the best groom for their daughter further accentuates this practice, mostly among urban educated families. Subsequently, failure to comply with the groom's (and his family's) demand for dowry has resulted in harassment, wife battering, suicide, bride burning, and other atrocities on women which, according to some sources, are gradually increasing. Because of the deeply entrenched value of maintaining a matrimonial status and the marital home at any cost, a lack of support groups under conditions of revolt, and economic dependence, women continue to make few attempts to alter the situation (Sriram and Bakshi, 1988).

(14) *Urban-rural structural characteristics*: In rural India, though agriculture is the main occupation, there are not many large landholdings. Therefore, it is difficult to maintain joint families today. A large number of rural families among the Scheduled Castes (SCs) are nuclear, whereas the educated SC families, especially in urban areas, are still living largely in joint families. This is also seen among upper-class professionals who own large businesses. In the case of some low-caste groups, modernity has helped to sustain the joint family. In urban slums, a majority of labor classes have nuclear families. Female agricultural laborers in some rural areas, especially in states like Kerala, Bengal and Punjab, also have nuclear families (Gulati, 1983;

Saradomani, 1983). In contrast, as Gore (1968) has pointed out, wage-earning middle-class families are becoming more nuclear. The joint family, then, is in some ways thriving, and in other ways declining in modern India, irrespective of urbanization and industrialization. Kolenda (1987) concludes that Rajasthan (with large business communities) has the largest percentage of joint families, while throughout the rest of India the family types vary from 40 per cent nuclear to 60 per cent joint, and vice versa, depending on each particular region of the country.

Changes in Contemporary Indian Family

Indian family, like other families across the world, has undergone drastic charges in structure, functions, role relationships, and values. The most prominent causes of change are industrialization, urbanization, modernization, liberalization, increased education of women, adoption of Western values and lifestyles, individuation, migration, the impact of mass communications and the internet, and the threat of terrorist attack and the insecurities built into modern societies. One result has been a gradual trend to nucleation in modern Indian family, despite the fact that the joint family system still exists (Ross, 1961; Nimkoff, 1959; Ramu, 1968). According to Ramu (1988), "there is a gradual change in the family towards a nuclear pattern in which the conjugal pair is the critical unit". In this type of family the power has shifted from the traditional patriarch or 'Karta' to the main breadwinner. One outcome has been a significant shift in the father-son relationship, particularly in families where the adult son is the main provider for the family.

It is important to note, however, that in spite of the movement towards nuclear families in India and the establishment of family autonomy, families still continue to maintain their emotional ties. These links can be seen during times of family celebration and crisis. Many families, though nuclear in structure, behave like a joint family. Thus, a new pattern of family life has emerged. Families are often nuclear in residence and routine decision-making (daily life) but joint in ethics and in making long-term decisions (marriage, property matters, travel, common celebrations, etc). Sinha (1988) has emphasized that the contemporary Indian family is in a 'transitional' phase, where structural changes are not entirely accompanied by psychological changes. People wish to live in small, nuclear family units while continuing to draw strength from the extended family, particularly during times of need and difficulty.

Nuclearization in the family system has brought with it not only structural but psychological, attitudinal, and behavioral changes, especially in families that have women who work outside the home. Exposure to Western ideals and norms, as well as the women's movement, which has pressed for equal rights and status, have served to modify the traditional values, ideals, and role-relationships in family life. Thus, although the extended family sentiments of unity, sharing, mutual dependence, conformity to family norms, and a sense of responsibility towards kin continue to influence family living in India to some extent, there are signs of rapid change. These changes are more evident in urban areas. The presence of the computer and satellite TV in Indian households has had a profound impact on the economic, social, and psychological life of family members. The electronic media promotes individual aspirations of consumerism, while at the same time erodes traditional values.

The New Economic Policy (NEP), implemented by the Government of India (1991), brought about marked changes in the values and attitude of people. The emphasis on quick money and shooter benefits has started to dehumanize and destabilize Indian society, including family life. As a result of the adverse work conditions of the poor, the disproportionate burden on working women, and the overall value crisis in Indian society, it is feared that family relationships are in danger of eroding. Mishra (1995: 30) summarized the current state of affairs with regard to the changing Indian family and its influences on family members as follows:

> Family in India, particularly in the urban educated clan, is undergoing transformation. The economic, social and cultural forces are reinforcing individualism and changes intrinsic to the traditional family system are leading to structural changes. Family members are questioning the roles, obligations and relationships which have been nourishing the inherently social texture of the Indian family. The tensions experienced in the course of pursuing personal (individual) goals and familial goals are becoming an important source of stress. This situation calls for a perspective which views individuality and relatedness as mutually constitutive and complementary. Such a solution shall constructively utilize indigenous values in which family happens to be a value in itself rather than a mere instrument for personal growth.

Another change observed in contemporary families in India is the freedom from castes and family-based occupations, and the emphasis on personal accomplishment and greater autonomy in fulfilling individual desires and wishes. Modern parents are deliberately trying to shape their children's lives in a different way. Stricter childrearing styles, coupled with greater expectations on the part of the parents, are creating excessive demands on children. With the increase in the number of employed mothers, the ecology of the family is changing dramatically, including the area of childcare. Sinha (1984, 1988) suggests that there are unstable and contradictory patterns of childrearing which generate anxiety and conflict in the growing child. The elderly (i.e., grandparents) in these changing circumstances also do not have much of a role to play in the child's socialization, as parents today are the main socializing agents. There are other external agencies which are also assuming much of the socialization role of children, including day-care centers, pre-schools, crèches, and even peer groups and the neighborhood, but again not optimally.

Recent changes in the nature and types of marriages, childrearing, and employment are resulting in a differentiation in the parental and marital roles. The nuclear family structure is assumed to favor a sharing of roles rather than a hierarchical structuring of roles, a liberal rather than conservative attitude, role diffusion rather than role differentiation, and an overall equalitarian/equalitarian world view. According to Conklin (1988), there is a greater emphasis today on mutual decision-making and the sharing of power in many Indian homes. Married couples see themselves as partners in childrearing and providing for the family. Although this trend has empowered women, it has not always contributed to marital happiness and stability, even though there appear to be more benefits than liabilities.

Other problems faced by contemporary families in India are occupational health hazards, disability, chronic/terminal illness, AIDS, substance abuse, unemployment, dowry, family violence, atrocities against women, and gender discrimination, to name a few. Families in India are experiencing numerous challenges which need to be addressed on a local, state, and national levels. These challenges are summarized as follows:

- Urbanization at an unprecedented rate.
- Breaking down of the traditional joint family system.
- Increasing number of nuclear, single-parent, women-headed, dual-earner, and migrant families.
- Families are in distressed conditions due to economic deprivation (poverty), social marginalization, alcohol dependence, and chronic illnesses such as cancer and AIDS.
- Growing number of elderly persons and families of the mentally ill with only elderly caregivers to assist.
- Increasing influence of mass media in shaping the attitudes, values, belief systems, and aspirations of people.
- Absence of clear-cut role models.
- Changes in the status, role, and employment of women.

- Loose kinship networks and a decrease in family and community cohesiveness.
- The gap between men and women's roles both inside and outside the family.

Stressors Associated with Families

Contemporary Indian parents appear to be ill-prepared to cope with the demands of parenting and family life, partly because many of them have grown up in a hierarchically structured and extended kinship network (Singh and Singh, 1996; Singhal and Mishra, 1994). Further, when things go wrong in families (Saraswati and Pai, 1997), modern parents get anxious when their grown-up children and adolescents breach established social codes. Intergenerational conflicts occur more frequently in families on issues related to marriage, career choices, and separate living arrangements. This can result in a falling back on tradition, which can breed yet more conflict. So, the key concern now is the stress created by changing family composition and dynamics in the family, with differential expectations, values, competencies and coping styles between parents and children. Clinical practitioners have expressed concern regarding implications for mental health, especially in terms of the tensions experienced by family members because of a weakening of social support from kinship groups and the community. Hence, at this critical juncture of transition in India, family life education would play a vital role in building a healthy nation.

Importance of Family Relationships in Modern Society

Family relationships are considered to be the building blocks of any society, and despite the multitude of changes, the family in India continues to provide strength and stability. India is proud of its heritage of nurturance, love, compassion, self-lessons, tolerance, generosity and understanding in family life. It is important to examine the major components of the Indian family system in order to gain a greater understanding of and appreciation for the whole.

Husband-Wife Relationship

In India, the institution of marriage is considered divine. The relationship between husband and wife extends far beyond the sexual cohabitation part of it, giving birth to children, and establishing a family. It is the sacred duty and religious obligation of the couple to develop and maintain mutual love, care, respect, sacrifice, and tolerance within the family environment. This is intended so that each family member can enjoy family life and learn the skills necessary to enter into a fulfilling relationship beyond the family and *jati* (group) in forming a stable and prosperous society.

As a part of marriage, sex is also considered to be sacred. However, the sexual relationship is so personal, confidential, and significant that it is never thought of as the foundation of the marriage or family. In the family system the husband-wife relationship is not based on total equality. The husband is usually older (by age) than the wife and is expected to be his wife's superior and receive symbolic and actual deference from her. There is no great expectation that the couple should share thoughts and tastes as one finds in Western society. The husband dominates the wife in making decisions in the family, and the roles of man and woman are markedly segregated. A woman is expected to be indulged in all the household affairs and remain within the house, whereas the man is expected to handle all crucial decisions of family life and all external matters of the family. However, in recent times, a monumental change has occurred in the role of men and women, at least among the educated. A wife is often referred to now as 'Dharmapatni' or 'Arddhangini', i.e., the "equal half" of man. No religious ceremony is complete without the presence of both the husband and wife together. Still, the wife, in every way, is expected to be a 'Pativrata' – one man's follower (acknowledging her husband's will and authority in all respect). She is supposed to fast (without food and water) as a gesture of worshipping her husband (an incarnation of God) during certain occasions such as 'Karwa Chauth', 'Savitri Amavasya' and 'Teej' which come once in a year. The wife takes food from the plate of her husband after he finishes eating, but the reverse does not take place. Being a dutiful and loyal wife is given top priority in Indian families even today, and the more a woman is obedient and gives selfless service to the household, the more she is appreciated and held in high esteem within the family.

In India, the relationship between husband and wife is culture-specific. She puts on vermilion and bangles as a mark of marriage and living with her husband. Moreover, she is expected to wear gold ornaments on her ears, neck, and wrists. The neck palm of the head and feet are also painted in local herbs (Mehendi) for special occasions that include Hindu weddings, and pujas such as Dussera and Diwali. However, the misery of the Indian woman starts once she becomes a widow. The presence of a husband is vital to the well-being of an Indian wife. A widow leads a life of destitution, often wearing white clothes and no jewelry. She has to maintain a vegetarian diet, cannot laugh openly or socialize with anyone other than close family members. In addition, she is expected to sleep on the floor, cannot participate in any auspicious occasions, and is supposed to chant only God's name. In some regions of the country, a widow is even expected to die alive as *sati* (sitting on the funeral pyre of her husband). The right to a happy life is lost with the death of her husband.

In sum, significant social changes have affected the conjugal relationship in India in recent decades. Families in India (especially more educated and urban) are moving towards equality and partnership in family life. Yet, an underlying tinge of male supremacy is still present within all castes and religions in India.

Mother-in-Law and Daughter-in-Law Relationship

The relationship between mother-in-law and daughter-in-law is often problematic and remains a controversial subject in India. In the traditional joint family system, the central figure of the household is the mother-in-law. She is a disciplinary figure and the implementer of family rules and regulations with the newly wedded bride or *bahu* in the family. It is the mother-in-law who transmits the values of her family and introduces each member of the family to the new entrant into the household (i.e., the daughter-in-law). Traditionally, a girl after marriage typically moves into the house of her husband's family (i.e., her in-laws) and directly comes under their authority. Her movements, behavior and living style are regulated by the in-laws. Without the permission of the mother-in-law she cannot even talk or visit her natal family. Today, the raising incidents of bride burning, widow atrocities, and death of the newly married women clearly reveal the dehumanizing relationship between married women and their in-laws in Indian families. A decrease in moral values and increase in greediness, consumerism, and a sense of false vanity and status in the society have exhilarated the system of dowry to a level where it impinges upon many people in the society. Dowry (bride price) is given and accepted by all castes today and has become a mandatory principle of marriage. The dowry system, coupled with the excessive rights and powers of mother-in-laws, has created a great deal of pain and conflict in families today. These social practices are in dire need of removal or change.

The main cause of friction between the mother-in-law and the daughter-in-law is jealousy, possessiveness and self-centeredness. In Indian families, among all castes and *jatis*, the mother-son relationship is a pivotal one. There is a strong, tender, unchanging and dependable bond between the mother and the son even when he becomes an adult. Her authority over her son's domestic life continues even after he gets married and sometimes even extends to the regulation of his sexual relationship with his wife (Karve, 1953). Though a bit more liberal attitude is found in families today, yet the trend of mother's authority in all vital decisions over his adult son's conjugal life still exists. This can be a major source of conflict between the mother-in-law and the daughter-in-law, as the young wife feels that her husband is solely her possession and the older woman (mother-in-law) should not try to meddle in or control the life of her married son. The son, in turn, can easily feel torn between his mother whom he cannot cross and his wife whom he really does not want to make unhappy.

If, on the other hand, the daughter-in-law does not believe in trying to strengthen family bonds, she becomes a real problem to the entire family. A newly married woman has multiple roles to play in the family. As a wife, daughter-in-law, and sister-in-law, she occupies a central place in the extended family system. Though it is sometimes difficult and strenuous, her caring behavior and ability to remain compromise, adjust, and be flexible can help elevate the family life to a peaceful and happy existence. Of course, this process is facilitated when mother-in-laws are also willing to be accepting, caring, and adaptable.

Role of Extended Family Members (Brother-in-Law, Sister-in-Law, Aunts/Uncles, and Cousins)

It may be said that the extended family kin which is normally found in a joint family is another source of support, especially in time of adversity and to individuals who are vulnerable. The network ties among uncles and aunts, cousins, in-laws, etc. provide a buffer against the effects of stress (Cassel, 1976; Cobb, 1976; Dean and Lin, 1977; Kaplan, Cassel and Gore, 1977). Therefore, the supportive functions of the extended family are important for the preservation of mental health, especially in the face of adversity. This is evident during critical life events such as deaths, accidents, hospitalizations, or any other traumatic events that impact the stability of the family unit. Historically, in India, the role of the extended family members has been very important; this tradition continues even in the present-day situation with families-in-transition.

Grandparents and Grandchildren's Relationship

In a typical Indian family, there exists a unique and special bond, that is, the relationship between grandparents and grandchildren. Throughout the ages, grandparents have had a significant impact on child development, providing support for the family unit as mentors, role models, and caregivers. They are also referred as silent saviours, offering a second line of defense and safety net to their grandchildren. Their nurturance, companionship, comforting behavior, and role as a discipline figure in the family contributes enormously to the socialization of grandchildren. Research indicates that in such a special relationship, there is a reciprocal beneficial impact on both generations, including preserving the psychological well-being of the grandparents. As storytellers, playmates, caregivers, etc., grandparents are of benefit not only to the grandchildren, but also to the family as a whole.

Conclusion: The Family as a Context for Health and Well-being

To conclude, it can be stated that the family has been the pivotal institution around which Indian society has derived its strengths and forged its future. The well-being of a nation or a society depends largely on the well-being of its families. What occurs in the family affects society and vice versa. Thus, the family unit provides the foundation that helps maintain the physical and psychological integrity of individual members.

To achieve the goal of family well-being, family resources, responsibilities and problems must be considered. Family life education is one key element in strengthening support systems for individuals, families, and the community, by making each aware of roles, responsibilities, and rights. It further empowers family members to be responsible, caring, and conscientious, while allowing them to reach their maximum potential for a better family life. Family life education is important for all those who recognize the family's role in ameliorating problems in the community through proper socialization of the family members. The concept of family life education is a rather a new concept to our society, and requires in-depth knowledge and understanding about the whole issue of family system, dynamics, and problems. A holistic approach may be necessary to strengthen contemporary Indian families, especially with regard to areas such as marriage and mate selection; maintaining harmony in the family; parent-child/adolescent and extended family relationships; interface of women and work; family stress; and the need for appropriate and effective education and prevention programs in urban, rural, and tribal areas. As stated in proclamation by the United Nations, when announcing 1994 as the International Year of the Family, by strengthening families we ultimately strengthen children, adults, the nation, and finally humanity.

References

Bharat, S. (1986). Single-parent family in India: Issued and implications. *The Indian Journal of Social Work*, 49(4), pp. 367-376.

Bronfenbreanner, U. (1979). *The Ecology of Human Development.* Cambridge Mass. Harvard University Press.

Cassel, J. (1976). The contribution of the social environment to host resistance. *American Journal of Epidemiology*, 104, pp. 107-122.

Chatterjee, S. (1988). Rise in female-headed families. In S. Chatterjee (ed.), *The Indian Women's Search for an Identity*. New Delhi: Vikas.

Chekki, D.A. (1974). *Modernisation and Kin Network.* Leiden: E.J. Brill.

Conklin, G.H. (1988). The influence of economic development on pattern of conjugal power extended family residence. *Journal of Comparative Family Studies*, 19, pp. 187-206.

Cobb, S. (1976). Social support – as a moderator of life stress. *Psychosomatic Medicine*, 38, pp. 300-314.

Dean, A. and Lin, N. (1977). The stress-buffering role of social support: Problems, prospects and systematic investigations. *Journal of Nervous and Mental Diseases.*

Desai, A.R. (1980). *Urban Family and Family Planning in India.* Bombay: Popular Prakashan.

Dube, Leela (1974). *Sociology of Kinship in India*, Bombay: Popular Prakashan.

Gore, M.S. (1968). *Urbanization and Family Change*, New Delhi: Popular Prakashan.

Gulati, L. (1983). Male migration to the Middle East and the impact on the family: Some evidence from Kerala. *The Economic and Political Weekly*, 22(44), pp. 41-46.

Kapadia, K.M. (1972). *Marriage and Family in India*, Bombay: Oxford University Press.

Kaplan, Cassel and Gore, M.S. (1977) Social support and health. *Medical Care*, 15, pp. 47-48.

Karve, I. (1953). *Kinship Organization in India.* Poona: Deccan P.G. College and Research Institute.

Kolenda, P. (1987). *Regional Differences in Family Structure in India*, Jaipur: Rawat Publications.

Laxminarayan, H.D. (1982). The rural family in transition. In J.K. Augustine (ed.), *The Indian Family in Transition* (pp. 44-45), New Delhi: Vikas.

Mishra, G. (1995). Reflections on continuity and change in the Indian family system. *Trends in Social Science Research*, Vol. 2, No. 1, (pp. 27-30).

Murmu, D. (1982). The tribal family in transition. In J.S. Augustine (ed.), *The Indian Family in Transition* (pp. 55-167), New Delhi: Vikas.

Mullati, L. (1989). The Bhakti Movement and the status of women: A case study of Veerasaivism. New Delhi: Abhinava Publications.

Mullati, L. (1995). Families in India: Beliefs and realities. *Journal of Comparative Family Studies*, 26(1), pp. 11-25.

National Commission on Self-Employed Women (1989). Report of the working group on Employment of Woman, New Delhi: Planning Commission.

Nimkoff, M.F. (1959). Some problems concerning research on the changing family in India, *Sociological Bulletin*, 8(2), pp. 32-38.

Nyes, F.I. and Gecas, V. (1976). The role concept: Review and delineation. In F.I. Nye (ed.), *Structure and Analysis of the Family* (pp. 3-14), Beverly Hills.

Paolucle, et. al. (1977) *Family Decision-making: An Ecosystem Approach.* New York: John Wiley and Sons.

Parsuraman, S. (1986). Migration and its effect on the family. *The Indian Journal of Social Work*, 47(1), pp. 1-14.

Ramu, G.N. (1968). Untouchability in rural areas. *The Indian Journal of Social Work*, 29, pp. 147-158.

Ramu, G.N. (1988). Martial roles and power: Perception and reality in an urban setting. *Journal of Comparative Family Studies*, 19(2), pp.207-228.

Ross, A.D. (1961). The Hindu family in its urban setting. Delhi: Oxford University Press.

Saradamani, K. (ed.). (1985). Women, work and society: Proceeding of the 1st symposium. Calcutta: Indian Statistical Institute.

Saraswati, T.S. and Pai, S. (1997). Socialization in Indian context. In *Asian Perspectives in Psychology*, H. Kao. and D. Singha (eds.), pp.74 and 92. New Delhi: Sage Methodology Series.

Singh, L.B., Singh, A.K. (1996). Alienation: A symptomatic reaction of educated employed youth in India. *International Journal of Psychology*, 31(2), pp. 101-110.

Singhal, R. and Mishra, G. (1994). Achievement goals: A situational contextual analysis. *International Journal of Intercultural Relations*, 18(2), pp. 239-258.

Sinha, D. (1984). Some recent changes in the Indian family and their implications. *Journal of Family Welfare*, XXXIV (4), pp. 3-12.

Sinha, D. (1988). The family scenario of developing country fits implications for mental health. *Health and Cross-cultural Psychology: Towards Applications* (pp. 48-70). Sage Publications.

Sinha, M. (1999). Reflections. *Social Welfare*, Vol. 45, No.11, February.

Sivamurthy, M. (1988). Household headship in India: Trends and implications. *The Journal of Family Welfare*, 34(4), pp. 3-11.

Sriram, R. and Bakshi, A. (1988). Family violence against married women. *Social Change*, 18(3), pp. 45-48.

3

Marriage

Its Impact on Family Life

Dibya Prava Pradhan

Marriage is an institution that regulates the relationship between a man and woman, which provides for the creation of a family. Until recent times Hindu marriages in India have been viewed as sacramental and irrevocable. There are changes in Indian marriages today that are affecting family life in many ways. This chapter is an attempt to understand the historical basis of Indian marriages, forms, functions, preparations, rituals, and ceremonies associated with marriage, including achieving harmony and happiness in marriage and family life. It also offers some suggestions for needed changes in marriage and family life in contemporary Indian society in light of traditional views and current realities.

Historical Background

India is a vast and ancient country. The dawn of Indian civilization dates to a remote past. Since then different races have come and settled here and contributed to the formation of a varied and composite culture. This cultural heritage has been manifested in different social customs and institutions. Marriage is one such institution, and it is important to examine marriage in Indian society in its diverse forms. Experts have defined marriage in a variety of ways. According to Hurton and Hunt (1968), "marriage is the approved social pattern whereby two or more persons establish a family". Westermark (1936) defined marriage as the "...more or less stable connection between male and female, lasting beyond the mere act of propagation till after the birth of offspring". Lowie (1950) saw marriage as "a contract for production and maintenance of children", whereas Lundberg notes that "marriage consists of the rules and regulations which define the rights, duties and privileges of husband and wife, with respect to each other". In Mazumdar's (1966) view, marriage is a socially sanctioned union of males and females. It has been devised by societies throughout the ages as a means for sanctioning the union or mating of men and women for purposes of (a) establishing a household; (b) entering into sexual relations; (c) procreating; and (d) providing care for the offspring. Finally, according to Anderson and Parker (1964), "marriage is the sanctioning by a society of a durable bond between one or more males and one or more females established to permit sexual intercourse for the implied purpose of parenthood". From these definitions, we understand that some writers have put an emphasis on marriage as a social pattern for establishing family, some as a stable connection between male and female, some as a contract for production and maintenance of children, and some as rules and regulations defining the rights and duties of the wife and husband. In India, marriage is considered a holy performance of religious duties. The union of the two souls is sacred and indissoluble in life and continues even after death. Marriage is considered a union between two families rather than two individuals. It is an important event in the life of every person, irrespective of caste, creed, religion or social status.

For every Hindu, marriage is considered to be one of the essential *sanskaras* (sacraments); thus, every Hindu must marry.

According to Mannu (IX-26), "to be the mothers were women created and to be fathers men, the 'Veda' ordained that 'dharma' must be practiced by man together with his wife". He further states (IX-46) that, "He only is a perfect man who consists of his wife, himself and his off-spring". Similarly, Mahabharata (*Adi Parva*, 74: 40-41) declares that, "Those who have wives can fulfill their due obligations in this world, those who have wives truly have a family life, those who have wives can be happy, those who have wives can lead a full life".

It is established from the religious texts that for Hindus, marriage is a sacramental union. In India, according to traditional Hindu law, marriage is a sacrament and not a civil contract. It is a *sanskara* or purificatory ceremony obligatory for every Hindu. The Hindu religious books have accepted marriage as a duty because an unmarried man cannot perform some of the most important religious rites. For every Hindu, marriage is obligatory, for having a son to repay the paternal debt to perform a *yajna* and other religious and spiritual duties, along with the life partner (Dharmapatni or Sahadharmini), for which marriage is the first and essential step.

The institution of Hindu marriage occupies a unique place in the life of every Hindu. It binds the wife and husband to perform *dharma* and to fulfill other duties concerning physical, social, and spiritual requirements. Hindu marriage strengthens spiritual advancements. It has social value besides being the source of individual pleasure. Grahastha ashrama (household life) is the basis of the 'ashrama' scheme and marriage is the foundation of grahastha ashrama. Procreation is considered as necessary to pay one's debt towards parents as well as ancestors in the family. Moreover, from this point of view, Hindu marriage has a very important place without which a man cannot advance towards the attainment of *moksha* (liberation of soul). Because of this unique feature, it has been said that probably no other people have endeavored to idealize the institution of marriage as much as Hindus have done. Even in the patriarchal society of the Rig-Vedic Hindus, marriage was considered a sacramental union. Thus, not only historically, but even, today, most Hindus regard their marriage as a holy sacrament.

Hindu Marriage

Marriage is essential in life. But, with the change of time and trend of the society it has developed in different forms. In Vedic times marriage was left to the choice of the persons concerned. Then, there came the practice of giving dowry in marriages. In later Samhitas there is clear evidence of giving a bride price. In Smriti eight kinds of marriages are recognized, out of which only four are said to have a religious character. These types of marriage are highlighted as follows:

1. *Brahma marriage*: This form of marriage is considered to be the highest and most valued in Indian society. In this system, the bride and bridegroom first receive the required education in ashrama. Secondly, if they agree to get married, the father of the bride gives his daughter to the bridegroom as a gift. Under this system, the girl is decorated with clothes and ornaments and is offered to a learned and gentle bridegroom. Even now, this form of marriage is most prevalent.
2. *Prajapatya marriage*: In this form of marriage the father offers his daughter to the bridegroom and the couple is blessed with the enjoyment of married bliss and fulfillment of *dharma*. This custom is more or less similar to Brahma marriage.
3. *Arsha marriage*: This was a common form of marriage in ancient India. In this the father offered his daughter to a rishi in exchange for a cow or bull and some clothes. These articles did not signify any price but symbolized the promise of the rishi to lead a domestic life.
4. *Daiva marriage*: Also an older form of marriage, in which the girl was well adored or decorated. The bride was then offered to the priest (*pundit* or *purohit*) who conducted a *yajna* function. The man not conducting the function of a

purohit or *pundit* was not offered the bride. Thus, the performance of certain functions was necessary for this type of marriage.

5. *Asura marriage*: In this type of marriage the bridegroom had to pay the bride price to her father or guardian in exchange for their daughter. There was no fixed limit to the price. The amount depended upon the status of the bride's family. The money was regarded as the value of sacrifice by the girl's parents. One such example was marriage between Pandu and Madri.
6. *Gandharva marriage*: The basis of this form of marriage was mutual affection and love of the intending bride and bridegroom and not money or gift. The example of this is the marriage of king Dushyanta with Shakuntala. In this form of marriage, religious ceremony can be performed after the sexual relationship between the two lovers has been developed. In Kamasutra this form of marriage has been categorized as an ideal type of marriage. According to Taittariya Samhita, the nomenclature of this form of marriage is after the Gandharvas among whom this type of marriage was prevalent.
7. *Rakshasa marriage*: This form of marriage was named because of its degenerated types and was prevalent in the age when women were considered to be the prize of a man. By invading, bridegrooms took the brides forcibly after killing or wounding her relatives. It was forcible abduction of females.
8. *Pishacha marriage*: This was the most degenerate type of marriage in which a man entered into a sexual relationship when the woman was sleeping, drunk or even unconscious.

In sum, most of these marriage types are rare if not non-existent in India today. However, all these forms cover every mode of Hindu matrimonial union between a man and woman. Of the above eight the first four are ancestral customs of old and are approved by the Dharmasastra.

In addition to the above, we may also classify some other forms of marriage, such as polygamy, polyandry, monogamy, companionate and experimental, prevalent in Indian society on the basis of numeric variation.

Polygamy

In this type of marriage a man marries more than one woman. Polygamy is a broader term and includes polyandry and polygamy. In India it is found among both Hindus and Muslims. Some of the Muslim and Hindu rulers of India were known to have a large number of wives. Under this type of marriage the husband cannot pay full attention to each of his wives, and it may result in jealousy, enmity and quarrel.

Polyandry

In this form of marriage one woman marries more than one man at a given time. This type of marriage is widespread only in few areas in Asia, including Tibet, the Malay Peninsula, Polynesia, among the Todas of Malabar, the Singhalese, and the Mundas. In Hindu mythology it is found among the five brothers called Pandavas who all had the same wife. Polyandry in India is of two types: (a) *fraternal polyandry*: In this, a woman is regarded as the wife of all brothers. The children are treated as the offspring of the eldest brother. (b) *non-fraternal polyandry*: In this, it is not necessary that all husbands of a woman should be brothers. The woman lives with her different husbands in turns, and while she is with one of them, the rest have no right to her. If a child is born, any husband can be chosen as the child's social parent through a special ritual.

Monogamy

In this type of marriage, one man is married to one woman at a time. A man cannot marry another woman and vice versa while the wife/husband is alive. This is the most acceptable and common form of marriage in India today. It also has more advantages than any other form of marriage. In this system there is sincere devotion and maximum affection given to everyone in the family.

Companionate Marriage

This marriage is based on an understanding between two persons that the marriage may be dissolved by mutual consent as long as they do not have offspring. One of the disadvantages of this system is that it may lead to quick divorce. It may also make it easier for people to marry only on the basis of sex.

Experimental Marriage

This type of marriage has been referred to as cohabitation. It allows two people to test their compatibility before they settled down as permanent life partners. This approach is thought to reduce the chances of divorce. By cohabitating they come to know each other intimately, including their vices and virtues. They may enter into marriage permanently if they feel that they have compatible personalities, lifestyles, values, and goals. However, cohabitation may not be a microcosm of real life and may include a set of rules and expectations that are far different than marriage itself.

Muslim Marriage

Muslims also emphasize the necessity of married life and its benign influence. Islam is one of the four scriptural religions that was brought into India and has contributed notably to Indian culture and civilization. However, the institution of marriage among Muslims is strikingly different from that of Hindus.

The Quran regulates marriage laws for Muslims throughout the world. It sets a Muslim marriage as a contract entered into primarily for procreation. This concept of marriage differs considerably from the Hindu concept of marriage, which again, views marriage as more of a sacrament. Following are the criteria for a valid Muslim marriage:

1. *Competence of parties*: The bride and bridegroom must be sound in body and mind and shall not have entered into any illegitimate affiliations. Muslim law also contains a provision for a boy and girl below the age of 15 years. Here, the consent of their respective guardians is necessary. Marriages of minors without adult consent are held as void. Marriages can still be valid apart from any religious ceremony being performed.
2. *Proposal and acceptance*: As in a contract, in a Muslim marriage, the proposal and acceptance must be carried on in the same meeting between both parties. The proposer must put the proposal of marriage either before two males or before one male and two females. In case, the proposal is made in one meeting but acceptance is granted in another, such a marriage is invalid. The two persons before whom the marriage is proposed act as witnesses. If the witnesses are absent, marriage becomes irregular but not void. But, the practice is different among Shia Muslims where the presence of witnesses is not necessary.
3. *Marital capacity of the parties, i.e., the bride and bridegroom:* Parties must have the mental capacity to understand the marital contract and the purpose and importance of marriage. Mentally deficient individuals are not permitted to enter into the marriage contract.
4. *Absence of certain impediments*: In order to void a Muslim marriage, the contract should be agreed upon in the absence of certain impediments. These impediments are of two types. The presence of some impediments makes a marriage void, whereas others are totally prohibited and their presence makes a marriage irregular but not void.

On the following grounds, a Muslim marriage becomes void:

1. Polygamy of the female
2. Marriage with near relatives
3. Marriage with idol-worshipers

Likewise, on the following grounds, a Muslim marriage becomes irregular:

1. Marriage of male with the filth woman
2. Marriage with follower of other religion
3. Marriage performed in the absence of witnesses

Christian Marriage

Christianity is another prevalent religion in India. It was brought to India in two main movements separated by more than a millennium. The first movement occurred in the early centuries after Christ when Christian travelers came and settled in Kerala State. They made converts among the inhabitants and established Christian faith. The second wave began in the 16th century when Europeans seized political control over trade centers in India and eventually over the whole country. They brought with them their traditions and social customs, including Christian beliefs and practices. Although marriage is not an essential condition for a Christian, marriage among Christians around the world and in India is the norm. The purposes of marriage among Christians are:

1. To regulate and control sexual impulses
2. To ensure healthy procreation
3. To develop mutual love among men and women
4. To reflect the relationship between Christ and his universal Church

Many Christian priests regard the institution of marriage as a blessing from God. The establishment of family is thus an important objective of the Christian marriage. A Christian marriage is not merely a civil contract like the Muslim marriage; rather, it is a religious sacrament as among Hindus, which binds the husband and wife to lead a united life throughout the trials and tribulations of life. Christian marriage provides flexibility as far as the choice of life partner is concerned. A great deal of freedom is given to both boys and girls in choosing their life companions. The settlement of Christian marriage is not like the arranged marriages among

Hindus; rather, it springs from mutual understanding of love and affection. In many cases, a long period of courtship between spouses precedes to final settlement of marriage, and during this period both the partners try to understand each other and find learn more about their partner. In the Christian system, only blood relations may prevent marriage to solemnize. Christians are free to marry anyone except a close blood relative (i.e., brother, sister, nephew, niece, first cousin). Love holds a crucial place in a Christian marriage. Most Christian marriages take place within the confines of the local church where a priest performs the marriage rites in the presence of family members and friends.

In India, on an appointed day, both the parties belonging to two sides gather in church and exchange finger rings, coconut and money as a symbol of their expression of the acceptance of marriage. The bridegroom's parents host a feast in honor of the other party. Now, the betrothed bride and bridegroom are free to meet each other, but they are not yet expected to enter into sexual relations.

The church enters the picture again when, three weeks before the wedding day, a notice is posted in front of the church informing people about the marriage. If anyone has any objection regarding the marriage, they can file a complaint after paying the prescribed fee. If the church upholds any of the objections submitted before it, the proposed marriage cannot take place. If it is not so, a particular day is fixed and the marriage is solemnized. Christians in India differ in their system of marriage from both the Hindus and the Muslims. Unlike the arranged Hindu marriage, the Christian marriage is a regularized type of love marriage. There are some provisions regarding Christian marriage made by the Indian Christian Marriage Act of 1862. It classifies Christians into two groups: those who are entitled to marry, and those who are not entitled to marry.

The Act also gives power to the central as well as state governments to appoint a registrar to formalize (legalize) the marriage; however, a magistrate can also perform the same functions. The rules for solemnization a Christian marriage are listed as follows:

1. A Christian marriage can be solemnized anytime between 7.00 a.m. and 7.00 p.m. (rule 10).
2. Every Christian marriage should be solemnized in a church only (rule 11).
3. Either the bride's party or the bridegroom's party should inform the priest and complete the form as provided in the schedule (rule 12).
4. The marriage should be publicized before it is solemnized. The particular marriage proposal should be put on the notice board every Sunday at least three weeks before the marriage to be solemnized (rule 13).
5. In case the marriage is solemnized at a place other than a church, the registrar should be informed about it, who will publicize the marriage (rule 14).
6. In case either of the individuals marrying is a minor, the registrar should be informed about it (rule 15).
7. Consent of the parents is essential in case of a minor spouse (rule 16).

Thus, every Christian marriage is registered. According to the Christian Marriage Act, there are also some rules regarding marriage for native Christians. These are listed below:

- At the time of marriage the boy should not be less than 15 and the girl less than 13 years of age.
- At the time of marriage no other spouse of either of the parties should be alive.
- There should be at least two witnesses at the time of marriage and the party to marry should take the oath of marriage before the registrar. In case of any violation the defaulter is to be penalized.

In sum, Christian marriages in India are closely linked to the local church and in some ways follow a more formal protocol than either Hindu or Muslim marriages. The actual marriage ceremony tends to be a single and relatively brief event, as opposed to the process followed in a Hindu marriage, which can take place over a period of several days.

Tribal Marriage

Another major segment of the Indian population is the tribal community. Most of the tribals usually live in hilly or forest areas throughout India. Though all of them are known as tribal people, they vary from region to region. Tribal people belong to different sub-castes such as Ho, Santhal, and Munda. Like other communities, marriage among tribal groups occupies a significant place, even though marriage traditions and ceremonies are different across the country. However, some similarities do exist. As a whole, marriage patterns include:

1. *Marriage by service*: In this form of marriage a bridegroom willing to marry a girl renders services to his prospective father-in-law for a period of four to five years. This type of marriage is prevalent among tribes, which are incapable of giving a bride price due to poverty. During the period of service the bride's father offers his daughter in marriage if he is satisfied with the man's services. Otherwise, he replaces him with another young man.
2. *Marriage by capture*: One of the most prevalent ways of procuring a bride is by kidnapping her with the motive of marriage. In this form of marriage, if a young man applies vermilion on the forehead of the bride, she becomes his wife. Excessive bride price is also the cause of such types of practice.
3. *Marriage by purchase*: In the early tribal societies this form of marriage was most prevalent. There is much similarity between this type of tribal marriage and the 'Asura' marriage among Hindus as described in the scriptures. The amount paid is not related as the brideprice but is rather compensation to the bride's parents. Today, the brideprice is becoming so high that only a small number of people in tribal communities can pay it. Because of this, there has been a trend towards other forms of marriage.

4. *Marriage by consent and elopement*: In this form of marriage a girl runs away with a young man after giving consent to marry him. After the marriage is recognized she returns to her parents. No brideprice is paid in this type of marriage. This resembles the 'Gandharva' marriage mentioned in the Hindu scriptures.
5. *Marriage by exchange*: In this custom of marriage, daughters are exchanged. A man gives his daughter for marriage to the son of another man, who in exchange gives his daughter to marry the son of the former.
6. *Marriage by intrusion*: In this system the girl does not come out of the house of her lover after she intrudes, despite the torture and insults she may experience. If she does not leave the house for a long period of time, she is considered to be married to that young man.
7. *Probationary marriage*: In this form, the bridegroom stays in the bride's house for certain period, and if the bride and bridegroom decide to marry during this period, their marriage is solemnized. Otherwise, he has to pay compensation to the bride's parents before leaving the place.
8. *Marriage by test*: Under this system, the bravery of the bridegroom is tested and the marriage performed only after he qualifies. In Hinduism, this can be illustrated by the marriage of Draupadi after Arjuna passed the test.
9. *Sorrrate*: In this type of marriage one marries the unmarried sister of his deceased wife.
10. *Levirate*: In this form the woman marries the younger brother of her deceased husband.

Functions of Marriage

It is true that marriage is an important event in one's life, it has also tremendous influence on individual health and well-being. This is because marriage serves a number of vital functions, including the following:

1. *It regulates the sex life of individuals*: Marriage is a powerful instrument for regulating the sex life of an individual.

Sexual impulses are powerful throughout a considerable period of life. They need to be controlled and regulated to avoid confusion and disorder in the society. Marriage is the safest and most suitable forum in which sexual relations can take place.

2. *It contributes to healthy social relationships:* Incest taboos exist in most societies. They support healthy family boundaries and procreation. In the absence of such taboos, relationships in the family would become confused, and the organizational and functional efficiency of the family is lost. Most societies around the world also have values and norms, which discourage extra-marital and pre-marital sexual relationships.
3. *Marriage leads to the establishment of family:* Sexual satisfaction offered by marriage typically results in self-perpetuation. It is in this close knit unit that children are born and brought up. The marital relationship has an enormous influence on the development of children. Inheritance and succession follow the rule of descent.
4. *It provides economic cooperation:* Marriage makes division of labor possible on the basis of one's biological sex. Partners distribute and divide work and then perform it. In both rural and urban areas of India one may observe divisions of labor based partly on sex, with an increased number of women working outside the home in multiple environments.
5. *It contributes to emotional and intellectual stimulation of life partners:* Marriage brings life partners together and helps them develop a more intense love and affection towards each other. It deepens their emotions and strengthens the companionship between two people. It also helps them learn from each other and develop an intellectual cooperation.
6. *It aims at social solidarity (unity):* Marriage not only brings two individuals of the opposite sex together, but also their

extended family members. Friendship between groups is reinforced through marriage. It is often suggested that by encouraging marriage between different groups, castes, races, religions, and cultural and linguistic communities, we can establish social and cultural solidarity in society. It is possible to minimize the social distances between groups and strengthen their communal spirit.

Preparation for Marriage

Marriage at the right time and with the right person is very important. However, two people must also be prepared for this monumental event. Although the couple may be very much in love and appear to be compatible, the question remains whether they are socially and emotionally mature enough for marriage, and that they have the knowledge, skills, and individual qualities to make their marriage happy and satisfying. Some of these skills and characteristics include empathy and a lack of self-centeredness, good overall physical and mental health, a readiness for sexual exclusiveness, positive parental role modeling (both past and present), and a willingness to take on the many responsibilities of supporting a family and being a loving and supportive spouse.

There is also a circumstantial preparedness of marriage. Some of these include financial security, family and parental support (both emotional and sometimes economic, the maintenance of clear boundaries (i.e., psychological, emotional, and to a certain extent social) between one's new marriage and family and one's family-of-origin, and timing of the marriage and the establishment of a family in the lives of the individuals. History has shown, probably in most cultures of the world, that someone can marry the 'right' person but perhaps at the 'wrong' time in their lives. For instance, an ill-timed marriage can occur because the couple is not ready economically, or in terms of personal maturation and life situation (e.g., one or both of them still completing their studies).

Selection of Life Partner

The selection of mates in Indian society is generally made by parents or elders. It is widely believed that these individuals have the life experience to make wise and careful decisions for these younger adults. However, some have contended that, in making the selection of mates, parents are often moved more by their own caprices and personal desires rather than by that which is in the best interest of their child. Moreover, the opinions and desires of the adult child are frequently ignored by parents and other family members. Parents may force upon the girl someone who she does not like at all, or upon the boy a woman whom he might have despised. Indeed, sometimes, parents in India encourage or demand the marriage of their son or daughter to one who is not a suitable match on biological or psychological grounds, but whose status and wealth would add greatly to the family's prestige. It is, therefore, recommended that parents, before contracting a marriage, should consult their sons or daughters and make known the reasons for their choice. It is also important that parents secure the approval of the choice of mate by their son or daughter so that the marriage is regulated by some degree of choice rather than by coercion.

Today, in India, there is among young adults a strong desire for (and expectation of) a perfect marriage. The vision of the perfect marriage entertained by young people is completely unrealistic. They want their partner to be beautiful and their relationship to be characterized by unmitigated love, devotion, and fidelity as well as comradeship, emotional expressiveness, and total openness. Further, young adults want to make sure that marriage gives them everything they expect and need, and that in no way it stifles their personality. They forget that there are natural shortcomings in any human relationship. Before two people agree to unite themselves in the bond of marriage, they must be ready to commit to something larger than themselves, and something that in many ways requires a loss of the self – the institution of marriage.

Arranged Marriages in India

Parents generally arrange the marriage of their adult children in the vast majority of cases in India even today, often with the assistance of marriage bureaus. Some of them insist on using the horoscope in selecting the most appropriate mate for their children. Here, they follow certain age-old principles of matching by following ten principles, such as: dasa melaka (like rasi), tara, nadi, guna, barna, barga, mandala, and so forth. *Gotra* (like Nagesha, Bharadwaja, etc.) is another aspect taken into consideration while searching for the match. For instance, two persons of the same *gotra* are forbidden to marry. If someone appears to be a good match for their son or daughter, then family members visit one another's home and conduct an interview. Generally, the boy is expected to go with his parents to the girl's house. After the interview, if the boy's side approves of the relationship, they write to the girl's parents. The girl's side may respond positively or negatively. If both accept the proposed match, further talks are held to finalize the details, such as venue, conduct of the marriage, and sharing of expenses for the wedding ceremony. These negotiations are vital, and many weddings are not settled because of disagreements that occur at this stage. Generally, most of the expenses for the wedding are to be taken care of by the girl's side of the family, and as mentioned previously, a demand for dowry has become the practice among many greedy parents. Once all of the aspects of this negotiation phase of mate selection are agreed upon, the girl's parents have to arrange for the wedding at mutually suitable place and on a mutually acceptable date. In addition, there is a ceremony of engagement when the settlement of marriage is confirmed. However, Indian youth in contemporary society often prefer to make their own marital choice for a mate based on love, with their parents' and family's blessing, rather than have an arranged marriage *per se*. These marriages are sometimes referred to as love marriages or free choice marriages.

Free Choice Marriages in India

Many free choice marriages in India today contain no religious ceremony and are only registered in the local government office. Moreover, some love marriages are settled on their own, generally without the consent of the parents. However, these marriages are comparatively few. In India, love marriages have generally not been successful. The romantic fallacy brings many lovers together these days because of less parental control in the choice of mates and greater freedom of choice. These changes can, to some extent, be attributed to an ever-present democracy and market-driven economy, and other social forces such as emancipation of women and increased nucleation in the family. Movement towards equality of the sexes in Indian society has played a major role in both personal and marital choice, especially among more educated families. However, a marriage which is based exclusively upon the vagaries of romantic idealism without consideration of money, social position, cultural dissimilarities, and parental objections, faces a tremendous handicap from its very beginning. Many young men and women are convinced that romantic happiness is the sole criterion of marriage. But, when the romantic attraction starts to fade and reality sets in, many of these love marriages become vulnerable. The incidence of conflict and unhappiness in these modern love marriages is believed to be relatively high.

Marriage Rituals and Ceremonies

Before the marriage is legally confirmed, certain ceremonies must first be performed. These ceremonies differ from place to place and community to community. Hindu marriages, while often playful and joyous occasions, are also serious, complicated, and often lengthy events.

Traditional Hindu wedding customs, or *vivaha*, date back 3,500 years. Each ceremony contains a deep philosophical meaning and purpose. The *vivaha* is performed in Sanskrit, one of the world's most ancient surviving languages. Marriage in the Hindu religion is the 13th of the 16 ceremonies in a person's life. It is a sacrament and as such is solemnized in accordance with the Vedas – the holy scripture of the Hindu religion. Because people's wealth and status differ and every state within India has its own traditions, languages, and manner of dress, marriage customs and ceremonies also vary. The Hindu marriage ceremony can last for hours, days or even weeks. Although the wedding itself is held on one day, there are a number of ceremonies that are usually held on separate days preceding the wedding. After the preliminary arrangements the majority of the wedding ceremonies will take place in a *mandap* (the four pole canopy at center stage). The sacred fire in the *mandap* symbolizes not only the illumination of the mind (knowledge and happiness) but is also a clean and pure witness to the ceremony as it progresses.

The ceremony itself is a collection of rituals performed by the bride, bridegroom, and their respective parents and close relatives. The priest chants *mantras*. He will also uses the following items in this ceremony specially collected for this purpose: fresh flowers to signify beauty; coconut to signify fertility; rice, jaggery and other grains to signify the food necessary for sustenance of human life; *ghee* (purified butter) to feed the sacred fire; and *kumkum* (vermilion) or red powder placed on the bride's forehead to signify good luck and to say that her soulmate (husband) is with her.

Major Stages in the Hindu Marriage Ceremony

Worship of Lord Ganesh

The wedding day starts with a prayer invoking Lord Ganesh, whose divine grace dispels all evils and promotes a successful and peaceful completion of the ceremony.

Grahashanti (worship to the nine planets)

This ritual is a prayer to the nine planets of our solar system. Ancient Indian scriptures indicate that various celestial bodies have an influence on the destiny of every individual. The effects of the nine planets are considered to be the most profound in this respect. During this puja the gods associated with these planets are asked to infuse courage, peace of mind and inner strength to the bride and groom to help them endure life's sufferings.

The Welcome

When the bridegroom arrives at marriage *mandap* (pandal), the father of the bride welcomes him by offering garland, applying sandal paste on the forehead and washing the right foot of the bridegroom with milk and honey either himself or by barber associated in the function. Then, the bridegroom is escorted to the *mandap* holding a new white cloth over his head.

Arrival of the Bride

The bride is escorted to the *mandap* by her maternal uncle, cousin sisters, sister-in-law (brother's wife) and friends.

Vagdana (oral promise)

In the presence of the people gathered for marriage, the names, *gotras* and *pravaras* of the bride and bridegroom are announced along with proclamation that they are ready for marriage. This is also known as 'sankalpa'.

Kanyadaan

Consent of the parents is obtained for the wedding to proceed. The bride's parents give their daughter to the groom by putting the bride's right hand on his hand (*hasta melap*, joining of hands) while reciting a sacred verse. The elders of the house place an auspicious white cotton cord around the couple's shoulders to protect them from evil influences. This also symbolizes the couple's bond. The groom holds the bride's hand and they both take vows to love, cherish and protect each other throughout life.

Ganthibandhan (tying the knot)

The priest ties the wedding knot as a symbol of the permanent union between the bride and the groom as husband and wife.

Agnipuja (evocation of the holy fire)

The priest sets a small fire. *Agni* (fire) is the mouth of Vishnu and symbolizes the illumination of mind, knowledge, and happiness. The remainder of the ceremony is conducted around the fire.

Laja Homa (putting puffed rice into the sacred fire)

Three obligations are offered to the sacred fire. The brother of the bride puts puffed rice into the bride's hand. *Mantras* are chanted. The bride prays to Yama, the God of death, to grant long life, health, happiness, and prosperity to the bridegroom.

Mangalfera (walking around the fire)

The couple walks around the sacred fire four times. This symbolizes obstacles in life that they will overcome together. These four rounds stand for four basic human goals, which are:

Dharma - righteousness
Artha - monetary accomplishment
Kama - energy and passion in life
Moksha - liberation from everything in life

Saptapadi (seven steps)

The bride and groom take seven steps together around the fire, facing the north. It is said in Hindu mythology that if two people walk seven steps together, then, they will remain lifelong friends. They exchange sacred vows at the beginning of each encircling walk. At the end of each walk, the bride's brother signifying wealth and prosperity fills the open palms of the bride with puffed rice. The seven steps and their promises are:

1. Let us take the first step to provide for our household – keeping a pure diet and avoiding those things that might harm us.

2. Let us take the second step to develop our physical, mental, and spiritual powers.
3. Let us take the third step to increase our wealth by righteous and proper means.
4. Let us take the fourth step to acquire knowledge, happiness, and harmony by mutual love, respect, and trust.
5. Let us take the fifth step so that we may be blessed with strong, virtuous, and heroic children.
6. Let us take the sixth step for self-restraint and longevity.
7. Let us take the seventh step to be true companions and remain lifelong partners by this wedlock.

Legally, the marriage is now final and binding. Before the seventh step is taken marriage is incomplete and may be revoked. Thus, the performance of 'saptapadi' is an essential condition of Hindu marriage.

Soubhagya Chinha (blessing the bride)

The bridegroom blesses the bride by putting *kumkum* or *sindoor* (vermilion powder) at the parting of her hair or on her forehead and by giving her a sacred necklace (*mangal sutra*). The *mangal sutra* represents the couple's togetherness, love, and sacred union.

Aashirvad (blessing)

Then, the priest blesses the Nedded couple. Flower petals and rice are given to the guests to shower them on the couple with blessings. After this, the ceremony comes to an end. Guests are invited to enjoy a sumptuous meal with the newly weds.

Vidai (bride's departure)

The farewell to the bride by her family and friends is a very emotional episode. The bride leaves her parent's home with tears of joy and sorrow to begin a new life with her husband and his family.

Sacred Beliefs and Values in Hindu Marriage

1. The marital bond is said to be indissoluble and irrevocable. Nobody can dare to dissolve or distort it. Both the bride and bridegroom are bound to each other until death. The belief is that the wife is also supposed to be with her husband even after death. Each partner is to adjust and compromise with each other in all aspects of their life.
2. Marriage is a social duty to family and also to the community.
3. The ideal of 'pativrataya' (devotion towards husband) associated in marriage.

The wife is expected to be devoted to her husband alone. It implies that fidelity and service to the husband are the main purpose of life. As a river merges into the ocean, the wife merges fully with her husband. This means that she must sacrifice her life to her husband even after his death. For Hindus, women aspire to marry. They know that unmarried women, especially as they get older, always face hardship in Indian society.

Making Adjustments in Marriage

Adjustments in marriage are inevitable and necessary. The relationship that a man has with a woman in marriage is perhaps the highest form of relationship because it involves physical, emotional, spiritual, and social aspects of life. Marital adjustment is an adjustment of two personalities from different families and often socio-cultural backgrounds. Koos (1958) indicates that "...adjustment in marriage is the achievement of the expectations the couple have of their marriage". According to Burgess and Locke (1950), "the basic factors in marital adjustment are personality characteristics, cultural background, social participation, economic status, response pattern, and sex desires". Kapur (1972) notes that marital adjustment is that state of relationship in marriage in which there is an overall feeling in husband and wife of happiness and satisfaction with their marriage and with each other. These days, however, there are greater problems of adjustment in marriage than perhaps ever before in Indian society, and for a variety of reasons.

Many tensions in marriage arise out of the personality structures of husbands and wives that make them more or less incompatible at the outset. A couple's sources of conflict may include differences in basic temperament, clashing philosophies of life (disparity of values), contrary personal behavior patterns, psychopathic tendencies, cultural differences, differences in social status, ill-health, problems with in-laws, and disparities in age. However, one of the major adjustment problems in marriage has to do with the couple's financial situation.

Many couples find financial adjustments very difficult, particularly if the wife was working when they were married and then stopped with the arrival of the first child. Not only is their total income reduced, but also the husband's earnings must now cover a wider area of expenses. The couple's financial situation can pose a threat to their marital adjustments in two important areas. First, friction may develop if the wife expects her husband to share the workload. During the early years of marriage, when the expensive labor saving devices and domestic help are most needed, the family usually cannot afford such luxuries and the wife may want her husband to help share the burden of running the home. This frequently causes friction, especially when the man considers homemaking woman's work. The second common threat has to do with the couple's desire to acquire material possessions as a stepping stone towards social mobility and a symbol of the family's success. If the husband is unable to provide a certain standard of living for his wife and family, frictional attitudes may develop. Marital tensions can also arise when the wife comes from an upper class family and is not able to adjust to a lower level of living.

Another adjustment problem in marriage is sexual adjustment. In some cases this is the root cause of crisis in marriage. Usually, the couple has had less preliminary experience related to this adjustment than to others, and they may be unable to adapt to each other's sexual needs and desires. If they have difficulty in achieving sexual harmony, they may also find it hard to create a good relationship at the emotional, mental or spiritual level.

Parents are often imbued with personal ambitions and the desire for their children's happiness, and consequently they often insist upon imposing their decisions upon the reluctant children. They are of the opinion that the daughter-in-law is too extravagant, uncooperative or unsuited to her task as a wife or mother. Parents and in-laws can criticize in such countless ways, which may play havoc in marital life. In India, due to the prevalence of joint family system, interference from in-laws is pervasive. Their narrow mindedness, uncertain temper, and involvement in the couple's affairs tend to increase the intensity of conflict. Some married women have even committed suicide because of irreconcilable differences with their in-laws.

A final adjustment that has to be made in marriage is when both husbands and wives have their own careers and wish to work outside the home. These dual-career marriages can be a breeding ground for jealously, resentment, and unhealthy competition. These couples need to have a great deal of flexibility, understanding, cooperation, and support if they are going to cultivate a happy and satisfying marriage while also maintaining a career life.

Conclusion

Change is the only constant in the world today, and it is happening at an ever-increasing pace in Indian society. Many inventions and discoveries in the field of science and technology, facilitation of education for all, advancement in information technology and mass media, widespread industrialization, expanded trade and commerce, women's liberation, the acceptance of democratic ideals, and the impact of western civilization – all have had an immeasurable influence on marriage and family life in India. Accordingly, the age-old notions and values regarding marriage have undergone a sea change. Thus, every effort must be made to enable young men and women to meet life with more adequate knowledge and resources., especially with regard to the establishment and maintenance of their own marriages and families. This can best occur through education on a widespread scale. In earlier times people in trouble would go to their parents, teachers, gurus, relatives or intimate friends for comfort and enlightenment. But, today, young people struggle to begin and maintain happy homes with a sturdy sense of independence. As the generation gap increases, young people feel that their elders are incapable of understanding their particular problems. However, all family members, no matter how young or old, have much to offer one another. And, each of them faces their own unique set of problems and challenges at each phase of life. Hence, family members, supported by their local communities, are in the best position to remedy their own ills and prevent difficulties before they have a chance to develop. Truly, therefore, it is time for family life education in India to "come of age".

References

Anderson, P. and Parker, E. (1964). *Society*, New York: Van Nosterdand Company.

Bhushan, V. and Sachdeva, D.R. (1995). *An Introduction to Sociology*, Kitab Mahal.

Burgess, E.W. and Locke, H.J. (1950). *The Family: From Institution to Companionship*, New York: American Book Co.

Das, G. (1988). *Indian Society and Social Institutions*, King Books.

Devadas, R.P. and Jaya, N. (1984). *A Textbook on Child Development*, Macmillan India Limited.

Fernandes, M. (1997). 'Marriage: A Lifelong Partnership' in *Alive*.

Hurlock, E.B. (1985). *Developmental Psychology: A Life-Span Approach*, Tata McGraw-Hill Publishing Company Ltd.

Hurton, C. and Hunt, A. (1968). *Sociology*, New York: McGraw Hill.

Kapadia, K.M. (1966). *Marriage and Family in India*, Bombay: Oxford University Press.

Kapur, P. (1972). *Marriage and Working Women in India*, New Delhi: Vikas Publishing House Pvt. Ltd.

Kishan, K. (1997). 'Fitness For Marriage' in *Alive*.

Koos, E.L. (1958). *Marriage*, New York: Henry Holt and Co.

Landis, P.H. (1954). *Your Marriage and Family Living*, New York: McGraw-Hill Book Co.

Lowie, R.H. (1950). *Social Organisation*, London: Routledge and Kegan Paul.

Lundberg, G.A., Schrag, C.C., and Larsen, Otto, N. (1958). *Sociology*, New York: Harper and Brothers.

Madan, G.R. (1984). *Indian Social Problems: Social Disorganization and Reconstruction*, New Delhi: Allied Publishers Limited.

Manu (Translated by Ramshankar Ray) (1927). *Manu Samhita or Manu Smriti*. Cuttack: Dharma Grantha Store.

Mazumdar, H.T. (1966). *The Grammar of Sociology*, Asia Publishing House.

Malinowski, B. (1932). *Crime and Custom in Savage Society*, New York: Harcourt Brace.

Mohan, D. (1972). *Pre-marriage Counseling: The Indian Family in the Change and Challenge of the Seventies*, New Delhi: Sterling Publishers.

Pothen, S. (1987). *Divorce: Its Causes and Consequences in Hindu Society*, New Delhi: Vikas Publishing House Pvt. Ltd.

Prabhu, P.N. (1963). *Hindu Social Organization*, (fourth edition), Bombay: Popular Prakashan.

Singh, K. (1998). *Indian Sociology, Society, Social Institutions and Problems.* Lucknow: Prakashan Kendra.

Westermark, E. (1936). *The Future of Marriage in Western Civilization*, London: Mcmillan.

4

Stages and Tasks of the Family Life Cycle

N. Jaya

The family life cycle provides a longitudinal view of family life over the years. It identifies particular problems, potentials, rewards, hazards, vulnerability, and strengths of each phase of family experience from the beginning of family life, till the end of it. Each stage of the family life cycle has certain specific developmental tasks to be performed by members in the family. The successful achievement of the family developmental tasks leads to present satisfaction, approval and success with later family tasks, whereas failure leads to unhappiness in the family, disapproval by the society, and difficulty with later family developmental tasks. Family's function at the frontiers of modern life and an individual pushes his/her way through the wilderness of family confusion and cultural conflict. Thus, understanding the various stages and tasks of family life cycle and successfully navigating the family is a goal worth the struggle.

One frequently quoted definition of family is that it is a unit of people usually related, usually living together, working together to satisfy their necessities, and relating to each other to fulfill their wants. The family is a group of persons united by ties of marriage, blood or adoption, constituting a single household, interacting and intercommunicating with each other in their respective social roles of husband and wife, mother and father, son and daughter, brother and sister, creating and maintaining a common culture (Burgess and Locke, 1953).

The family is a small social unit consisting usually of husband, wife and children, but sometimes excluding one of these members or including grandparents, even non-related friends. The family is the unit which gives an individual strongest sense of community, and which, more than any other institution, lends stability and sincerity to life (McCormack, 1974).

Hence, family has been the chief social institution since time immemorial. Families have survived war, peace, prosperity, panic, depression and recession in various forms and combinations. Although the family today is extremely vulnerable, it is also malleable to withstand the pains of change and stress (Billingsley, 1975). Families cope with the pressures exerted on them by changing to meet new conditions. A family performs the following basic tasks that are essential for its survival and continuity:

1. Providing shelter, food, clothing, health care, etc., for its members.
2. Meeting family expenses, and allocating and sharing such resources as time, space, and objects according to each member's needs.
3. Determining who does what in the management, and care of the home and its members.
4. Assuring each member's socialization through the internalization of increasingly mature roles in the family and beyond.
5. Establishing ways of interacting, communicating, expressing affection and concern.

6. Bearing and rearing children, involving participation of family members appropriately.
7. Relating to school, temple, church, work, community life, in-laws, relatives, guests, friends, mass media, etc.
8. Maintaining motivation, rewarding achievement, meeting personal and family crises, setting attainable goals, and developing family loyalties and values.

All families perform the above basic tasks as long as they live. Each family performs its functions in its own ways, which may differ from those of others. There was a time when family members spent most of their time together. Today, family members are scattered and their work and play activities are more individual than family-based.

Decades ago family members knew what was expected of them and they were specifically prepared for the roles they played. Both men and women had learned their roles in their own homes before they married. Children had their place in the scheme of things and knew what was expected of them from the beginning. The family lived according to relatively rigid rules that were traditionally established and maintained by social and moral pressures of the entire society.

In contemporary society, both men and women, have a wide variety of expectations of one another as their roles have become more complex and flexible. These expectations differ from couple to couple and family to family. When a home is seen as a good place to grow up and not merely as a roof over one's head, life is lived at much deeper level. The potentialities of such a home environment are unlimited, but its problems, especially for transitional generations, are also unlimited.

The Family Life Cycle

There is something predictable about family development that helps an individual to know what to expect from any given family at any given stage. This process in families is similar to that of each individual who grows, develops, and matures with successive changes and readjustment. Hence, families follow a universal sequence of family development. The concept of 'family life cycle' has been vividly described by Duvall (1977) as under:

> The family life cycle, used as a frame of reference, affords a longitudinal view of family life. It is based on the recognition of successive phases and patterns as they occur within the continuity of family living over the years. It opens the way for study for the particular problems and potentials, rewards and hazards, vulnerability and strengths of each phase of family experience from beginning to end.

Families mature as their children grow up through childhood into adolescence, and finally into adulthood and make homes of their own. Families that once expanded to accommodate the requirements of growing children must later contract as they release these same children as young adults. The bustling years when family life runs at a hectic pace eventually give way to the long, slow moving years of the 'empty nest' period when middle aged and aging parents face the latter half of their marriage together as a pair. With the prolongation of life, these later years present new opportunities and problems.

Stages in the Family Life Cycle

The family life cycle, as depicted by Duvall (1977) consists of eight stages. These include:

1. Married couples (without children) – 2 years
2. Child bearing families (oldest childbirth – 30 months) – 2.5 years
3. Families with preschool children (oldest child 2½-6 years) – 3.5 years
4. Families with school-age children (oldest child 6-13 years) – 7 years
5. Families with teenagers (oldest child 13-20 years) – 7 years
6. Families launching young adults (first child gone to last child's leaving home) – 8 years

7. Middle-aged parents (empty nest to retirements) – 15 + years
8. Aging family members (retirement to death of both spouses) – 10 to 15 years

There are also a number of advantages of the family life cycle concept. These include:

(i) Description of life from cradle to the grave.
(ii) Analysis anticipating the possible happenings in later stages in family life.
(iii) Knowledge of a family's position in the life cycle helps in anticipation of vital factors.
(iv) Helps in understanding systematic qualities of the family.
(v) It is possible to study that life is continuous, flowing from one stage to another, without a break/pause.
(vi) Provides advantage point basic to family development study.

Developmental Tasks of the Family Life Cycle

In the family life cycle, each stage has certain developmental tasks to be performed by members of the family. Whatever culture in which an individual grows up, he/she faces the developmental tasks peculiar to it at every stage of life span. According to Havighurst (1953), a developmental task is a task that arises at or near a certain time in the life of an individual, the successful achievement of which leads to one's happiness and to one's success with later tasks, whereas failure leads to unhappiness in an individual, disapproval by society, and difficulty with later tasks. These growth responsibilities are jobs to be done by an individual as he/she develops.

The concept of 'developmental' task satisfies the search for a frame of reference that deals dynamically with the challenges of human development. This framework keeps personal responsibility in the hands of the developing persons, but still allows room for the helping roles that family members, school personnel and community workers might play. The developmental tasks faced by individuals as they progress through the

Table 1

Developmental Tasks of an Individual from Birth to Death

	Infancy (birth to 1 or 2 years)	Early childhood (2-3 to 5-6-7)	Late childhood (5-6-7 to pubescence)	Early adolescence (pubescence to puberty)
1	2	3	4	5
I. Achieving an appropriate dependence indepndence pattern	-Establishing oneself as a very dependent being -Beginning the establishment of self-awareness	-Adjusting to less private attention; -Becoming independent physically (while remaining strongly dependent emotionally)	- Freeing oneself from primary identification with adults	-Establishing one's independence from adults in all areas of behavior
II. Acquiring an appropriate giving receiving pattern of affection	- Developing a felling for affection	- Developing the ability to give affection - Learning to share affection	- Learning to give as much love as one receives, forming friendships with peers	- Accepting oneself as a worthwhile person really worthy of love
III. Relating to changing social groups	-Becoming aware of the alive as against the inanimate and the familiar as against the unfamiliar -Developing a rudimentary social interaction	-Beginning to develop the ability to interact with age mates -Adjusting in the family to expectations it has for the child as a member of the social unit	-Clarifying the adult world as over against the child's world -Establishing peer groupness and learning to belong	-Behaving according to a shifting peer abode

Late adolescence (puberty to early maturity)	Maturity (early to late active adulthood)	Aging (beyond full powers of adulthood through senility)
6	7	8
-Establishing oneself as an independent individual in an adult manner	- Learning to be interdependent-now learning, now succouring others, as need arises - Assisting one's children to become gradually independent and autonomous beings	-Accepting graciously and comfortably the help needed from other as powers fail and dependence becomes necessary
- Building a strong mutual affectional bond with a possible marriage partner	Building and maintaining a strong and mutually satisfying marriage relationship -Establishing wholesome affectional bonds with one's children and grand children -Meeting wisely the new needs for affection of one's own ageing parents -Cultivating meaningfully warm friendships with members of one's own generation	-Facing loss of one's spouse and finding some satisfactory sources of affection previously received from mate -Learning new affectional roles with own children, now mature adults -Establishing ongoing, satisfying affectional patterns with grandchildren and other members of the extended family -Finding and preserving mutually satisfying friendships outside the family circle
- Adopting an adult patterned set of social values by learning a new peer code	-Keeping in reasonable balance activities in the various social, service, political and community groups and causes that make demands on adults -Establishing and maintaining mutually satisfactory relationships with the in law families of spouse and married children	-Choosing and maintaining social activities and functions appropriate to health, energy and interests

Contd...

Contd...

	Infancy (birth to 1 or 2 years)	Early childhood (2-3 to 5-6-7)	Late childhood (5-6-7 to pubescence)	Early adolescence (pubescence to puberty)
1	2	3	4	5
IV. Developing a conscience	-Beginning to adjust to the expectations of others	-Developing the ability to take directions and to be obedient in the presence of authority -Developing ability to be obedient in the absence of authority where conscience substitutes for authority	-Learning more rules and developing true morality	
V. Learning one's psychosocial biological sex role		-Learning to identify with male adult and female adult roles	-Beginning to identify with one's social contemporaries of the same sex	-Strong identification with one's own sex mates -Learning one's role in heterosexual relationships
VI. Accepting and adjusting to a changing body	-Adjusting to adult feeding demands - Adjusting to adult cleanliness demands - Adjusting to adult attitudes towards genital manipulation	- Adjusting to expectations resulting from one's improving muscular abilities - Developing sex modesty		- Reorganising one's thoughts and feelings about oneself in the face or significant bodily changes and their concomitants - Accepting the reality of one's appearance
VII. Managing a changing body and learning new motor patterns	- Developing a physiological equilibrium - Developing eye hand coordination - Establishing satisfactory rhythms of rest and activity	- Developing large muscle control - Learning to coordinate large muscles and small muscles	- Refining and elaborating skill in the use of small muscles	- Controlling and using a new body

Late adolescence (puberty to early maturity)	Maturity (early to late active adulthood)	Aging (beyond full powers of adulthood through senility)
6	7	8
- Learning to verbalize contradictions in moral codes as well as discrepancies between principle and practice, and resolving these problems in a responsible manner	-Coming to terms with the violations of moral codes in the large as well as in the more intimate social scene, and developing some constructive philosophy and method of operation -Helping children to adjust to the expectations of others and to conform to the moral demands of the culture	-Maintaining a sense of moral integrity in the face of disappointments and disillusionment's in life's hopes and dreams
-Exploring possibilities for a future mate and acquiring 'desirability' -Choosing an occupation -Preparing to accept one's future role in manhood or womanhood as responsible citizen of the larger community	-Learning to be a competent husband or wife, and building a good marriage - Carrying a socially adequate role as citizen and worker in the community - Becoming a good parent and grandparent as children arrive and develop	- Learning to live on a retirement income - Being a good companion to an ageing spouse - Meeting bereavement of spouse adequately
- Learning appropriate outlets for sexual drives	-Making a good sex adjustment within marriage -Establishing healthful routines of eating, resting, and working, playing within the pressures of the adult world	- Making a good adjustment to failing powers as ageing diminishes strengths and abilities
	-Learning the new motor skills involved in housekeeping, gardening, sports and other activities expected of adults in the community	- Adapting interests and activities to reserves of vitality and energy of the aging body

Contd...

Contd...

	Infancy (birth to 1 or 2 years)	Early childhood (2-3 to 5-6-7)	Late childhood (5-6-7 to pubescence)	Early adolescence (pubescence to puberty)
1	2	3	4	5
VIII. Learning to understand and control the physical world	- Exploring the physical world	- Meeting adult expectations for restrictive exploration and manipulation of an expanding environment	Learning more realistic ways of studying and controlling the physical world	
IX. Developing an appropriate symbol system and conceptual abilities	- Developing preverbal communication - Developing verbal communication - Rudimentary concept formation	- Improving one's use of the symbol system - Enormous elaboration of the concept pattern	- Learning to use language actually to exchange ideas or to influence one's heaves - Beginning understanding of real casual relations - Making finer conceptual distinctions and thinking reflectively	- Using language to express and to clarify more complex concepts - Moving from the concrete to the abstract and applying general principles to particular
X. Relating oneself to the cosmos		- Developing a genuine, though uncritical, notion about one's place in the cosmos	- Developing a scientific approach	

Late adolescence (puberty to early maturity)	Maturity (early to late active adulthood)	Aging (beyond full powers of adulthood through senility)
6	7	8
	- Gaining intelligent understanding of new horizons of medicine and science sufficient for personal well-being and social competence	- Mastering new awareness and methods of dealing with physical surroundings as and individual with occasional or permanent disabilities
- Achieving the level of reasoning of which one is capable	- Mastering technical symbol systems involved in income tax, social security, complex financial dealings and other contexts familiar to Western man	- Keeping mentally alert and effective as long as is possible through the later years
-Formulating a workable belief and value system	- Formulating and implementing a rational philosophy of life on the basis of adult experience - Cultivating a satisfactory religious climate in the home as the spiritual soil for development of family members	- Preparing for eventual and inevitable cessation of life by building a set of beliefs that one can live and die with in peace

years from birth to death are innumerable. It would be impossible to list all of the growth responsibilities to be achieved by any one person. Yet, there are certain categories of tasks that allow us to catalog the more common developmental tasks within our culture. These are detailed in Table 1.

Family Developmental Tasks

In addition to developmental tasks of individuals in their respectable stages, there are also family developmental tasks. A family developmental task is a growth responsibility that arises at a certain stage in the life of a family, the successful achievement of which leads to present satisfaction, approval and success with later tasks. However, failure to achieve one or more of these tasks leads to unhappiness in the family, disapproval by society, and difficulty with later family developmental tasks (Havighurst, 1953). It is revealing that family development follows an orderly sequential change in growth, development, and dissolution or decline throughout the entire family life cycle. Some of the reasons these tasks are important are listed as follows:

- Keep the family in focus throughout its history.
- See each family member in interaction with all other members.
- Watch the ways in which individuals and the family units influence one another.
- Recognize what a given family is going through at any particular time.
- Highlight critical periods of personal and family growth and development.
- View both the universals and the variations among families.
- Beam in on the ways in which culture and families influence each other.

More specifically, understanding family developmental tasks helps us to:

- Get a broader view of family life than that afforded by experience in any one family.
- Collect the fallacies and distortions that prevail on family tasks.
- Focus on the normal aspects of family living rather than on the atypical, abnormal forms more often reported.
- Recognize the family as the hub of society around which all other institutions and groups have revolved in every culture known to man throughout all of history.
- Learn more about the contribution of family life to human development.
- Keep up with changes in families resulting from their adaptation to changing social conditions.
- Foresee predictable problems and potentials in families as they change in form and function over the years.
- Establish reliable bases for making individual and family decisions about matters that occur and reoccur through out the life span.
- Adopt family plans for future family situations in a given home.

There are also many characteristics of family developmental tasks. Some of these are:

- Basic to a given stage of development in the family life cycle.
- Directed to meet the requisites for family well-being and continuation of life.
- Represent growth responsibilities to be accomplished at each stage to satisfy biological requirements, cultural imperatives and one's own aspirations and values.
- Exert internal pressure on the family to change.
- Changes of family's sense of identity, reputation in community and own aspirations to meet the new challenges as a family unit.
- Shift as the family grows and changes.
- Constantly modified by interplay of forces within and outside the family.

Developmental Tasks of Stage 1: Married Couples

Marriage is a critical transition point for couples. It involves moving on from their families and from the orientation phase of their development to the unfamiliar husband-wife relationship. At this stage, husband and wife concentrate their attention on the interpersonal relationship within the marriage and their major goal of adjustment to life as married partners. The developmental tasks of the young married couple are as follows:

Husband	*Wife*
1. Becoming established in an occupation: —Getting specialized training. —Assuming responsibility for getting and holding job. —Working towards security and advancement in work.	1. Making a home and managing the household: —Getting settled in her home. —Establishing and maintaining household routines. —Learning the many skills of home making and housework.
2. Assuming responsibility for the support of the family: —Earning the family income. —Planning for the long pull of family support through the years.	2. Becoming a financial helpmate in establishing the home: —Working until her husband is established. —Seeing work as secondary and possible intermittent.
3. Establishing mutually satisfying sex relationships: —Awakening his wife's sexuality. —Developing competency as a husband.	3. Becoming a satisfying sex partner: —Learning her sex role as wife. —Responding effectively and participating in their mutual fulfillment.
4. Assuming hostess and companionship roles as a married woman: —Planning for recreational activities as a couple. —Accepting and refusing social invitations. —Entertaining their friends, associates and families.	4. Becoming domesticated as a married man: —Sharing leisure time with his wife. —Developing mutual interests. —Cultivating joint activities. —Getting into the young married set.

Family Developmental Tasks of the Married Couple

A couple must establish their marriage as a functioning unit of society if they are to continue as a couple. The family developmental tasks of the married couple include:

(a) Finding, furnishing and maintaining their first home.
(b) Establishing mutually satisfactory ways of supporting themselves.
(c) Allocating responsibilities that each partner is able and willing to assume.
(d) Establishing mutually acceptable personal, emotional, and sexual roles.
(e) Interacting with in-laws, relatives, and community.
(f) Planning for possible children.
(g) Maintaining couple motivation and morale.

Finding, Furnishing and Maintaining Home

Finding and furnishing a suitable home to call their own is an exciting but difficult task for many first married couples as their income will be lower now than later in the family cycle. Their desires and dreams are often beyond their resources. Their unrealistic expectations of what comes with marriage have been built up over the years by personal fantasies and romantic myths. The young couple may risk spending more than they earn, buying too much on credit, and getting into debt, with multiple monthly payments for things they bought on the installment plan. Before they realize how much their regular costs will be for food, rent, utilities, fuel, car expenses and all the rest, they are overcommitted. They usually struggle to meet the high cost of living with resources more modest than either of them had as single persons.

Supporting Themselves and Their Household

In most families, both husband and wife work, at least until the first baby comes. Some husbands prefer full-time homemaker wives, but most young men find that the household can be supported with less strain when there are two paychecks helping to support the family. Decisions about spending the family income tend to be more cooperative and democratic when both of them work. Husband and wife together make their financial plans, shop together for what they need, read labels, enquire about the warranties, and are increasingly aware of the quality of the goods they buy.

Allocating Responsibilities

Some husbands have little interest in housework, and they do not expect their wives to work outside homes. Increasingly, young married couples allocate their responsibilities on the basis of their interests and competence. Educated married partners tend to believe in equalitarian relationships, but in actual practice the husbands usually have a greater voice in the family decisions. Working class couples say that the husband should be the dominant one, but their working wives have a relatively powerful say in household and financial decisions. New consumer goods make housekeeping more interesting for both men and women than it once was. Husbands and wives today are adept at meal preparation with the help of convenience foods, packaged products, modern kitchen equipment and outdoor grills. Laundry too has become familiar ground for both husband and wife.

Becoming One – Emotionally and Sexually

Getting married means working out comfortable roles as husband and wife. It involves getting through to one another as fully and as freely as possible in the many dimensions of their relationship. It includes establishing the continuity of a mutually satisfying sexual relationship that cements the pair bond and gives the couple a sense of unity to the marriage.

Interacting with In-laws and Relatives

When a man and a woman leave their parental homes and set up their own home, they experience a basic shift in roles.

Simultaneously, they find themselves in three families – the wife's family of origin, the husband's family of origin, and the family they are establishing as their family of procreation. Each of their relatives on both sides of the family are now part of a larger kin network which must be remembered on special occasions and relied on from time to time throughout the family life cycle.

Developmental Tasks of Stage 2: Childbearing Families

The childbearing stage in the family life cycle begins with the birth of the first baby and continues until the first-born is in preschool. During this period, the husband and wife have their first experience as parents. They enter the stage as a married couple and leave it as established parents with one or more children. During this segment of the cycle, family life proceeds at a rapid pace through a series of overlapping phases. These involve the changing nature of the parents' roles, their tasks of settling down as parents, the child's developmental progress, and the appearance of family developmental tasks. Some of these tasks may be unfulfilled, some are left incomplete, and all are swiftly replaced by urgent new demands on the attention of the young family.

The first phase of the childbearing family stage is one of rejoicing. The man has come through the crisis of the birth of his first child with a sense of relief and satisfaction. The woman emerges from the first fatigue of childbirth with a feeling of accomplishment, a sensation of being part of the process of creation itself. By the third day mother and baby have made their first efforts to learn to live together. With the homecoming of mother and baby comes the end of the first flush of elation and realization that parenthood is an awesome responsibility. Now, the care of the newborn is totally one's responsibility. The coming of the first child is a crisis in that it calls for reorganization of the family. Roles must be reassigned, personal needs must be met in new ways, and family values

Figure 1

Developmental Tasks of Father and Mother in Stage 2

Father	*Mother*
Reconciling conflicting conceptions of role.	Reconciling conflicting conceptions of roles.
Making way for new pressures made upon him as a young father.	Accepting and adjusting to the strains and pressures of young motherhood.
Learning the essentials of baby and childcare.	Learning how to care for her infant with competence and assurance.
Conforming to the new regimes designed as most healthful for the young family.	Establishing and maintaining healthful routines for the young family.
Encouraging the child's full development.	Providing full opportunities for the child's development.
Maintaining a mutually satisfying companionship with his wife.	Sharing the responsibilities of parenthood with her husband.
Assuming the major responsibility for earning the family income.	Maintaining a satisfying relationship with her husband.
Maintaining a satisfying sense of self as a man.	Making satisfactory adjustment to the practical realities of life.
Representing the family within the wider community.	Keeping alive some sense of personal autonomy through young motherhood.
Becoming a family man in the fullest sense of the term.	Exploring and developing satisfying sense of being a family.

Child

Achieving physiological equilibrium following birth.

Learning to take food satisfactorily.

Learning the know how and the where when of elimination.

Learning to manage his body effectively.

Learning to adjust to other people.

Learning to love and to be loved.

Developing systems of communication.

Learning to express and control feelings

Learning foundations for self-awareness.

must be reoriented. The parents may want a child but still be dismayed to discover what they are like. One interpretation is that their first child forces the young parents to take the last major step into the adult world, as they encounter the developmental tasks that go with being responsible for another human being. Parenthood, even more than marriage, demands maturity in both the husband and wife. The developmental tasks of this stage are presented in Figure 1.

Family Developmental Tasks of the Childbearing Families

The developmental tasks of the family in the childbearing stage are basically concerned with establishing the young family as a stable unit, and mutually supporting the developmental needs of mother, father and baby in ways that strengthen each one and the family as a whole. These include:

(a) Adapting housing arrangements to the little child.
(b) Meeting present and future costs of childbearing.
(c) Assuming mutual responsibility.
(d) Facilitating member's role learning.
(e) Communicating with one another in the family.
(f) Planning for future children.
(g) Relating to relatives and others.

Stimulating Optimum Infant Development

The means of stimulating optimum infant development are presented in Figure 2.

Developmental Tasks of Stage 3 : Families with Preschool Children

While the first child is between two-and-a-half years of age, the preschool family typically has a second and possibly a third child, making a total of three to five persons, with the possibility of from three to ten interpersonal relationships. The possible positions in the family are husband-father, wife-mother, son-brother, and daughter-sister – each with its

Figure 2

Means of Stimulating Optimum Infant Development

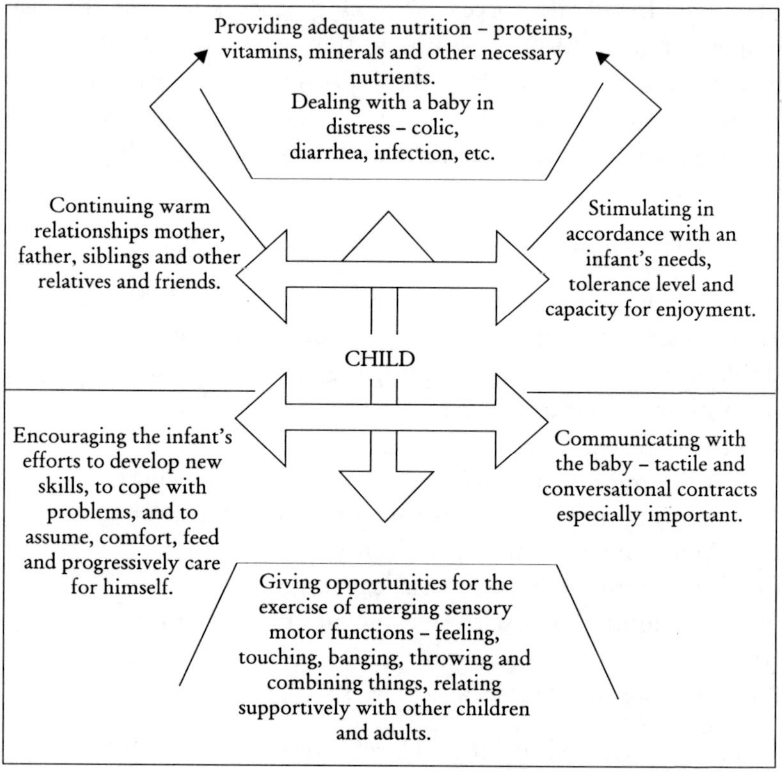

own developmental tasks. While the adults struggle with their childrearing and personal tasks, the preschool child faces the crisis of initiative (expanding imagination) versus guilt (developing conscience).

Developmental Tasks of Families with Preschool Children

The developmental tasks of families with preschool children are no doubt exciting, enlivening and exasperating. They are outlined below in Figure 4:

Figure 3

Developmental Tasks of Preschool Child in the Family

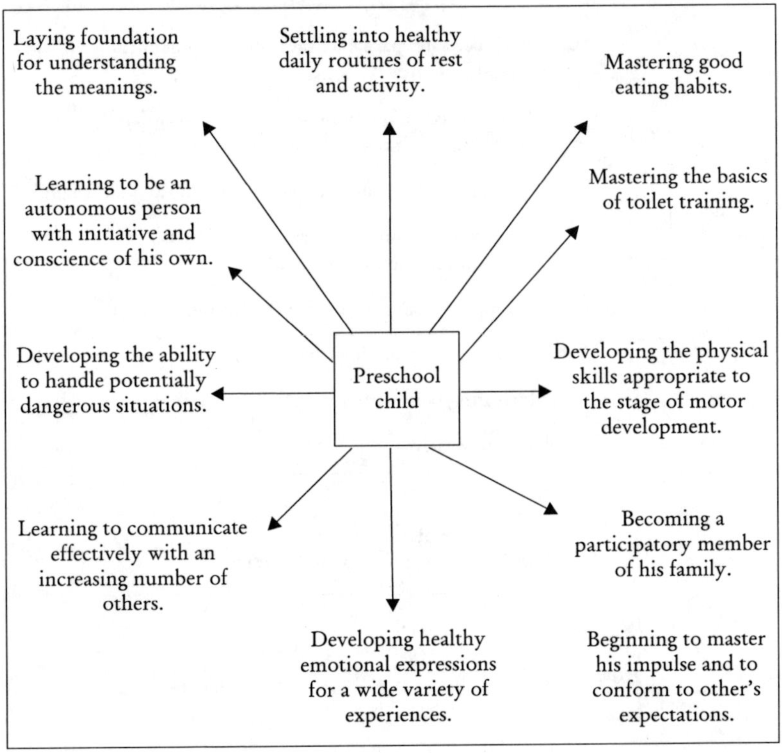

Developmental Tasks of Stage 4: Families with School-Aged Children

When the first child goes to school at about six years of age, the family enters a new stage of its life cycle. This stage, which is characterized by the presence of school-aged children, continues until the child becomes a teenager at 13 developmental tasks of parents in this stage are depicted below in Figure 5.

Parents know well that they are needed throughout the bustling years of this stage. But, on the whole, this is a less hectic time than before, since household routines have become

Figure 4
Family Developmental Tasks with Preschool Children

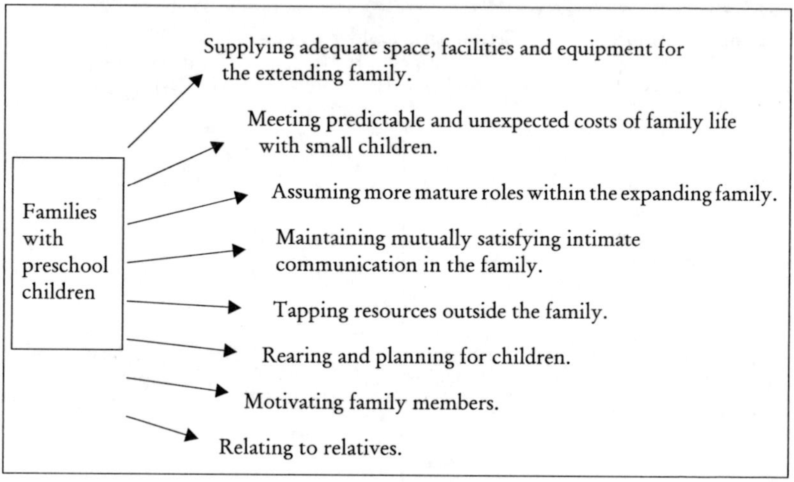

Figure 5
Developmental Tasks of Parents

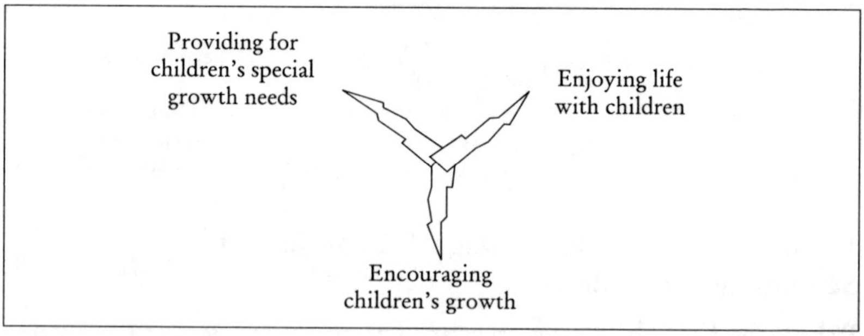

established and the children are growing at a less rapid rate than they did as infants or preschoolers.

Developmental Tasks of the School-Aged Children

1. Learning the basic skills required of school children:
   - Mastering the fundamentals of reading, writing, calculating and problem-solving.

- Understanding of cause and effect relationships.
- Developing concepts essential for everyday living.
- Continuing to develop the ability to reason and to do reflective thinking.

2. Mastering the physical skills appropriate to their development:
   - Learning the games, sports and the various roles in activities pursued by children of their age and sex in one's community.
   - Developing abilities needed in personal and family living.
3. Developing a practical understanding of the use of money:
   - Finding socially acceptable ways of getting money for what they want to buy.
   - Learning how to buy wisely the things they most want with what they have, to stay within their available resources.
   - Learning the value of saving for postponed satisfactions.
   - Reconciling differences between wants and resources and accepting the fact that others may be poorer and richer than they.
   - Acquiring a basic grasp of the nature and function of money in everyday life in the family and in the larger community.
4. Becoming an active cooperative member of the family:
   - Gaining skill in participating in family discussions and decision-making.
   - Assuming responsibilities within the household and finding satisfaction in accomplishment and belonging.
   - Becoming more mature in giving and receiving affection and gifts - between themselves and their parents, siblings and relatives within the extended family and to take the initiative in enriching them as they become able.

5. Extending their abilities to relate effectively to others, both peers and adults:
   - Making progress in their ability to adjust to others.
   - Learning to stand up for their rights.
   - Improving their abilities both to lead and to follow others.
   - Meeting basic social expectations - learning simple conventions, rule, customs, courtesies, and standards of their families and groups.
   - Learning genuinely cooperative roles with others in many situations.
   - Making and keeping close friends.
6. Continuing the learning involved in handling their feelings and impulses:
   - Growing in their ability to cope with simple frustrations.
   - Exploring socially acceptable ways of releasing negative emotions effectively.
   - Becoming more mature in expressing feelings in ways and at times places appropriate within their culture.
   - Gaining skills in sharing their feelings with those who can help.
7. Coming to terms with their own sex role, both now and as it will become:
   - Learning what is expected as appropriate for boys, for girls, for men, for women, for married people, for parents and for other adults.
   - Clarifying knowledge about the nature of sex and reproduction.
   - Adjusting to a changing body in the pubertal growth spurt as teen years approach (accepting the new size and form, functions and pubertal growth).
   - Thinking ahead wholesomely to what it will be like to be grown up as a man or woman.
8. Continuing to find themselves as a worthy person:

- Identifying with his own age and sex in appropriate ways.
- Discovering many ways of becoming acceptable as a person, gaining status.
- Growing in self-confidence, self-respect, self-control, and self-realization.
- Extending the process of establishing their own individuality.

9. Developing a conscience with inner moral controls:
   - Distinguishing right from wrong in a variety of situations.
   - Learning that rules are necessary in any social enterprise.
   - Developing the ego strength for principled moral behavior.
   - Trying to live according to appropriate social and moral values.

Family Developmental Tasks at the School-Aged Stage

By the time, the eldest child is in school, the husband and wife have been married seven years or more, have been parents for at least six years, and have settled into familiar ways with each other and with their children. The developmental routes

Figure 6

Family Developmental Tasks

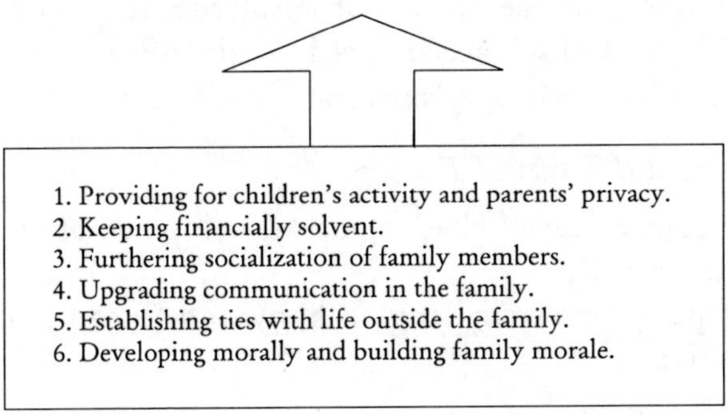

traversed by the oldest child are gone over again by the younger children – each in his turn, each in his own way. Family developmental tasks at this stage are presented in Figure 6.

Developmental Tasks of Stage 5: Families with Teenagers

A family enters the teenage stage of the family life cycle when the oldest child becomes 13 and leaves it when the first child departs for marriage, work, or higher education, etc., as a young adult. Adolescence is a period of strain in most families. As teenagers strive to establish their identity and to emancipate themselves from their parents, the parents tend to feel that their children undervalue them and the adolescents believe that adults generally depreciate teenagers. During the teen years, young people gradually come to understand themselves as members of their own generation. They must explore and draw on the resources within and beyond their families for all they require to accomplish the developmental tasks that lead into effective adulthood.

Developmental Tasks of Teenager's Parents

Success in the developmental tasks of adolescence is profoundly influenced by the ways in which parents perform their own developmental tasks at this stage. When the parents accept themselves as they are, with all their weaknesses and strengths, and when they accept their variety of roles at this stage of development without undue conflict or sensitivity, they set a pattern for a similar sort of self-acceptance in their children. The developmental tasks of teenager's parents are illustrated in Figure 7.

Developmental Tasks of Teenagers

The teenagers have challenging developmental tasks as highlighted below:

1. Accepting one's challenging body and learning to use it effectively.

Figure 7
Developmental Tasks of Teenager's Parents

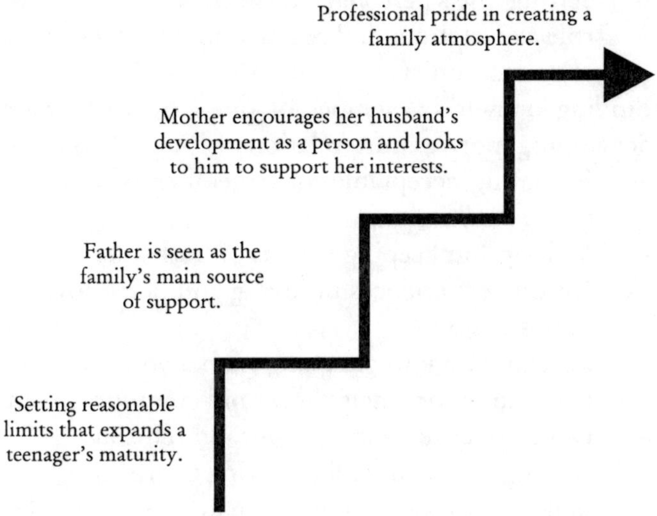

- Coming to terms with the new size, shape, function, and potential of one's maturing body.
- Accepting differences between one's own physique and that of age mates of the same and other sex as variations that are normal and to be expected.
- Understanding what pubertal changes mean and wholesomely anticipating maturity as a man or as a woman.
- Caring for one's body in ways that assures its health and optimum development.
- Learning to handle oneself skillfully in the variety of recreational, social, and family situations that require learned physical skills.

2. Achieving a satisfying and socially accepted masculine and feminine roles:
   - Learning what it means to be a boy or a girl in one's culture.

- Anticipating realistically what will be involved in becoming a man or a woman.
- Setting one's personal course within the leeway of sex role expectations and practice allowed by one's family and community.

3. Finding oneself as member of one's own generation by developing more mature relations with one's age mates:
   - Becoming acceptable as a member of one or more groups of peers.
   - Making and keeping friends of both sexes.
   - Getting experiences in loving and being loved by the opposite sex.
   - Learning how to get along with a wide variety of age mates in school, neighbors, and community settings.
   - Developing skills in inviting and refusing.
   - Solving problems and resolving conflicts.
   - Making decisions and evaluating experiences with one's peers.
4. Achieving emotional independence of parents and other adults:
   - Becoming free of childish dependence upon one's parents.
   - Developing more mature affection for parents as persons.
   - Learning how to be autonomous, capable of making decisions and running his own life.
   - Growing out of the dependence of childhood and the impulsive independence of adolescents and attaining a mature interdependence with others.
   - Learning to be an adult among adults.
5. Selecting and preparing for an occupation and economic independence:
   - Seeking counsel and getting specific knowledge about work within the limits of real possibilities.

- Choosing an occupation in line with interests, abilities, and opportunities.
- Preparing oneself through schooling, specialized training and personal responsibility to get and hold a position.
- Apprenticeship experiences wherever possible along the lines of future vocational interests.

6. Preparing for marriage and family life:
   - Enjoying the responsibilities as well as the privileges of family membership.
   - Developing a responsible attitude towards getting married and having a family.
   - Acquiring knowledge about mate selection, marriage, home making, and childbearing.
   - Learning to distinguish between infatuation and more lasting forms of love.
   - Developing mutually satisfying personal relationships through process of becoming involved with a loved one.
   - Making decisions about engagement, marriage, completion of one's education, and the multiple demands on young people of marriageable age.
7. Developing the intellectual skills and social sensitivities necessary for civic competence:
   - Developing concepts of law, government, economics, politics, geography, human nature, and social organizations that are relevant to the modern world.
   - Gaining awareness of human needs and becoming motivated to help others attain their goals.
   - Acquiring problem-solving methods for dealing effectively with modern problems.
   - Becoming involved in causes and projects outside oneself and becoming a socially responsible person.
8. Establishing one's identity as a socially responsible person:
   - Attaining a mature set of values and ethical controls appropriate to one's culture.

- Developing a workable philosophy of life that makes sense in today's world.
- Implementing worthy ideals and standards in one's life.
- Assuming social obligations and responsibilities that express one's feelings of relatedness to others and society at large.
- Learning to see oneself in relation to the universe and to the whole human race.

Family Developmental Tasks at the Teenage Stage

While mother, father, teenager, and younger/older siblings are working through their own individual developmental tasks in the midst of social pressures that often thwart and hinder them, the family as a whole is busy with its own developmental tasks during this stage. These tasks are outlined below in Figure 8:

Figure 8
Developmental Tasks of Families

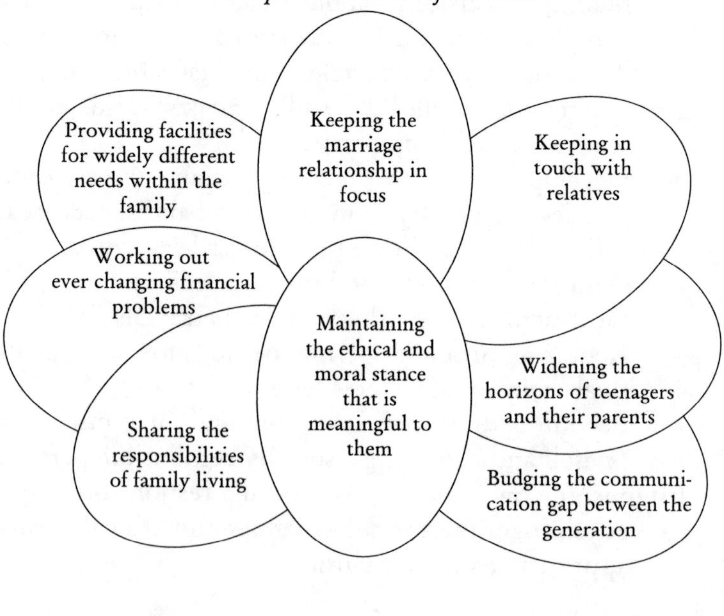

Developmental Tasks of Stage 6: Families Launching Young Adults

The young of the family are ready to be launched in the later teen years. This stage in the family life cycle is characterized by the young person's departure from home to take on full-time job or attend college, and to eventually marry.

The launching stage is marked by the simultaneous release of the family's child(ren) and the recruitment of new members by marriage. Positional developmental tasks continue for the parents in their many family roles and functions. The primary goal in this stage is the successful launching of children into the adult world and the reorganization of the family into a new entity.

Most families today play active roles over a considerable period of time in getting their young people successfully launched into the world. While the first child is busy getting established as an autonomous young adult, there may be one or more younger children still in the family – each with his or her own developmental tasks to accomplish. Therefore, the family's tasks involve not only assisting the young adult to become successfully independent, but also maintaining a secure home base in which the other members of the family can thrive. These tasks are summarized as follows:

1. Rearranging physical facilities and resources.
2. Meeting the expenses of launching center families.
3. Reallocating responsibilities among grown and growing children.
4. Coming to terms with themselves as husband and wife.
5. Maintaining open systems of communication within and beyond the family.
6. Reconciling conflicting loyalties and philosophies of life.
7. Widening the family circle through release of young adult children and recruitment of new members by marriage.

Developmental Tasks of Stage 7: Middle-Aged Parents in the Empty Nest

The family life cycle in the middle years begins with the departure of the last child from the home and continues to retirement of the husband (or wife) and then death of one of the spouses. This period may last months or years. Developmental tasks of this stage are highlighted below in Figure 9:

Figure 9

Developmental Tasks of Middle-Aged Parents and Families

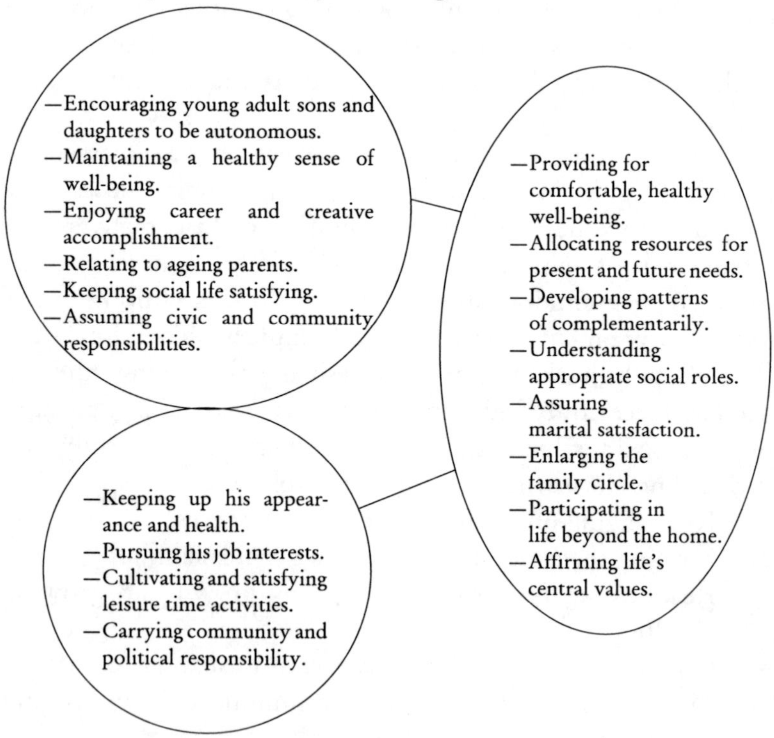

Developmental Tasks of Stage 8: Aging Family Members

The final stage of the family life cycle begins with the man's retirement, continues through the loss of the first spouse, and ends with the death of the second. The aging couple continues to be family to their grown children, grandchildren, and great grandchildren. The pair faces together the family developmental tasks of the final stage of the family life cycle. These tasks are summarized below in Figure 10:

Figure 10
Developmental Tasks of Aging Couple

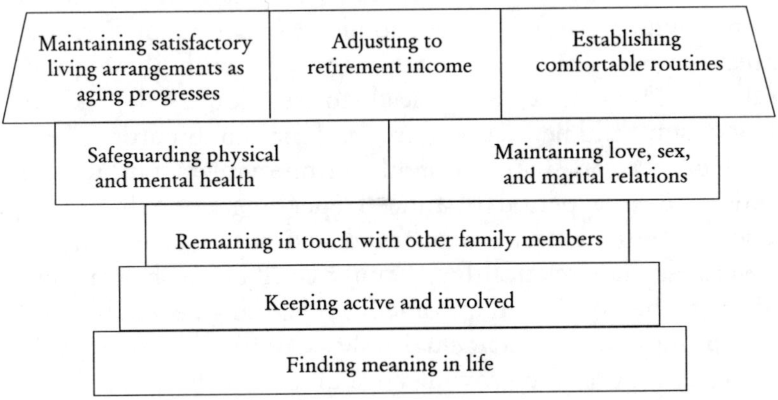

Success in these developmental tasks lies in each individual's, as well as the couple's, ability to remain curious and concerned about life, and to retain patience in the present and faith in the future. Those who find the aging years delight ful are self-educable, self-sufficient, and aware of all that is taking place about them. They smile and stand straight. They listen and they give of themselves to others of every vintage.

Conclusion: Developmental Crises and Satisfactions in Marriages and Families

The dynamic quality of family development is an ever-present challenge. There are rarely two days that are alike in most families. The family no sooner gets nicely settled into one stage of the family life cycle than another is upon them with new demands, stresses, and satisfactions. It may seem that anything can happen, and some satisfactions are more prevalent at some stages of the family life cycle than at others. Knowledge of family development helps us know what to expect throughout the life cycle.

Every family is to some extent vulnerable to anxiety and harassment and beset with complexities that arise both from within the family and from the social forces that impinge upon it. In times of social unrest families are called upon to protect themselves to safeguard the nation's security. In periods of unemployment, inflation, economic depression, or terrorist threat, some families are unable to cope with these harsh realities. Hard times may lead to self-doubt, depression, alcoholism, child neglect or abuse, and marital discord.

Conflict can shatter a family in one violent outburst or erode it over a period of time. Depending upon how it is handled, conflict between husband and wife can destroy or strengthen their relationship. Family conflict can help relieve the inevitable tensions that come from learning new habits and attempting new developmental tasks. Conflict, constructively managed, exposes the growing edge of a relationship so that it can be dealt with productively. It can redefine a situation and leave the marriage stronger than it was before. Constructive quarrelling is directed at the issues, problems, and dilemmas facing the pair, rather than at one another's egos. As time goes on, a couple learns what to expect of one another and how to solve their problems so that conflict is neither frequent or painful.

Desperation in families living beyond their means may break forth in disintegrating ways. A working class husband can become abusive and domineering, while contributing neither material nor emotional support to the family. His wife carrying more than her share of family responsibility becomes discouraged, than desperate. Insufficient income causes unhappiness, dissatisfaction, worry, and hopelessness and can result in physical symptoms that are actually an expression of anxiety. Lower class families have less access to professional help because (i) they are less likely to recognize their real problems;

(ii) they do not know where to go for help; and (iii) help is not readily available to them. Destructive quarreling and chronic complaints build up until the man leaves home or the couple separates.

Relatively affluent couples can also become discouraged in their efforts to find satisfaction with one another. Today, as men and women demand happiness as their right, and because divorce is more acceptable and employability is a greater possibility for the women, many married couples can afford to maintain two separate households. Hence, disintegration of middle and upper class marriage is increasing even in India. Destructive conflict is rightly feared as harmful to the participants and to their relationship. Explosive outbursts or aggressive silences are threatening and belittling. They leave the marriage weaker than it was and the spouses farther apart than ever. In time, the two become alienated and break up, unless they have the will and the ability to strengthen their union.

Successful marriage depends upon the willingness of mature adults to work towards a lasting commitment to each other and to their partnership. Marriage involves the risk of failure and the loss of some privacy and autonomy in exchange for the warmth of a companionship with a familiar mate over the years. Parenthood has become a courageous leap of faith into the future that only the brave should attempt. Its responsibilities frighten those who are immature who prefer pursuing their own personal goals to taking on the burden of dependent youngsters. Couples who enjoy their nurturing roles, who know what to expect of their children and of themselves, and who have positive attitudes about the developmental crises that come to all families may be expected to raise their children with less strain than less confident and competent parents. The satisfactions more than outweigh the stresses for those who want a stake in creating the culture of the future through their own sons and daughters.

Thus, the future of India is built in families. There, the citizens of tomorrow are nurtured and the culture is translated into action. Apart from millions of decisions by couples to bring forth children they will nourish, teach, and launch against the void, the human race has no wisdom, no advance, no community, no grace, and no future. Families function at the frontiers of modern life. Today, people push their way through the wilderness of family confusion and cultural conflict. Road building is strenuous work, but the dream of a nation of vital, happy families producing generation after generation of strong and creative people is a worthy one, and a goal worth the struggle.

References

Bell, N.V. and Vogel, E.F. (1989). *Modern Introduction to the Family.* The Free Press, New York, pp. 45-48.

Burgess, Ernest W. and Locke, Harvey J. (1953). *The Family: From Institution to Companionship*, Second Edition. American Book Company, New York.

Duvall, E.M. (1977). *Marriage and Family Development*, Lippincott Company, Philadelphia, pp. 47, 137–461.

Eshleman, J.R. (1985). *The Family*, Allyn & Bacon Inc., Boston, pp. 149-151.

Havighurst, R.J. (1953). *Human Development and Education.* Longman Co., New York.

Kapadia, K.M. (1988). *Marriage and Family in India*, Oxford University Press, Bombay, p. 309.

Skolnik, A.S. and Skolnik, J.H. (1983). *Family in Transition*, Little Brown & Co., Boston, pp. 409 and 453.

5

Parenthood

Changes and Challenges

Yamuna T.V.

To be a parent is the most challenging task in modern-day society. Parenting is a complex issue, and with changing times, it is facing numerous challenges. This chapter offers an in-depth examination of parenthood, explores specific issues involved in parenting, and sheds light on the redefining role of fathers in contemporary India. Further, it discusses the nature of positive parenting and makes some suggestions for how parents can deal more effectively with the children and youth of today and enhance their competencies for a better life.

Being a parent is one of the most challenging but rewarding jobs anyone could ever adopt. It is the longest task and responsibility that an individual will ever perform. Parenting is an active process that demands that individuals use their skills and knowledge to plan, give birth, raise, and provide for children. The parenting process includes protecting, nourishing, and guiding the child. It involves a series of interactions between the parent and the child throughout the life span. Unlike in earlier times, parenthood in contemporary India is, generally speaking, a chosen and planned act. The reasons for choosing the role of parenthood are numerous and varied. Some of the basic reasons identified specific to Indian society are:

- *Social expectation and pressure:* To have children within a year or two after marriage is common and expected. When couples do not have a child after some period of time, others tend to believe that something is wrong with the marriage relationship, or perhaps that one of them has a physiological problem that is preventing pregnancy or childbirth.
- *Social status and identity:* Society identifies a mature and growing marriage as an institution that includes children. Having progeny stimulates the development of responsibility, selflessness, and increases social contact, improves socialization, and provides an accepted adult status.
- *Recognition:* Parenthood allows adults to receive recognition and eligibility to partake in rituals, functions, and ceremonies.
- *Religious and moral beliefs and obligations:* Bringing children into the world is considered a divine duty of life. Many religious teachings encourage multiplying and replenishing the earth to ensure continuity and spread of one's religion.
- *Escape from loneliness and isolation:* Children fill voids and help us overcome feelings of loneliness. They are a source of love, warmth, and affection.
- *Security during old age:* Children provide health care, support, security, and comfort during old age.
- *Biological and psychological expression:* The process of childbearing and rearing provides people with a sense of pleasure and achievement. Being a parent contributes to feelings of competence and accomplishment.
- *A source for counteracting sorrow and difficulties:* Being involved in childrearing activities helps parents find solace from grief and sorrow that are a natural part of life.

- *Economic assets:* Children are often valued for their contribution to the family's economic well-being. Members of large families especially tend to share responsibilities for the common welfare of the family.
- *Ensure identity:* Children as descendants which ensure parents' own identity. They continue the family name and frequently pass on the family business or occupation to the next generation.
- *Attain moksha (salvation):* In Hindu families there is the belief that begetting a son ensures *moksha* or *mukti* (salvation) and guarantees that parents will reach heaven and become one with God, provided that proper funeral rites are performed for them by the son.

Foundation for Parenthood

Mahabharata and Ramayana are the two great Hindu epics that reflect the ideologies and symbolize this great world religion. These epics are relevant even today. They explain, through story sequences, the ground realities of human relationships within and beyond the family unit. The relevance of these epics to everyday life is seen through numerous characters and situations in these stories.

In earlier times, before electricity made its way into the towns and cities, listening to stories from the epics narrated through classical music, dance, and *harikatha* (story telling and explaining the meaning of the story by relating its relevancy to everyday happenings for better understanding) was the chief source of entertainment for people. Sculptures depicting the sequence of the epics were found around the exterior and interior walls and on the pillars of the temples. Abstract concepts were literally concretized so that they could be understood in verbal and pictorial forms. Included were characters, situations and sequences that depicted marital and parental roles, as well as many other aspects of human relationships. These structures highlighted joys and sorrows present in all relationships, showed paths a person should take to live a healthy and prosperous life, and illustrated ways of achieving harmony with family members and others. They illustrated both rivalry and positive relationships between siblings. These stories, told and retold over the centuries in India, have instilled in the minds of people the importance of parenting and the key role it plays in life and society.

Besides, they illustrate the importance of progeny, early childhood care, parent-child separation, proper and ineffective discipline, parental efforts to facilitate and maintain good sibling relationships, and the consequences of positive and negative approaches to parenting. Thus, the cultural and religious doctrines found in the epics have had a profound influence on Indian family life for thousands of years.

Contemporary Indian Family Life

In contemporary India, the foundation for parenthood practice begins very early in life. Children in their early childhood years receive encouragement and appreciation for their activities in their playtime. Role playing as mother/father or caregiver provides children with their first experience in handling infants (toys) in the cradle, cuddling, bathing, feeding, soothing the crying baby and putting it to sleep. These behaviors are strengthened when children are given the opportunity and responsibilities of being caregivers to younger siblings (or cousins in joint families).

The expectant mother in India, even in poor families, is given a great deal of care, respect, and attention by family members. Ceremonies related to one's first pregnancy are performed. These ceremonies, along with announcing the arrival of a member to the community, enable the female members of the community to visit the expectant mother to greet, bless, and advise. Generally, the first baby is delivered in one's maternal home. Arrival of a male child, rather than a female child, causes particular rejoicing due to the belief that the parents attain *moksha* (salvation) if the son performs their funeral rites. Moreover, sons are expected to protect and offer comfort to parents during old age and continue the family line. The female child receives less attention because her presence in the parents' home lasts only until her marriage, after which her duties and responsibilities are transferred to her husband's home. However, she receives extra care, consideration, and attention before and after her marriage.

Elaborate rituals and festivities mark every important event related to the developmental milestone of parenting, starting with *punyarjanam* and *namakaranam* to performance of the marriage (see Table 1).

Table 1

Rituals Performed in Order to Fulfill Parental Responsibilities

Rituals	*Age*
Punyarjanam (purification) *Namakarnam* (naming ceremony)	10th day
Annaprashtanam (feeding rice/solid food)	7th month
Tonsuring, and earlobe punching	12th month
Formal introduction to learning alphabets	before age 2
Attainment of menarche	11-14 years
*Upanayanam** (wearing sacred thread) (boys)	9-11 years
Mate selection, engagement marriage	age vary
Seemantham	7th month of first pregnancy

**Upanayanam* is performed only in certain communities.

Childbirth and baby care techniques are part of rearing a daughter that carry over to her adult married life. The last trimester of the first pregnancy is generally spent in the maternal home. It is considered obligatory on the part of parents of a daughter to extend complete assistance in the delivery and continue such assistance until the baby is five months old. This cultural phenomenon provides a highly beneficial and personalized education for young mothers with regard to parenthood and childcare. Grandmothers and other caregivers also offer their expertise in teaching the mother and helping to care for the newborn. Besides exposing the young mother to the nuances involved in childcare, she is taught ways of coping with her new role as mother.

Assistance with parenting and childcare occurs best in a joint or extended family system. In situations where the young mother is employed, parents continue their assistance in caring for children for long periods, ranging from a few months to several years depending upon the situational need. If they are unable to provide such assistance, a woman experienced in childcare is appointed. Because of these protective systems within the culture, perhaps the need for professional parent education is not seen as needed. However, in recent years, particularly in metropolitan areas, parent education classes have been initiated in an effort to extend parenting knowledge and skills to new parents who reside mainly in nuclear families, and who often do not have the help of extended family members.

Stages of Parenthood

Just as children go through the stages of development, parents also go through the stages of parenthood that require appropriate parenting stage responsibilities (see Figure 1). These stages involve changing tasks and roles of both parents and children. These tasks, roles and, responsibilities have been highlighted by Galinsky (1987) and are briefly described in this section.

Image Building (Conception to Birth of the Baby)

The young parents dream and build images of ideal parenting and of what they want to become before the baby is born. Friends, siblings, parents, grandparents and others provide advice and share their experiences. Many people make judgements about what kind of parents these individuals will or should be, suggesting for example, that "I will never scold my child", "My child will have everything that is needed", or "My child will learn music, which I missed as a child". During this period, mothers also have fears about child death or disability. Fathers may worry about death of the spouse during childbirth and about their role as a father, as well about upcoming expenses and the family's financial needs. Parents are also reminded of their past and how they were parented, which may trigger feelings of both joy and sorrow.

Nurturing (Birth to 18 Months)

Parents build an attachment with the child and identify themselves as a parent, assess and understand what kind of parent they really are. Grandparents, parents-in-law, friends, and relatives find out how the parents handle this new role. They may offer advice, suggestions, and extend help in baby care or in household chores.

This stage is critical in building trust, bond and close attachment between the parent and the child. Trust emerges as the child's basic needs for warmth, food, dryness of nappy, safety, eye contact, and touch are satisfied. The child's belief and trust of the parent as a dependable source forms the basis and establishes a firm foundation for all future relationships for the rest of the life. Numerous personal adjustments must be made by the mother to meet demands of the baby in terms of resting period, feeding schedule, managing the soiled clothes, maintaining contact, and giving personal attention when the baby is at play and shows initiations to become mobile.

The parents worry and sometimes doubt their parenting methods, questioning themselves, "Are we spoiling the child?" Parents can experience doubts, and feelings of helplessness and uncertainty in caring for the baby. They may feel jealous, competitive with others who play a role in the child's life, and consider that other caregivers may not do a good job of baby care, or develop fear that the child may love other caregiver more than them.

Authority (18 Months to Age 5)

The parents become persons-in-charge when the child begins to talk and walk. This is the period when the parent sets new rules for the child's action and behavior, decides when to say 'yes' and when to say 'no', and prepares the child for separation, e.g., to be away for schooling. This is also the 'what' stage, the child is being exposed to new environments, and becomes very inquisitive to absorb the new information. Thus, this is the first trial period that tests the limits of parental patience. Exercising utmost care to discipline, maintaining consistency, and avoiding ambiguity in giving directions helps the child to conceptualize what is expected of him. During this stage, parents may seek assistance and guidance from professionals or experienced persons.

Interpretation (Age 5 to Puberty)

The child's question from 'what' turns to 'why' and 'how'. This requires explaining each of the queries; the numbers of such queries grow as the child's language skills grow and understanding expands. The queries may range from natural calamity to other normal aspects of nature; birth to death, etc. Parents will have to respond satisfactorily with convincing replies.

The child experiments with rules and social norms, examines the quality of treatment he/she receives and the relationship maintained within the family. The type of parenting used in such situations plays a significant role in determining the sort of adult the child will become. Acceptance, appreciation and affection expressed by parents equip the child to develop a positive attitude and approach towards life. It is at this stage that children make harsh conclusions and judgements about parental intentions and actions as they struggle to understand relationships, meaning or realize that other people also have feelings. This stage necessitates parents to interact with the child in an age-appropriate manner. They may need to frequently revisit and revise their parental roles as the child continues to mature.

The child may show a special interest in materialistic possessions, and might experiment with unique clothing and accessories of dress, appearance and/or behaviors. Parents can attempt to alter adverse behaviors that occur by making rules age-appropriate, modifying expectations when necessary, and by serving as a role model for the child to follow.

Preparation for Independence (Teen Years)

The parents of teenagers face challenges over their authority as parents. A teenager fights with parents in making decisions, and on issues considered as personal matters. Although the teen is taught to say 'no' and expected 'not to do' during certain situations, parents should expect experiments with the rules as the teenager examines the consequences, parental authenticity, and how authority impacts on the teenage, on parents and others. Some experimentation is done in the absence of parents; many times the teen will try to destroy the evidence of such attempts.

Teenagers begin to show that they are 'grown up' and are 'capable' of handling difficult situations themselves, that they are different than their parents in many ways, and that their problems and needs are not well understood by the parents. During such times, teenagers need parental guidance to make decisions and to make tough choices. They require careful and sympathetic listening, brief counseling and independence to prove that they are capable of making certain decisions and able to accept the consequence of such decisions. Some typical sentences repeated often by teenagers in this stage are:

'You don't understand'.
'My problems are different'.
'I cannot explain everything to you'.
'I am not a small child'.

Distancing (Adulthood)

Parents experience a certain distance to be established and maintained by their children as they get a strong hold on their newly acquired independence. Children, who sought permission to go out from their parents during the earlier stages, now inform the parents where they have been and with whom they have been, if inquired. The parents of young adults need to equip themselves to accept the probable separation from their child arising out of their departure to fulfill their educational pursuit or pursuit of employment. The parents are expected to select suitable mates, oversee the marriage ceremony, and ensure that adult children are settled in life.

Distance between parents and grown-up children continues even when they live together at home. Additional relationships in the family through marriage of their sons and daughters are established. Restraining from counseling and advising, being courteous to the grown-up son/daughter, and maintaining a cordial relationship with the son/daughter-in-law, and non-interference in their married life and in their relationships is expected and appreciated.

Grandparenting (Above Age 55)

The role of grandparenting is more supportive in nature than in previous stages, irrespective of it being short-term or long-term (surrogate), and any attempt to exert authority in childcare and disciplining may be treated as interference. The grandparents are expected to baby sit, tutor, drop off and pick up the children from school, accompany them to the park, and give alternative home remedies. They are expected to give suggestions, counseling and guidance, and advice only on issues sought by the young parents and youngsters at home.

Single Grandparenting

In cases where a spouse dies, the surviving spouse has to make many new adjustments; for example, sharing of views and news gets restricted. Advice and counseling may be treated as old fashioned and traditional. Grandchildren have less time to spare to listen to elaborate talks, discussions, and enumeration of incidences and experiences. Hence, they expect the grandparent to be brief or avoid such talks. However, a grandparent, who keeps abreast with the current ways of living and who is not critical of new trends, would be better accepted by the younger generation. In failing to do so, grandparents may have to seek the company of their own age peers, or face being isolated, neglected and avoided by the younger generation.

Specific Issues in Parenting

Warmth, physical closeness, and nourishment during nursing enable the infant to develop attachment and bonding towards the mother. Results from an empirical research study, conducted by Harlow and Harlow as early as 1969 with monkeys, revealed that soft contact comfort was the most important and critical variable in the development of attachment. More attachment occurred between young monkeys and a makeshift terry-cloth mother that did not feed them, than with a wire mother that fed with a nursing bottle. Monkeys reared in isolation and monkeys reared with wire mothers were unable to form healthy adult relationships and were unable to care for their own offspring. This study showed that familiarity, security and control facilitate attachment. A child, who feels secure in a familiar situation, will develop attachments to adults providing that security. An infant is highly dependent and helpless; it is with the adult's help and assistance that the baby develops a secure and safe feeling in the new environment. If a child is able to elicit the right parental response when in distress or need, he/she will feel secure with the parent. Play stimulation (vocal and physical) enhances and facilitates attachment (Ross and Goldman, 1977). Besides this, the mother who is sensitive to the wants and needs of her baby; who responds quickly; accepts parenting responsibilities cheerfully; respects the baby's autonomy and responds willingly to baby's signals, is more likely to develop a very strong enduring parent-child attachment with her child (Ainsworth, Bell and Stayton, 1971; Golombok, 2000). Concrete, positive parental behavior facilitates attachment. A child, who has secure attachments with parents, is more likely to develop healthy relationships with others throughout the life span (Jensen and Kingston, 1986).

The first elements of good parenting probably begin in infancy and involve the characteristics identified above: dealing with feeding, toilet training, and crying. The need for attachment gradually lessens as the child grows up, acquires language skills, makes friends, and becomes independent to meet his or her individual needs.

When the fact of "I am going to be a parent" is communicated to the expectant parents, the news generally generates joy, happiness, and enthusiasm besides anxiety, tension and also responsibilities with which that they have to live. Many new parents are given an advice, "Don't worry, you will pick up parenting skills, once the child arrives". Though this is true, much of the uncertainty and anxiety could be reduced if new parents become educated about infancy and childhood prior to the actual experience. The information is especially important for first-time parents; it helps them know what to expect and ways to solve commonly occurring problems.

After the birth of the first child, young parents normally experience a variety of problems. Such problems may affect their involvement in parenting. Some of the initial problems that affect new parents are:

- Loss of sleep, disturbed sleep schedule, extra work, fatigue and exhaustion.
- Strain on the marital relationship, inability to spend time together changes in interest and preferences, and changes in sexual relationship.
- Doubt regarding performance as a parent, demands of new responsibility, strain on emotions, particularly when the baby's health and growth schedules are affected.

- Less freedom to travel, to go out and socialize.
- Loss of career opportunities, loss of income and increased economic burden.
- Misunderstandings and conflicts of interests between spouses.
- Differences in parenting styles and resultant disagreements over these differences.

However, many of these problems get diluted, if the:

- Parents are well adjusted as a husband-wife unit, are highly motivated and eagerly looking forward to parental responsibilities.
- Father is cooperative and willing to share responsibilities of childcare.
- Parents have a good support system from their parents in caring for the newborn.
- Mother had easy labor and delivery.
- Parents have adequate financial security.
- Child's health is good.
- Mother is able to manage duties of motherhood, a career, and housekeeping, while continuing to nurture the marital relationship. It is important for her to be able to shift among these roles.
- Parents have adequate exposure/knowledge to parenting, infancy and early childhood development.
- Postpartum depression and anxiety are absent.

Children imitate parents and other adults whom they admire and respect. Parents discuss how to imbibe appropriate behavior in their children, make all efforts to increase their effectiveness as parents, and help facilitate positive growth in the child. However, generally, they follow a "do what I say, not what I do" approach. Children are keen observers and tend to internalize the actions modeled by their parents. They mimic, duplicate or emulate the behaviors they observe. When they are engaged in a similar situation, they imitate the internalized actions; for example, parents remove their footwear at the door before entering the house so the child also takes off the footwear by the doorway before stepping into the house. Thus, parents need to model correct actions or adopt the behaviors which they would desire in their child, rather than simply telling the child what is correct or incorrect behavior.

Facets of Parenting

Parenting is a complex issue. It is dependent on intrafamilial factors. Some aspects, which play a role in determining the parenting performance, are discussed in this section.

Family Structure

The structure of the family, i.e., single or joint/extended family, decides the number of adjustments parents need to make while exercising parenting skills. In a joint/extended family, the senior (or other) members may interfere when parents are disciplining the children. They may support the new parents by serving as a caregiver or surrogate parent during short-term or long-term absences of the parents.

Family Situation

The family situation at the time of birth of the baby decides the type of reception the child receives upon arrival and thereafter. If the parents were eagerly looking forward to have the baby, the parenting is more likely to be positive and exuberant, than in situation where the arrival is unwanted or unexpected. The familial situation during the expected period of arrival or after the arrival of the baby, namely, economic gain or loss, death, injury, promotion in the job etc., influences greatly the quality of the parenting the newborn receives.

Family Reputation

The position and status the family enjoys in the neighborhood, community and society will be extended to the baby. A child from the family of well or ill repute gets the same treatment, recognition and the status in the social system as other family members.

Family Relationships

The relationships maintained between the spouses, with their respective parents, with the other family members and between the siblings bear a strong influence on the parenting.

Ordinal Position and Sex

In the Indian context, a first-born boy enjoys better parental care than a girl and other later-born children. The last-born is more likely to be pampered in a smaller family and neglected in large family, and often they become dependent on older siblings for guidance in making important decisions.

Experience and Exposure to Parenting Skills

Parents who had adequate exposure to baby and child care during their own childhood and adolescence, such as taking care of younger sibling or niece/nephew, may find parenting easier than those who have had little or no exposure to child care.

Parental Expectation

If the child is unable to meet the standards set by parents, normal harmonious parenting may get jeopardized.

Child's Inborn Abilities and Disabilities

The parents of a child, born with certain gifts or disabilities/ deformities, are more likely to face greater parenting stress, strain and effort than parents of children who are normal. One parent or family may blame the other for the child's condition. The financial burden alone can overwhelm the young family faced with the physical challenges associated with disability.

Temperament

Individual parent's temperament and that of the child's and other family members can determine the nature of the relationship between the parent and the child.

Financial Situation

Parents, who are economically well placed and possess adequate financial support, will be in a position to meet the needs of their child by affording better care, opportunities and facilities for the child's optimum development and growth.

Educational Status

Parents with higher education tend to understand the problems and needs of their children; they are more likely to make correct attempts to solve their problems and fulfill their requirements. Typically, educated parents maintain realistic standards, aspirations, and better relationship with their children.

Employed Mother

The employed mother faces many challenges in providing quality parenting; however, she can be helped through the cooperation extended by her spouse and by other family members in sharing household chores and in discharging parenting responsibilities. However, the cultural, traditional, and regional practices in each community set standards and limits for the parents to conform to the norms.

Aspects of Parenting Practice

To strengthen parenting skills, parents need to understand and learn about themselves (e.g., how they were parented, their expectations for the child, etc.) and also about child development. In this section, an attempt is mode to discuss the aspects that would strengthen efforts of parenting (DeBord, 1997).

Caring for Self

Parents should fulfill their own needs adequately. Further, they need to master skills necessary to manage the household, seek and accept support when required, and recognize strengths and weaknesses in each other, as well as in themselves. They should set goals for raising the child and establish a good relationship with the spouse and with those who play a role in childrearing process.

Acquisition of Knowledge

Understanding children and their distinctive needs in each stage of development is important. Each child is unique in abilities, responses, and also the way in which the world is perceived. Adequate knowledge of the developmental milestones of children and their changing and varied needs contribute to less conflict in helping the children grow, to feel secure, and to be happy and healthy.

Nurturing

Each child has specific wants and needs that require nurturing. By meeting the needs of the child, a positive relationship can be built, which consistently sends messages of love and support. Expressions of love and affection, listening to the child's ideas, feelings, problems and difficulties, kindness, and sympathy, help the child to feel connected to the family and society.

Guidance

Children need and desire guidance to develop personal strengths. This can be accomplished by a steady, but warm, authority. The parents using authority and parental power must identify, introduce and enforce reasonable limits while gradually giving freedom by encouraging the child to become more and more responsible. The use of good judgement to set limits to protect the child and showing concern for others' welfare contribute to enhance child's personal strengths. Children need guidance to be engaged in meaningful activities and to use their time in meaningful way. Their growth as individuals depends on their ability to make decisions and face the consequences of their own decisions.

Motivation

Parents who take their parenting responsibilities seriously and look for ways to teach throughout their children's lives are more likely to bring up children who become confident, skilled learners and persons with high educational standards. Motivating through methods that are appropriate to the age and level of understanding of the child enable him/her to learn about self, others, and the surrounding world.

Parenting responsibilities in an individual's life

Expectant parenthood

↓

Arrival of children

↓

Adjusting to new role,
Learning about child care

↓

Training in habits,
Disciplining,
Educating

↓

Career guidance,
Supporting to settle in jobs

↓

Mate selection
Marriage

↓

Supporting the new family,
Assisting in rearing grandchildren

Harmonious Relationship

Parents with genuine interest in parenting build healthy relationship with school, neighbourhood, and community groups. They notice and speak up about the child's needs, problems and work to bring about a positive change. Parents, who locate, seek and weave a thread of compatible harmony between home and community resources, increase the quality of the community on the whole.

Parenting Styles

The styles of parental responses and interactions with their children can be classified into three types (Baumrind, 1971). The styles followed by parents may not fit into any one category, as parents combine the styles depending on the situation, age and sex of the child. Further, parenting styles shift as parents gain knowledge about the parenting process through various sources, relate their own experiences, and receive responses/feedback from the child and from significant others around them. The three parenting styles are permissive, authoritarian and authoritative.

Permissive Parenting

Permissive parents give too much freedom, set no limits or boundaries, and provide no guidelines for the child to follow socially accepted norms. They employ little or no punishment. Often these parents are uninvolved in parenting and spend little time with their children, giving excuses of stress and work. Such parents allow their children to face difficult situations in which they have little or no experience or skill to manage on their own and to contend with the consequences. Permissive parenting may result in children who have less self-control, become aggressive and irresponsible, and have low self-esteem.

Authoritarian Parenting

Authoritarian parents are demanding, strict, give punishment, and do not allow choices or the freedom to express various opinions. They dislike questioning of their authority, set very high standards, and demand that their standards be satisfied. These parents value submission, obedience and tradition, while discouraging independence and individuality. This parenting style may produce a child who lacks self-confidence, curiosity and creativity, self-control and who has low self-esteem. Under such parenting style, the child will exhibit difficulty in making one's own decisions and behaving in a socially approved manner under given circumstances.

Authoritative Parenting

Authoritative parents employ explanations, discussions, reasoning; they balance their parenting style by using punishment and rewards appropriately. Punishment is never harsh or physical. Instead, it is given by way of deprivation of an opportunity or gifts. Moreover, punishment is used only when ample evidence of willful wrongdoing is observed. When children correct their behavior, they are rewarded. Rewards include praise, a pat on the shoulder; a smile or a nod. Generally, the reward is proportionate to the positive behavior that is being reinforced. Such parenting style results in children who have good self-control, high self-esteem, self-confidence, responsibility, independence and control over their emotions.

Practical Suggestions to Understand and Prevent Misbehavior in Children

Effective parenting is often challenged by misbehavior of children. Understanding why children misbehave is important to respond effectively. Children misbehave when they:

- are sleepy, sick, need fresh air, exercise and food,
- are puzzled or unsure about what is expected of them,
- need attention and love, or need to feel secure,
- want to fulfill their curiosity,
- are not physically and mentally ready or able to follow the rules,
- are bored,
- are angry, disappointed and frustrated, and
- want to assert independence.

Strategies and techniques to prevent a child's misbehavior are as under:

- Set rules that are age-appropriate, then help the child to understand the rule and why it is important.

- Encourage child-initiated activities.
- Extend love without imposing any conditions.
- Build confidence about the child's abilities.
- Provide opportunities to participate in household chores.
- Provide a separate space to maintain the child's personal belongings.
- Give the child freedom and also responsibilities.
- Encourage speaking clearly without fear or shame.
- Discipline in manner that is consistent and gentle.
- Allocate specific space for the child.
- Be a good role model.
- Explain to the child in age-appropriate language what is expected of him or her.
- Avoid displaying personal anxiety/fear about probable misbehaviors.

Fathering: Redefining the Role

From times immemorial, childrearing responsibilities have been borne by the mother. The mother is supposed to have a maternal instinct that is aroused automatically as soon as she conceives and becomes aware of it. The infant spends most of his/her initial time with the mother following birth and thus becomes highly attached to the mother and other caregivers. Mothers typically fulfill the role of primary caregiver, and thus meet the child's needs for basic security. Conversely, the father is viewed as a provider and protector, who aides in the socialization process, stimulates curiosity, and effects discipline.

Keen observation reveals that children yearn deeply for their father. An infant in the first months of life can tell the difference between a mother's and father's style of care. It is probably because they are born with a drive to find their father and fathers have the internal capacity, the instinct to respond (Pruett, 2001). When the father embraces his child, the baby sees a different face that stimulates curiosity and involves socialization. Through interaction and stimulation with their infants, the father encourages the baby to distinguish different sounds, faces and touches at an early age. He helps the infant to become more receptive to change, less fearful of new experiences and assists in establishing trusting relationships with others (Ballard, 1995).

An infant's capacity to recognize father's care early in life supports the importance of fathering to the healthy development of the child. A toddler explores every inch of his father's face and physique. The school-aged child longs to be with his or her father at work, to know his friends, to challenge his skills and strengths. Teenage boys may express the need for their father by competing with the father and confronting his values, beliefs, and limits. For some/many sons and daughters, it is only at the father's death that they realize the intensity and longevity of their need for him (Pruett, 2001). In addition to the child's contribution to the father-child relationship, the father's response to that relationship shapes it further. A father's care differs from that of mother's in many ways. Fathers spend more of their time with their children in play that involves noisy, boisterous activities. They engage the children in active exciting games on the spur of the moment. They encourage exploration. Mothers are more likely to talk or sing soothingly, combining play with the care taking routine (Berger, 1994).

Children from families where the father involves himself in childcare from the very beginning enjoy strength in dealing with stress and frustration, and are less rigid in their gender stereotyping. These positive behaviors become stronger and endure longer when they are complemented by the mother's support of her partner's active contribution. The experiences and relationships that mothers have had with their fathers powerfully shape their expectations about their spouses' role in the life of the child. A mother acts as gatekeeper to her child's world from the very beginning of her baby's existence and plays a significant role in encouraging and in promoting competent fathering.

At the present time, the joint family system that offered experienced, valuable support in child caring/minding is gradually fading, particularly in urban areas. Thus, fathers have to share and develop the right attitude towards parental responsibilities. Fathers generally have a positive, invaluable impact on children. Besides playing a beneficial role in stimulating and socializing children, a father's presence in their development reduces the likelihood of their suffering from potentially detrimental personal relationships that are crucial during the formative years. The importance of a father's role in childrearing is fully realized with his absence. Early sexual activity, drug use, high rates of school failure or drop out, and juvenile delinquency are the result of a father's absence (Jaya, 1998).

Fathers also play an important part in sex role development besides influencing pro-social behavior such as generosity, altruism, helpfulness, and problem-solving behaviour. Positive fathering brings the child and father closer, establishing a close and long lasting relationship, and leading to a happy child who is satisfied with life (Lambert, Cwik, and Bogeschneider, 1995).

Perhaps more than any other single factor, the absence of the biological father is the leading cause of many of this nation's problems, including crime, teen violence, drug use, juvenile delinquency, teenage pregnancy, mental illness, suicide, and poor educational performance. Among several other statistical correlations demonstrating the crucial role of the father in the proper and healthy development of children, educational problems among children and adolescents have been linked to the lack of a father in the home (Ballard, 1995).

The degree of acceptance or rejection a child receives from the father affects development as deeply as the presence or absence of a mother's love. Fathers are as important as mothers in childrearing. However, fathers face several barriers posed by socio-cultural practices that discourage competent fathering within and outside of the family.

Barriers to Competent Fathering

Fathering has received a setback due to several barriers set by social and cultural interplay, such as follows:

- Social pressure to delegate all childcare tasks to female members.
- Culture defines childcare tasks as women's tasks.
- Personal pride, inhibitions.
- Lack of knowledge about childcare.
- Lack of time to spare for children.
- Personal experiences of having received inadequate fathering during their childhood.
- Lack of a role model.

Suggestions for Positive Parenting

Positive parenting is the loving and supportive care provided by both parents. The parenting role has shifting its paradigm from fear-based to love-based. Positive parenting also can be termed 'conscious parenting', or always seeking the betterment of children in the long run. To achieve the goal of treating or rearing children in a way so that today's children can be tomorrow's healthy and successful adults, key issues involved are as follows:

— The happiness and harmony between father and mother are important prerequisites for a physically fit and mentally happy child.

— Maintaining harmony between parents and children is essential for positive parenting.

— Children should be allowed to explore and do things themselves to enhance their self-esteem, so that they might experience a happy, gratifying, and purposeful life.

— The parents' own behaviors, attitudes, beliefs, and values affect greatly the child's development. Hence, parents need to recognize their own belief system and how it can impact on the lives of their children. Further, they should attempt to keep in tune with the changing times.

- Children need unconditional love and support from their parents for healthy development. Rationalizing, reasoning, giving adequate time, and answering questions are essential on the part of parents. These childrearing practices promote the same future behaviors in their children.
- Support children emotionally at times when they need it most, so that they do not feel let down or alone. It seems likely that a child who feels emotionally isolated senses a breach of faith and trust on the part of the parents.
- Accept each child as an individual with his or her unique gifts and talents. Each child is different, hence comparison with others is unwarranted.
- Positive requests to children, without forcing them to do something, work wonders.
- Showing positive feelings and appreciation for even the small work done by the child will encourage the development of confidence and a secure self-concept (i.e., "I feel good about myself and about my abilities").
- Listen carefully to your children and provide support and guidance.
- The relationship of parents with other members of family, relatives, and neighbors affects the general environment to which children are exposed.
- Parent education, in terms of learning and practicing good parenting skills to rear and manage today's children, is essential. Modern-day children are more world-wise, having been exposed to many more situations than their parents, which may lead to a feeling of incompetence and helplessness on the part of the parents to manage their children.

Conclusion

Parenting is not an easy task. Becoming a parent is the easiest part, whereas, being a conscious and positive parent is a momentous task. Parenting is the most important role one faces in a lifetime. Parents who provide an encouraging environment for their children are rewarded when, as adults, their children realize a successful fit into the culture and society.

Parenting concepts are deeply rooted in Indian families, because of a strong, sustained tradition of educating and training young parents to accept, perform and establish enduring relationships and responsibilities with their children. Generally, the young mother is introduced to the nuances of parenting by way of the 'hands on' method at her parental home, and under the guidance of her mother or an experienced family member. This practice could be the reason why the need for professional parent education usually is not expressed.

Effective parenting enables children to build and develop positive behaviors and good, solid self-concepts that are important to functioning fully as a healthy adult. Parenting, as such, is greatly dependent on intra-familial issues that play a significant role in parental performance. However, parenting skills can be strengthened if parents learn about themselves as a 'parent' and about child development. Learning about the stages of human development helps parents understand about their ever, changing roles in the lives of their children and also what is expected of a parent at each stage. Finally, a father's love and influence is as important as a mother's in the life of a child. Fathers should overcome the internal and external barriers that exist to fulfill the duties of fathering.

Note

The concept of parenting and parenthood varies according to region, and varies within the rural, urban and tribal areas in India. This paper discusses general concepts about South Indian ways of parenting and parenthood.

References

Ainsworth, M.D.S., Bell, S.M., and Stayton, D.J. (1971). Individual differences in strange situations behaviour of one year olds. In H.R. Schaffer (ed.), *The Origins of Human Social Relations,* London: Academic Press.

Ballard, T., (1995). Supporting the role of fathers in families – Statement, for a Meeting at the White House. November 27.

Baumrind, D., (1971). Current patterns of parental authority. *Developmental Psychology Monographs*, 4(1).

Berger, K.S., (1994). *The Developing Person through the Life Span.* New York: Worth, pp. 188-189.

DeBord, K., (1997). *Parenting Types.* In www.parentsplace.com.

Galinsky, E., (1987). *Stages of Parenthood.* In www.parentsplace.com/family/fcs-447.htm.

Golombok, S., (2000). *Parenting: What Really Counts?* London: Routledge, p. 69.

Harlow, H., and Horlow, M.K. (1969). Effects of various mother-infant relationships on Rhesus Monkey behaviours. In B.M. Foss (ed.), *Determinants of Infant Behaviours*, (Vol. 4), London: Methuen.

Jaya, N., (1998). Why children come to the observation home repeatedly. *Vignana Chudar*, (Vol. 25), p. 5.

Jensen, L.C., and Kingston M. (1986). *Parenting.* New York: Holt, Rinehart and Winston, p. 321.

Lambert, J., Cwik, M.S., and Bogeschneider, K. (1995). *Effects of Involving Fathering.* A Report to the Wisconsin Governor's Commission on Families and Children. July.

Pruett, K.D., (2001). *Father Need: Why Father Care is as Essential as Mother Care for your Child.* In www.fathering.com.

Ross, H.S., and Goldman, B.D. (1977). Establishing new social relations in infancy. In T. Alloway, P. Pliner and L. Krames (eds.), *Attachment Behaviour*, New York: Van Nostrand.

6

Language Socialization in Contemporary Indian Families

Smita Sinha

Indian families are undergoing a state of transition. With the advent of modernization, industrialization, and globalization, changes are noticed in all spheres of human activity. Language interactions among family members are no exception. There is a gradual shift from yesterday's interfamilial interaction to that of today's in terms of language usages. This paper presents the transition in verbal behavior from that of older generation family member to present generations in the state of Orissa. The language behavior of the family members from a high socio-economic group as well as low socio-economic group was studied. Some remedial suggestions will be outlined that may improve the verbal communication within families, so as to increase the quality of life.

"With a sweet tongue and kindness, you can drag an elephant by the hair."

—A Persian proverb

A historical investigation into modern Indian families would reveal that in most extended families there are three generations of family members living together – grandparents, parents, and their children. Grandparents are the product of the pre-independent era, brought up under strict imperial government as children. This was the time when Indians were struggling for freedom from colonial rule. Although the parents are the product of the post-independence era, still the touch of the British rule had some influence on their upbringing. As children, today's parents heard stories of British India, and the strict sense of duty and discipline that was coupled with brutality that defined that era. Indian values were introduced from childhood through bedtime stories from ancient Indian literature such as Ramayana, Mahabharata, Panchatantra, etc. In contrast, today's children are the offspring of free India, influenced by mass media such as TV and films and peer group socialization.

Similarly, school teachers of earlier generations were strict, and physical punishment was an accepted means of inducing student discipline and assuring compliance with studies. In comparison, the school teachers of modern-day India are more open, friendly, and in most schools, physical punishment is completely banned.

Language serves as a powerful medium of communication in the family. It is through language man learns to socialize with other human beings. Language socialization is defined as "the process of socialization through language and socialization to use language" (Ochs, 1986). Children develop communicative competence through participation in social interactions. Socio-cultural and family values are transmitted to children through language. Values embedded in cultural patterns and social structures are expressed in "modes of speaking" (Peters and Boggs, 1986). Particular lexical items, intonation, style, or grammatical features mark the modes of speaking specific to a speaker, family, situation, or even to a generation of people. Since the family serves as the smallest unit of society, proper verbalization among family members enhances the quality of life, brings peace, happiness, and success both for each individual and also for family as a whole; whereas, improper language socialization in the family leads to misunderstanding, misery, failure, and sorrows. Broadly, it may lead to lack of interpersonal relationships and improper social development among family members. Hence, overall family peace and happiness are at stake.

Family Life and Communicative Behavior

"The most fundamental aspect of the family process is communication" (Bochner, 1976). Communicative behavior in the family can be seen in verbal or non-verbal symbols or messages. Pearson (1989) maintains that no universal laws about communication behavior in the family have been determined. It is not possible to offer a list of specific communication skills for highly satisfying relationships. Language, however, plays an important role in the communication among family members, thus enabling good relationships. An understanding of communication may not secure family success, but it will enhance the likelihood of happiness with family members. For Anderson (1959), communication is a process of understanding others. It is dynamic and constantly changing with situation.

> The family provides a unique communication setting. Families are organised, relational transactional groups, usually occupying a common living space over an extended time period and possessing a mixture of interpersonal images that evolve through the exchange of meaning overtime (Pearson, 1989).

Proper verbalization among family members promotes understanding, support, and increased satisfaction. It also helps to manage power and stress issues by supporting better decision-making abilities. Improper language interactions lead to misunderstanding, increase the likelihood of conflict, and can cause a loss autonomy and intimacy among family members.

Individual autonomy is defined as a state of being self-governed, self-determined, and independent. Intimacy refers to close relationships, associations, affiliations, or acquaintances with other people. As one becomes increasingly intimate with another person, he/she may feel less individual autonomy. Conversely, as one becomes more autonomous, he or she may feel less intimate (Pearson, 1989). In other words, autonomy and intimacy are inversely proportionate to each other, and a balance between one's autonomy and intimacy is required for a satisfying family life.

The family acts as a speech community. A speech community shares rules for the conduct and interpretation of speech (Hymas, 1972). Family members may develop a common code for expressing wants, needs, and emotions. Others outside the family might be unable to interpret the underlying meaning of an utterance, even though they know all the words. They may interpret what they hear according to the rules of speaking, and thus misunderstand the speakers' intention, perhaps perceiving insincerity or offence where none was meant. A form of address or a personal question, which may be perfectly appropriate or even mandatory for one family/generation, may seem absurd or even insulting to another family or generation. "Even though, the usage of each generation may necessarily come to include features that distinguish it from the last, they all still essentially speak the same language, since the social coherence of the speech community ensures an uneventful and gradual evolution" (Singh, 2000).

Each individual is a fountainhead, as he/she contributes to the building block of a social group, i.e., the family. Concepts such as sharing a language and belonging to a family come into being through acts of identity, which people make within themselves and with each other. In fact, a family and the linguistic attributes of its family members have no co-existential locus other than in the minds of the members, and they are interconnected only in the way they behave with one another.

The language of each individual represents the family or the social group to which he or she belongs. Chomsky (1956, 1975, 1980) and Skinner (1957) developed various theories on language acquisition and development of communicative competence. Children learn to speak at home by listening to the ambient language that surrounds them. They begin to understand the value of communication, develop the ability to communicate, and develop appropriate grammatical skills and particular communicative style. They also acquire a particular attitude about language and communication. Day (1982) believes that language attitudes are an integral part of communicative competence, which is the knowledge required to use a language appropriately in a speech community. It includes, in addition to grammatical knowledge, social knowledge, which acts to define the communicative process and to shape the way messages are realized in social situations.

Biological and Cultural Language

"A common language symbolized the unity of those who spoke it, expressed their uniqueness, highlighted the difference between them... legitimized their self-assertion and their struggle for autonomy" (Cooper, 1989:12). Communicative competence includes not only the mastery of grammar and lexicon but also rules of speaking. Wolfson (1983) equates rules of speaking with norms of interactions, which are culture-specific and largely unconscious. By unconscious, he means that speakers use language spontaneously and automatically; the vocabulary and suprasegmental or prosodic aspects of language such as stress, intonation, etc., come very naturally and in accordance with the culture.

Singh (2000) talks about biological and cultural languages. Language has a culture-specific aspect: different families have come to encode features that diverge from the biological base, but which have emerged from cultural evolution. In the process of normal language acquisition, the child's biological language is specified by the ambient language, but is influenced by the cultural language. In India, it is believed that members of the younger generation use language in accordance with their peer group identity, while displaying resistance to the authoritative language of the older generation. In other words, there is some kind of cultural influence depicted in their language.

Language Socialization in Indian Families

To determine language socialization in Indian families, a study was carried out in Bhubaneswar, the capital city of the state of Orissa. Data consisted of selected conversations with family members from 20 households where Oriya was spoken. Ten families each represented the upper class (category A) and the lower class slum areas (category B). Data were collected via tape recordings in the homes without the conscious knowledge of informants. This method was used in order to get accurate information and natural speech from family members. All family members were native speakers of Oriya – an Indo-Aryan language. Data for this paper were selected from longer recordings in an attempt to establish comparability across a similar range of interactive situations and a variety of speakers, as well as to be representative of speech interactions of the family members.

The data chosen for the present purposes were similar in the following respects:

(i) Speakers involved – grandparents, parents and children.

(ii) Settings – Living rooms, bedrooms and/or kitchens in family homes.

Data were analyzed to study the following linguistic variables:

- Politeness/impoliteness, based on the international contour of utterances and on the kind of lexical items used.
- Whether the speaker was commanding or submissive while articulating.
- Whether the speaker used abusive or derogatory language.

- Whether the speaker used harsh language that was considered as cold.

Every effort was made to analyze roughly equal amounts of data involving the full range of speakers and settings. The samples were composed of approximately the same proportions of talk for each family.

Sample Profile

All 20 children from families in category A had been born and had lived continuously in posh areas of Bhubaneswar, and were attending expensive English medium schools. The 20 children from families in category B had been born and had lived all of their lives in the slums of Bhubaneswar. Some of them were going to Oriya medium government schools, while others were school dropouts, having left school after failing in their final examinations. All the children were aged 13-15 years old.

Parents who were in category A earned high incomes and had achieved high educational levels afforded to the economically privileged. Both parents worked in these families. The children had been raised by grandparents and servants. The interviewees observed that these couples shared a friendlier and open relationship among themselves than couples in the category B.

In contrast, all the parents representing the category B had low incomes and no education. Both parents worked in low-paying jobs, such as laborers, maid servants, or rickshaw pullers. The male members normally got drunk at night. Further, there were reports of constant fights, verbal abuse, and use of filthy language between husbands and wives and with the children. Some of the families had access to television, which served as a source of entertainment.

The grandfathers of category A were educated retired men, who had held high paying jobs. Grandmothers were non-working housewives, who had dropped out of school. The grandfathers played the role as the family decision-maker, whereas the grandmothers were busy basically with childrearing and kitchen work. In other words, the grandparents followed the traditional segregation of work prevalent in Indian families in past eras. Conversely, all grandparents in the category B were uneducated, not having attended school. They lived with their children, and were completely dependent on them financially.

Occurrence of the following variables was calculated for contrastive purposes: politeness, harshness, impoliteness, use of abusive language, commanding language, submissiveness language, and language that was considered to have a cold tone.

Observations

Use of Honorific Terms in Address

All grandparents in category A used the word "tu", meaning 'you', as a non-honorific second person singular pronoun when referring to the parents and children. Fifty per cent of the parents used a slightly honorific term "tume" for children; whereas, the other half used the non-honorific term "tu". They used "aapana", a highly honorific second person pronoun, for father and "tu" for the mother as a gesture of love. The use of the honorific pronoun form, "aapana", suggested the distance in the relationship, as well as the respect for that addressee, whereas, "tu" symbolized 'love' as well as subordination in relationship. In category B all the members, irrespective of age, referred to one another as "tu".

Use of Honorific Terms in Reply

In Oriya, the reply 'yes sir' is "aagna" which is considered as a symbol of honour, civility, and polished behavior. The children of the category A did not employ this term when talking to their parents or grandparents. However, parents in the category A used the term frequently when talking to the grandfathers. No individual in category B used this term.

Use of Swear, Abusive and/or Unparliamentary Words

Ten per cent of the grandparents in category A used derogatory words, such as "sala", meaning wife's brother. This term is used as a derogatory one in Oriya when one is annoyed with a servant or some outsiders. Few parents used this word. Children used English swear words like "shit". All members in category B used swear words. Use of abusive or unparliamentary words was frequent and appeared to be the normal standard of language, as these words were spoken without any inhibition.

Use of Insulting, Harsh, and/or Pain-generating Words Combined with Cold Behavior

About 70 per cent of children used harsh words such as "mind your own business", "that's none of your business", "you can't dictate terms with me", "no need to poke your nose into my affairs', mainly with their parents, although sometimes with grandparents. They did not hesitate to offend or insult these elders in front of others. In contrast, when outside the home, these children behaved civilly with others, following the rules of good etiquette and mannerism. They were aware of their constitutional rights and the difference between egalitarianism versus authoritarianism.

Surprisingly, in the category B families, members did not speak in a harsh or cold manner to each other, nor used insulting words, even though fights were common over trivial issues. Instead, swearing or dirty language was used on a regular basis.

Deviation from Standard Variety

Older generations in the higher social class were closer to the norms of standard language in their use of certain linguistic variables. The shift from more formal to informal speech by the younger generation can be explained as the effect of upward social mobility on language use. Among the slum dwellers, there was a total deviation from standard Oriya. The dialectal variety used by them was distinctly different from the standard form.

Bilingualism

Children in category A used frequently English and Hindi, along with Oriya, in their interactions with other family members. This code switching and mixing is a unique feature in the speech of the youngsters, which was not observed in the speech of their parents or grandparents. No one was bilingual in the slums, thus there was no sign of code switching or code mixing, although, they understood Hindi.

Discussion and Findings

Findings from the study revealed that terms expressing one's status or honorific terms were used exclusively in category A families, and mainly by grandparents or parents. It is likely that these terms were missing in the language of those in category B because they had never been addressed or responded to with these words. Perhaps, they did not feel that terms which symbolize a high social standing or status were appropriate for their life situation. In terms of swear words usage, individuals in both categories used these terms during conversations. Swearing was employed on a typical basis in the lower income families, whereas, it was less common in category A families. Children in category A families used English swear words, which suggests the influence of television, movies, and other mass media on their language.

A striking feature found uniformly in the higher economic class was that children were less polite in their speech and mannerisms, as compared to children in the lower economic class. Children in category A families felt the freedom to express their need for autonomy and independence, as shown in some of their statements about parental interference in their lives. They were aware, however, of appropriate social etiquette, applying the rules outside of the home, while choosing not to use them in the home. None of this type of linguistic behavior was noted in the speech of children in category B. It may be that the simple struggle to survive negates issues with independence and autonomy. Further, children who are working have already achieved a level of independence. Parents who work in occupations requiring intense physical labor may not have the mental or physical resources available to try to monitor or interfere in their children's lives. In addition, fathers who are intoxicated after work would have dulled mental facilities which could create an attitude of not caring about what the children are doing (i.e., not interfering with their lives).

It was expected that the standard form of Oriya would be common among family members in category A, as these families had a history of privilege and high academic achievement. It was not surprising that a dialectal variation of Oriya was spoken in the slums, where educational levels were low. One tends to speak in the dialect to which one is exposed. It may be that children in category B families who were still attending school spoke a more standardized form of Oriya in the academic setting, while using the non-standard form at home.

Lastly, it was obvious that the educational and social experiences of children in category A families had contributed to the bilingualism displayed. Children from lower income families may not need to use other languages on an expressive level, whereas, it may be essential to understand Hindi and perhaps English.

Implication of the Study to Family Life Education in India

In general terms, differences were found in language usage between the two economic classes of families studied. All families face challenging situations. It is important for family life educators to know the various verbal and non-verbal interactional styles and expectations when dealing with disputes or problems in families from all economic classes.

Pearson (1989) makes a distinction between integrative, disintegrative, and descriptive verbal acts. While the integrative verbal act is a positive communication revealing one's feeling and ideas with understanding and empathy, disintegrative verbal acts disclose one's feelings as threat-inducing to one's partner or family member. Descriptive verbal acts are mere exchanges of information. For effective communication in families to occur, it is recommended that members engage in more integrative verbal behaviors.

Although Indian children are the 'building blocks' of the nation, they are more aggressive and impolite in their speech and behavior than in past generations, especially in the context of their families. Since parents today do not have a tendency to speak rudely to grandparents even during conflicts, where do the children pick up such features? They are influenced in part by movies, TV, and other aspects of the media. Modern parents need to find create and effective ways to teach children not to succumb to unhealthy external pressures, and also teach and model the proper way to speak politely and correctly to others. Specifically, parents and other adults in the family need to learn to use and then teach problem-solving, listening, and negotiation skills to their children, while at the same time provide understanding and support.

The older generation must demonstrate a sense of equality rather than a sense of power or control over their offspring through proper verbalization of words without hurting their feelings. The harshness in the behavior of children and adolescents is due in part to the growing dissatisfaction with such a competitive and impersonal world, coupled with lack of value-oriented education. Talking about these difficult issues begins at home, but in an environment where children will be carefully listened to and taken seriously by their caregivers. According to Phillips and Goodall (1983), talk is the substances of a loving relationship. Talk enables lovers to exchange feelings and make agreements about their day-to-day life. In this way, each married couple develops their own unwritten constitutions and agreements about how decisions are to be made and carried out, how disputes are to be settled, how rituals and ceremonies will be conducted, and how they will deal with each other and everyone else. These communicative behaviors will then be more caught by than taught to their children.

References

Anderson, S.A. (1959). The "concept" of communication. As cited in F.E.X. Dance (1970). *Journal of Communication*. 20, pp. 201-210.

Bochner, A.P. (1976). Conceptual frontiers in the study of communication in the families: An introduction to the literature. *Human Communication Research*, 2, pp. 381-397.

Chomsky, N. (1956). Three models for the description of language: Transactions on information theory, IT-2, pp. 113-124.

Chomsky, N. (1975). *The Logical Structure of Linguistic Theory*. New York: Plenum.

Chomsky, N. (1980). *Rules and Representations*. New York: Plenum.

Cooper, R. (1989). *Language Planning and Social Change*. Cambridge: University Press.

Day, R.R. (1982). Children's attitudes toward language. In Ellen Bouchand Ryan and Howard Giles' (eds.) *Attitude Towards Language Variation Social and Applied Context*. London: Arnold.

Hymas, D. (1972). Models of the interaction of language and social setting. In Gumperz, J.J. and Hymas D. (eds.). *Directions in Sociolinguistics: The Ethnography of Communication*. New York: Holt, Rinehart and Winston, pp. 35-71.

Ochs, E. (1986). *Language Socialization Across Cultures*. Cambridge: CUP, (pp. 276-320).

Pearson, July C. (1989). *Communication in the Family: Seeking Satisfaction in Changing Times*. New York: Harper and Row.

Peters, A.M. and Boggs, S.T. (1986). Interactional routines as cultural influences upon language acquisition. In B.B. Schieffeling and E. Ochs (eds.), *Language Socialization Across Cultures*. Cambridge: CUP, (pp. 80-96).

Phillips, G. and Goodall, H.L., Jr. (1983). *Loving and Living: Improve Your Friendships and Marriage*. Englewood Cliffs. NJ: Prentice-Hall.

Singh, I. (2000). *Pidgins and Creoles*. London: Arnold.

Skinner, B.F. (1957). *Verbal Behaviour*, New York: Appleton-Century-Crofts.

Wolfson (1983). *Rules of Speaking in Language and Communication* (ed.) Richards and Richards W. Schmidt. Longman.

7

Old Age and Family Life in India

Minoti Phukan

Older adults and their families are at a crossroads in Indian society. In past years the elderly were considered as asset within the joint family structure, where they were ensured of familial care and support. However, in recent years, the family structure has become a nuclear one, with females working outside the home for both financial and professional reasons. This phenomenon has resulted in a deprivation of care for the aged at home and has left them with a certain sense of insecurity. The elderly are no longer considered as 'assets' but rather as 'liabilities' for their adult children. This chapter discusses various problems experienced by older adults in India today, and needed adjustments within society and the family system. Suggestions are made for how the elderly can more successfully cope with the challenges of growing old in a society that no longer values and appreciates them as it once did. It also discusses obligations of family and community with regard to meeting the needs and enhancing the quality of life for elders.

Life is a progression from youth to old age. Increasing physical and mental declines mark our older adult years. People are defined as old according to both appearance and position. Old age in contemporary India is characterized by an objective condition of social, economic and family marginality, as well as by a role and identity crisis. It is also characterized by changes in intellectual capabilities. Another indication of old age is when the individual relinquishes his or her occupation. Older adulthood has become clearly distinguished as a specific stage of life, with retirement from one's work role as a milestone, whether it is forced or elective.

Parsons (1954) states that "...retirement leaves the older man in a peculiarly functionless position, cut off from participation in the most important interests and activities of the society". There are very few incentives for older persons to make productive contributions to society, and there are many obstacles to their engagement both socially and vocationally. Among men the transition from active adult status to retirement is often more traumatic than that for women. When relative poverty and deprivation accompany retirement, which is often the case in India, elderly individuals experience an even greater loss of identity and personal worth. Marriages and family life are significantly influenced by such changes in the status and role of the elderly person.

Scholars have employed different definitions of 'aged', 'elderly', 'aging', and 'old' and no one can claim to have a patent over this definition. The variety of definitions offered in the gerontological literature is almost as diverse as the number of writers (Bali, 2001). In India, there is no clear-cut demarcation of the age upon which a person can be called 'old', 'elderly' or 'aged'. However, definitions of the terms 'elderly' or 'aged' vary from society to society. Old age is generally determined by physical or mental condition rather than chronological age. Indeed, the idea of keeping a precise account of age is a relatively recent one in Indian society.

In rural India people are not classified as 'aged' by an absolute biological and chronological criterion, since most older people do not know their age. They are, however, generally aware of their relative age, which has to do with the category and activities appropriate to their contemporaries and the progress made through the life cycle of their kin in the adjacent generations. Age is sometimes determined by an association of a person's birth with special historic events, or geo-climatic, astronomical occurrence, eclipses, full moon floods, earthquakes, droughts, or with socio cultural events or festivals, rituals, and the like. Moreover, in rural areas, old age is identified as a period of life when one moves from more of a state of independence to dependency upon others. This transition may occur because of limited income, poor health, and/or disability. Among peasant communities, handing over property by an aging individual to others belonging to the younger generation (mostly sons) symbolizes the crossing of the threshold of age of a person (Bali, 2001). Among women, the transition to old age occurs with menopause. The physical and psychological problems associated with menopause, when coupled with the departure of children from the home, can be traumatic for a woman Indian society.

The welfare of the elderly was traditionally embedded in the structure of the joint family. With increasing occupational mobility and attendant migrations, the joint family structure, particularly among the more mobile, has undergone inevitable changes. These changes have been more adaptive than transformative. Instead of moving towards traditional nuclear families as in the West, India seems to be nucleating in the household sense (Bali, 2001). The joint family is giving way to the extended family with nuclear or small households as the primary units of residence. In India, providing social security and developing welfare services for the elderly on the part of the state is a recent phenomenon, as it was the responsibility of the family earlier to take care of its elders. Because of an ever-increasing female participation in the labor force, migration from rural to urban areas, longer life expectancy of older adults, changes in family structure, roles, relationships, work pressures, and demands on the time of potential caregivers in the family, it is becoming increasingly difficult for the family to take care of their elderly.

Problems during Old Age

The problems of old age are both complex and multifarious. According to Bali (2001), the main problem with the elderly in India is poverty. The majority of older people live in or on the margins of poverty. For those family members who work in the subsistence economy, their livelihood depends on the vagaries of the monsoon. The elderly continue to work as long as their physical abilities and health permit. They do not receive any pension, nor do they have any income security when they can no longer work. On the other hand, the small numbers of older adults, who are employed in the formal or organized sector, generally receive some pension when they retire. This pension is often very minimal. On retirement, they seem to loose a major source of their livelihood as well as their identity. Because the elderly have little or no money, they suffer from malnutrition and other health-related problems, leading to depression and other forms of mental illness. The high incidence of poverty among older people is also reflected in other measures of deprivation, such as housing and access to health and social services. This has significance for their quality of life in that the elderly have difficulties in having their basic needs met. However, health problems among older adults are the major problems. This issue is examined in more detail in the next section.

Health Problems

Ill-health is recognized as one of the pressing problems of the aged in India. Older people become more concerned about their physical well-being than they were younger, which may lead to certain psychological distress (Jayashree, 1990). Factors such as nutrition, exercise, sanitation, personal hygiene, and mental stimulation contribute to one's health status in old age. DeSouza (1982) describes four factors, which determine the overall health of older people. These are: (1) the nature and condition of their work: hard work combined with poor nutrition leads to the state of general disability, which may cause old people to suffer from what may be called deficiency illness'; (2) environmental conditions due to lack of basic amenities such as water, latrines and drainage result in an environment that is a health hazard; (3) eating an inadequate and unbalanced diet; and (4) the availability and quality of health services. With increased longevity come increased health problems. Findings from various studies (Shanas and George, 1976; U.S. National Survey, 1983) indicate a decline in physical and psychological health with increase in age. Hence, not only the probability of dying increases with age over the adult life span, but also the incidence of many chronic diseases and disabilities. Some of the common diseases during old age are:

1. Difficulty with vision including cataracts, glaucoma, and retinal disorders.
2. Hearing impairments and general sensory loss.
3. Respiratory diseases such as chronic bronchitis and asthma.
4. Diseases of the locomotors system: fibrosis, gout, rheumatism, arthritis, osteoarthritis, and osteoporosis.
5. Dental problems.
6. Degenerative diseases of blood vessels and the heart, like arteriosclerosis leading to high blood pressure and possible stroke. Cerebrovascular diseases are a major cause of death among the aged.
7. Increased incidence of diabetes.
8. Nutrition deficiency diseases, indigestion.
9. Gastro-urinary disorders: enlargement of the prostate.
10. Inflammation/pain at joints.

11. Accidents: Due to the loss of sensory functions like hearing, vision and touch, the elderly are prone to accidents resulting in fractures as a result of frequent falls.
12. Easily susceptible to colds and cough.
13. Insomnia.
14. General weakness.

Because of these health problems during old age, it is advisable for older citizens to have routine check-ups. But, people in general, and particularly in our country, may not take health-related matters seriously. In spite of standard medical advice that old people should have regular health check-ups, they are reluctant to comply. The non-compliance may be largely due to financial issues. How much will the medical examination and possible treatment cost? Who will pay if the elderly cannot afford the costs? In rural India, ignorance on the part of old people, lack of medical facilities or inadequate medical facilities, and a lack of initiative and interest on the part of extended family members are some of the factors that aggravate the deteriorating health status of old people.

Certain employers offer free treatment and medicines through government hospitals, dispensaries, company hospitals, and medical units to employees. Moreover, reimbursement of medical bills is available for treatment of certain diseases in reputed government or private hospitals in the country. But once retired, all these medical benefits cease. Therefore, treatment of medical problems is much more expensive for retired people, as compared to those who are presently employed. As a result, the health status of retired people may be allowed to deteriorate without medical intervention. Absence of the loving care offered by family members also has a negative impact on the health status of older people.

According to a survey conducted by Helpage, India, physical health problems were not cited as the major ones, but were linked to monetary and mobility issues. Instead, crammed living space in children's homes, and humiliation due to financial dependence were the major problems cited by the aged. In general, aged males have more complaints about different ailments being suffered by them than aged females (Sengupta and Chakravorty, 1982). Ahmed (2001) reaffirmed that aged females are biologically stronger than aged males. In the words of Kofi Annan, the Secretary General of United Nations, "There is also a significant gender discrimination to this portrait of humanity's 'coming of age', women nearly everywhere living longer than men. They face a higher risk of chronic illness and disability, discrimination, or marginalization. Women sometimes face a triple burden: child care, older care, and, of course, seeing to their own well-being. But these contributions to their families, community and the economy are often overlooked" (Jena, 2002).

Psychosocial Problems

Various types of psychosocial problems can emerge during old age. Many of the psychosocial problems could be analyzed within the context of family system. The shift from age-old joint family systems to nuclear families has created erosion in the interrelationships that existed in traditional joint family systems. Consequently, the status and authority of the old has undergone major changes. According to Mohanty (1989), changed physical and psychological capacities, circumstances, and opportunities tend to impose limitations necessitating substitution and reorganization in the behavior pattern of the old. The role as head of the household is realized no more, once the man reaches old age. He is not required or consulted when major decisions are made, either at home on a personal level, or in the society. These circumstances create a void in the mind of the old and thus the elderly suffers from distress. Certain psychological hazards keep operating during old age. These often involve the acceptance of some traditional beliefs and cultural stereotypes concerning older people (Hurlock, 1990). This acceptance, according to Hurlock, is hazardous as it makes the individual feel inadequate, discouraged, and inferior; they are no longer needed by their family or by society. Feelings of inadequacy can cause the elderly to refrain from doing any fruitful or productive work or to pursue new or old hobbies for personal satisfaction. Another traditional belief is that older people are somewhat forgetful, having trouble remembering old as well as new events, and often find it difficult to remember both existing and new names of the places, individuals, or facts.

All these factors create psychological stress in the lives of older people. They may find it very difficult to adjust to retirement in this highly competitive and work-oriented society. In order to cope, older people could get involved in voluntary works that benefit the society. This work would not only give them a sense of achievement, but also would generate self-respect and offer them some level of esteem in the society.

In Indian society, old people are offered due honor. Yet they may feel isolated or disenfranchised due to multiplicity of reasons. Initially, upon retirement, they have a feeling that they are unwanted, as their opinions and values are not considered appropriate by the present generation. They have plenty of time at their disposal, but others do not have the same to share with them. In the absence of pre-retirement planning, in most cases, old people cannot utilize their time in meaningful ways. Studies indicate that older people have more mental problems than the younger people. In addition, the aged feel insecure at the thought of being replaced by the younger generation which increases their mental discomfort. They start considering themselves inadequate. This further aggravates their mental depression.

Psychological depression is closely associated with retirement. About 93.4 per cent of survey respondents expressed their fear over retirement. It was found that 80 per cent of the respondents suffered from psychological depression due to the sudden loss of work and changes in the roles (Vijaya Kumar, 1997). Findings from the survey conducted by Helpage, India indicated that upper-middle class aged men listed having mental health problems. They mentioned not only the lack of work but also a family system in which they could utilize their productive potential and maximize their leisure time. They reported experiencing a general feeling of "talking to the wall", even when their spouses were alive. Lack of emotional support by family members is considered the second major problem across all economic groups and is described as "neglect", "feelings of insecurity", "considering oneself a burden", "experiencing feelings of loneliness in everything" and "old age is a disease" (Jena, 2002).

Economic Problems

Once the individual steps into old age, economic problems start dominating in their personal lives. Immediately after retirement, the individual is faced with continuing bills, and a diminished income. During old age, the major recurring expenditure is on health. It is believed that earning a good income ensures good mental and physical health. It is well known that the retired life is accompanied by a decline in economic status. In a study cited by Jena (2002), for example, economic problems were at the top of the list given to elderly males. However, there are variations. Vijaya Kumar and Suryanarayan (1993) concluded that variations in the economic conditions of the elderly mainly depended upon the nature of their employment. Other factors included the sex and marital status of the person, health, social obligations, and degree of control over their economic resources.

The previous factors clearly define the areas to which expenditures are incurred. Deteriorating health status may be regarded as the major source of financial depletion during old age. Sometimes medical costs become too heavy to bear. This is why pre-retirement planning for service holders, as well as pensioners and non-service holders, is crucially important. However, composition of the family and pattern of living also have an impact on the economic status of older adults. Living in a nuclear family and being the sole income earner for the family definitely creates a heavy burden for the elderly. On the other hand, older adults who are dependent on their children for their livelihood quite often consider themselves a burden on their offspring. These issues were much less of a concern in joint rural families than in urban families that were more nuclear in structure (Vijaya Kumar, 1997).

Financial problems in old age make life adjustment difficult. If they happen to become a burden to the next generation, the risk of being neglected increases significantly. In the Indian context, particularly in urban families, some adult children do neglect their older parents and relatives. However, if retired persons have a pension, own property, or possess a large bank balance, they are more likely to receive care and attention from the younger generations. Burk (1971) concluded that older adults who have enough money to live as they did before retirement adjust better to their changed lifestyle. However, according to Mohanty (1989), in India, retired persons in the middle and lower middle classes typically experience acute financial problems. After exhausting their savings within a few years after retirement, they become dependent on their children. Thereafter, these older people are often neglected and ill-treated because they become a burden on the family. At the same time, many still feel responsible for taking care of their adult children and grandchildren. One study by Vijaya Kumar and Raja Reddy (1993) found that 49 per cent of retired respondents shouldered the financial burden of the education and marriage of their sons and daughters – no small task when one is living on a restricted income.

Position of the Aged in Contemporary Indian Families

Historically, the elderly have been held in high esteem in Indian society. In recent times, however, their status has been changing rapidly. The honor once accorded to the old is becoming something of the past (Mohanty, 1989). One study conducted by Menachery (1987) on the status of retired persons in the Indian family revealed a considerable reduction in their status and position in the family after retirement, primarily because they were no longer the primary breadwinner. Family members' perceptions of adults also change as they get older and are no longer able to provide help for the family. Verman and Sharma (1983) found, for example, that the majority of respondents from the younger generation expressed negative feelings about aged family members. However, such feelings tended to decrease with an increase in the educational level of younger family members. There is, therefore, need to educate children about the importance of respect and care for older people in the family and community, and to regard them as valuable resources. Verman and Sharma (1983) conclude that, on the one hand, the aged need to come to terms with their changing status and reformulate their social and psychological roles, and on the other, younger people need to be sensitized to understand the need and problems of the elderly with greater empathy and tolerance.

An investigation by Sahoo (1999) suggests that Indian families function as safety-valves for the aged. Families help to moderate the stress that stems from aging. This kind of support system needs to be retained to prevent the deterioration of the quality of life of older adults. Indeed, as Chowdhury (1999) asserts, older people are a valuable asset to our society and have the potential to play a constructive role in nation-building. People of all ages need to be re-educated as to the value of the elderly in modern India and the positive contributions they can make.

Adjustment of the Aged

According to Roosevelt (1961), adjustment occurs when there is a balance among needs, stimuli and opportunities offered by the environment. When these elements are in balance, there is a greater likelihood that personal well-being and life satisfaction will be experienced. Older individuals can be said to be in a state of well-being if they (1) take pleasure from activities in daily life; (2) view life as meaningful and accept present life circumstances; (3) feel that they have achieved their major life goals; (4) have a positive image of themselves; and (5) primarily experience happy and optimistic attitudes and moods (Havighurst, Neugarten, and Tobin, 1968).

There are two major theories associated with the process of adjustment in old age. *Disengagement theory*, propounded by Cumning and Henry (1961), portrays aging as a process of gradual physical, psychological, and social withdrawal from the mainstream of society in preparation for eventual physical decline and death. Disengagement is a mutual process whereby society relinquishes the elderly from their roles at the same time that the older individuals are beginning to shift their attention away from work, social, and civic activities. Eventually, disengagement becomes mutually advantageous to both older persons and the larger society. Contrary to the disengagement theory, *activity theory* maintains that the most successful aging takes place in those who maintain a high degree of involvement in life and relationships. Havighurst (1968) has stated, however, that:

> From a social psychological perspective aging is better viewed, not as a process of engagement or disengagement, but as a process of adoption in which personality is the key element. The aging individual not only plays an active role in adapting to the biological and social changes that occur with the passage of time but creates patterns of life that will give him greatest ego involvement and life satisfaction.

Older people have to make adjustments primarily in two areas: working life and family life. Whether a service holder or not, with approaching old age, people start realizing that not only is their perceived usefulness lessens as they grow older, but their status in the family and world of work as well. Hurlock (1990) indicates that the most important adjustments centering on family relationships involve relationships with one's spouse, relationships with offspring, parental dependency, and relationships with grandchildren. How well husbands and wives adjust to each other in old age depends on many factors. Common interests, mutual friends, compatible personalities, and a similar or harmonious worldview are a few of the factors that contribute to adjustment. Adjustment in the family life during old age also has a lot to do with the degree of dependency – both economic and emotional – between aging parents and adult children. In India, aging parents tend to maintain a certain authority over their adult children, and an emotional dependency is common. However, when there is a reversal of roles in the family (i.e., older adults now becoming economically dependent on adult an child or children), their roles of authority often change, as does the level of respect given to the elderly. Intergenerational conflict then becomes more common, which can lead to various types of abuse and neglect.

Finally, older adults in the family also have to make adjustments with regard to their grandchildren. Although, they are often placed in caregiving roles, conflicts between older and younger generations often erupt because of the rapidly changing values, attitudes, patterns of dress and behavior, and loosening of moral standards of the young. Often, a gap between them is created that is too great to bridge (Hurlock, 1990). These conflicts can also become a breeding ground for problems between the elderly and their adult children.

Retirement and Old Age

The age of retirement in modern India is typically between 58 and 60 years. As in most societies, retirement from one's work or service is difficult for older adults in India. According to Choudhury (1992), the process of adjustment to a new environment can be a very demanding and unsettling one, and there is some evidence that the first year or two following retirement is a period of high risk for older adults. Their chances of becoming ill (e.g., heart attack or stroke), depressed, suicidal, abused, or exploited by others increases geometrically with age after retirement.

Retirement is a social process by which an individual is withdrawn from the labor force or his/her professional life. In India, the mandatory retirement age is 58 or 60 years of age. However, on retirement, a person does receive certain economic benefits from the government, and often from the public or private sector where he or she was employed. This process of retirement involves several stages (Atchley, 1976). The post-retirement period, beginning with the 'initial' stage, is characterized by involvement in a variety of self-selected activities. The second stage is characterized by 'disenchantment' when the individual may experience the beginning of a decline in economic well-being and meaningful activities, as well as poorer health. This realization may lead to depression and a fear of the future. The third stage is that of 'reorientation' in which a realistic plan of alternative is developed. It leads to the fourth phase of post-retirement – the 'stability' stage – in which a satisfying routine for the retirement years is established. The fifth and last stage is 'termination'. This stage involves coping with illness and the loss of many activities because of declining health or financial resources. During this stage, illness or disability may prevail and the individual may become dependent on others, often to the extent that institutionalization is necessary.

The transition from an active and 'productive' life to retirement, then, is a difficult one for most people. According to Shanas (1972), the transition to retirement involves two alternative assumptions: (1) the individual finds a substitute for lost roles or satisfaction provided by the job; or (2) the individual adapts to retirement by accommodating his or her lifestyle to changes in health and income status and to changes in daily routine resulting from an increase in free time. Either way, adjustment to retirement involves an ongoing process of accommodation and change that can put great stress on individuals and families.

Successful adjustment to old age, perhaps more than anything else, requires preparation. In this case, knowledge is power and planning is empowering. Although anticipated by the vast majority of people, there are many in Indian society who are completely ill-prepared for retirement and the process of growing old. Vijaya Kumar (1997) has offered the following principles that may be helpful in preparing for and adjusting to retirement. These include:

(1) Plan early.
(2) Maintain flexibility in the interest and social roles.
(3) Remain physically and socially active.
(4) Plan for a gradual transition from work to retirement.
(5) Provide for a 'trail run' before a final commitment is made to a new residence of lifestyle.
(6) Consult with spouse, friends and children about short-term and long-term retirement plan.

Pre-retirement plans may include the following issues:

(1) Construction of own (permanent) house.
(2) Arrangement of financial security.
(3) Settlement of daughters and sons.
(4) Securing jobs for sons.
(5) Selecting avenues for engagement in social activities.

In reality, however, the majority of aging adults in India engage in no pre-retirement planning. Vijaya Kumar (1997) concluded from his study that, due to the lack of pre-retirement plans, the majority of retired persons are suffering from multiple problems, which include economic hardship, psychological depression, low self-esteem, ill-health, loss of a spouse, conflicts with adults children (e.g., sons, daughters, and daughters-in-law), and social discrimination, to name a few. Because of these issues, retired persons may develop negative attitudes towards retirement. Post-retirement 'education', as well as group or individual counseling, may help individuals acquire knowledge about, and adapt more effectively to, the rigors and challenges of becoming old.

Conclusion

Most societies, including India, are concerned about the phenomenon of aging and how to help their elderly remain healthy and respected citizens. Traditionally, the family in India has been the key provider of affective and material care for the elderly. However, Indian families today are at a crossroads with regard to how the needs of older adults will be met. Seemingly juxtaposed are the traditional values associated with family centered, informal parent care, and the newer values of a more public commitment to providing efficient services for the elderly. Upon closer analysis, though, it may be possible for India to continue to expand public services for the elderly while at the same time reinstating a cultural tradition that emphasizes the integration of the elderly with the family and society (Bali, 2001). The responsibility for action does not rest with any one sector of the community. It calls for collaborative and cooperative efforts on the part of all concerned with care of the elderly in making the lives of elderly people socially meaningful and worth living. Families need to be better informed and equipped in every way to provide necessary support for its older family members. Further, elderly persons need to be show how to stage engaged in family and community, and how to take better care of their own lives (Chowdhury, 1999). Such a reorientation needs to begin on a community level, but with state and national support on both practical and economic levels. As the lives of older adults are transformed, perhaps, the notion of 'trickle down' will once again become prevalent in Indian society.

References

Ahmed, J. (2001). Adjustment Patterns of the Retired Elderly, Unpublished Doctoral Dissertation, Jorhat: Department of Child Development and Family Relations, Faculty of Home Science, Assam Agricultural University, Assam.

Alderin (1937). In Dhilon, P.K. (ed.) *Psychosocial Aspects of Aging in India*. New Delhi: Concept Publishing Company, pp. 32-34.

Atchley (1976). In Vijaya Kumar, S. (1997). Pre-retirement plans and post-retirement adjustments. *Research and Development Journal*. 3 (2), 12.

Bali, A.P. (2001). *Care of the Elderly in India: Changing Configuration*. Shimla: Indian Institute of Advance Study.

Burk (1971). In Path, R.N. and Jene, B. (eds.) (1989). *Aged in Some Socio-Demographic Dimensions*, New Delhi: Ashish Publications, p. 218.

Choudhury, N. (1992). In Nandhini, G.S. and Parvathi, S. (1996). Adjustment depression and sense of well-being among men and women senior citizens. *Journal of Psychological Researches*. 40 (122), 1.

Chowdhury, A. (1999). The status and prescription of aged in Orissan families. In J.K. Baral and A., Chowdhury (eds.) *Family in Transition: Power and Development*. New Delhi: Northern Book Centre.

Cumning, F. and Henry, W.E. (1961). *Growing Old: The Process of Disengagement*. New York: Basic Books Inc.

Dak, T.M. (1987) (ed.). *Aging in India: Challenge for the Society*. New Delhi: Ajanta Publication.

DeSouza (1982). In Sharma, M.L. and Dak, T.M. (eds.) (1987). *Aging in India: Challenge for the Society*. New Delhi: Ajanta Publications, pp.199-203.

Dwoeretzky, J.P. (1984). *Introduction to Child Development*. New York: West Publishing Company, pp. 580-581.

Havighurst, Neugarten (1968). In Roosevelt, E. *The Autobiography of Eleanor Roosevelt*. New York: Harper and Row, pp. 194.

Havighurst, Neugarten and Tobin (1968). In Roosevelt, E. *The Autobiography of Eleanor Roosevelt*. New York: Harper and Row, pp. 192.

Hurlock, E.B. (1990). *Developmental Psychology: A Life-Span Approach*. New Delhi: Tata McGraw Hill Publishing Company Ltd. pp.389-450.

Jayashree, V. (1990). Health problem and aging. *The Mind*, 16(1) Summer, 9.

Jena, M. (2002). Problems elders face in changing society. *The Times of India*, July 1, p. 6.

Jay Kumar, G.S. (1992). Health of the elderly. *Social Welfare*, xxxix, pp. 3-5.

Menachery, G. (1987). Status of the retired in the family after retirement. *Journal of Psychological Researches*. 31 (3). pp. 135-136.

Mohanty, S. (1989). Retired government servants and their problems of socio-psychological adjustment. In Pati, R.N. and Jene, B. (eds.). *Aged in India: Some Socio-Demographic Dimensions*. New Delhi: Archies Publications.

Nandhini, G.S. and Parvathi, S. (1996). Adjustment, depression and sense of well-being among men and women senior citizens. *Journal of Psychological Researches*. 40 (122).

Parsons, T. (1954). Age and sex in the social structure of the United States. In T. Parsons (ed.), *Essays in Sociological Theory*. Glencoe, Ill: The Free Press.

Roosevelt, E. (1961). *The Autobiography of Eleanor Roosevelt*. New York: Harper and Row.

Rosow, I. (1968). *Housing and Local Ties of the Aged*. New York: Free Press.

Sahoo, F.M. (1999). Psychological well-being of Orissan families. In J.K. Baral and A. Chowdhury (eds.) *Family in Transition: Power and Development*, New Delhi: Northern Book Centre.

Sengupta and Chakravorty. (1982). In Sharma, M.C. and Dak, T.K. (eds.) (1987). *Aging in India*. New Delhi: Ajanta Publications, p. 195.

Shanas and George (1976). In Jayashree, V. (1990). Health problem and aging. *The Mind*, 16(1) Summer, 9.

Shanas, E. (1972). Adjustment to retirement: Substitution or accommodation? In Carp, F. (ed.). *Retirement*, New York: Human Science Press.

Vijaya Kumar, S. (1997). Pre-retirement plans and post-retirement adjustments. *Research and Development Journal*, 3 (2), pp. 12-22.

Vijaya Kumar, S. and Raja Reddy, K. (1993). Problems of retired persons. In *Man in India*, 73(3), pp. 241-249.

Vijaya Kumar, S. and Suryanarayan (1993). Problems of retired persons. In *Man in India*, 73(3), pp. 241-249.

8

Contemporary Family Problems

G. Baradha

The range and variety of problems that Indian families face are vast. They are developmental and everyday problems faced by all families at one time or another. There are, however, family problems which are specific in nature, though this does not imply that other families do not have problems. This chapter analyzes the variedness of family problems in India experienced by family members at different stages of the family life cycle. It also discusses various coping strategies and suggests preventive methods at length. The need for understanding family problems has been emphasized in order to prepare family members to face these problems successfully so that they can have healthy and satisfying life.

Family living is a constant process from day-to-day, week-to-week, and year-to-year. It is unpleasant only when family members fail to do their share in making the business of home living easy and smooth. When difficulty arises in the family, it is no cause for alarm. On the other hand, conflicts that occur too frequently and that never seem to get worked out are matters for concern. At times every person is irritated and irritating, thoughtless and discourteous. However, living in an unhappy and conflict-ridden home is a breeding ground for personal illness and pathology.

The family in contemporary society is less organized than were certain earlier forms of the family. A generation ago, the family in India provided six distinguished services for people, including biological, economic, social, emotional, educational, and religious. Today, five of these (except emotional) are being largely transferred from the family to outside agencies or institutions. Some examples include:

— An increasing proportion of family tasks (e.g., laundry) is done commercially.
— Responsibility has been transferred from home to school for increasing portions of the child's education.
— Children's religious instruction has shifted from home to church/temple.
— Money issues include bank loans, need for supplementary income in addition to the male's income, etc. In past eras, family-based economic services were used.

Emotional support is still centered in the family, and the future stability of the family will depend largely on the strength of family bonds. Families in the contemporary society accept the challenge that intimacy and constancy are necessary for a satisfying and happy life. Each family is unique in its style of living and in the problems it faces. While some characteristics of the family are fundamental, many change as the family unit deals with challenges at different developmental stages. When the changes are sudden, causing disorganization and disruption in the structure of family and its functions, there is a problem in the family or we can say the family is in 'crisis'. A crisis is something that makes one strive for a different and unusual solution of the problem. Family problems and crises may be defined as a drastic change in the course of events. Crises are times of instability, necessitating, problem-solving skills, decision-making, and adjustments.

Sometimes the problems develop because of events outside the family, e.g., natural calamity such as hurricane, earthquake or flood, war, national economic depression or the closing of a plant where family members work. At other times, the problem occurs within family system due to the loss of a family member, conflict that erupts in family violence, divorce, or alcoholism. Internal problems or crises tend to demoralize a family, increasing resentment, alienation, and conflict. Sometimes, a crisis develops out of whole series of small internal and external events that build up to the point where family members cannot cope up with the series of events. Some examples are:

— First or unwanted pregnancy.
— Moving or shifting to a new place.
— Financial problems due to the company closing of industrial sites.
— Borrowing several lakhs/crores of money.
— Having a tough time with the new neighbors.
— Accidents.

All these can take place within early months of marriage, and both husband and wife may not be prepared to deal with the situation. The family may be in crisis overload – too many difficult situations with which to deal and few resources (emotional, economic, etc.) available for use. Some causes of family crises include: infidelity, alcoholism/drug abuse, death, divorce, family violence, i.e., child and/or spouse abuse, sexual abuse, economic distress, conflict in marriages, single-parent families, victimization, and disgrace in the family. Thus, any rupturing of family relationships, which forces reorganization of the family pattern, not only constitutes a family crisis but also is a threat to family unity. The internal crises in the family are the contemporary problems.

Crises in Different Stages of the Family Life Cycle

Duvall (1977) describes each family as having eight basic developmental tasks – responsibilities that must be accomplished to ensure the family's operation as a unit at all stages of its development. These are:

— Providing physical care.
— Allocating resources.
— Determining who does what.
— Assuming that members are socialized.
— Establishing interaction patterns.
— Incorporating and releasing members.
— Relating to society through its institution.
— Maintaining the morale and motivation of members.

The family life cycle divides the family experience into phases or stages, each with its own challenges, tasks, and problems. At various times in family life, events like parenthood, launching children, and retirement occur, which, according to Duvall, shake up a family, compelling the members to change the way they handle developmental tasks. These critical transition points are markers that occur just prior to each stage of the family life cycle as the family mobilizes for the next step in their development. Particular tasks and stressors accompany each stage – problems that cause feelings of anxiety, frustration, and depression; feelings with which family members must learn to cope. The dynamic quality of family development constitutes an ever-present challenge. Rarely are two days alike and predictable in most families. The family no sooner gets nicely settled into one stage of the family life cycle, than another emerges (with new demands and stresses). Knowledge of family development helps us to know what to expect throughout the life cycle and get prepared accordingly for success at each stage. Some examples of life stressors follow.

Moving/Shifting

Families in the early stages of the family life cycle tend to move or shift places of residence more often than families with school children. Moving can create various conflicts, such as social or emotional adjustments. Perhaps neighbors were friendlier in the old neighborhood, or may be the couple lived in closer proximity to relatives who offered a degree of social or emotional support before moving.

Monetary Challenges

Lack of monetary resources at any stage of the life cycle is difficult. In the first few years of marriage, prior to the birth of children, the couple is trying to settle into a new home. In the traditional Indian system, parents help their children establish the new home. In the middle and later years, couples face many challenges to economic stability including costs associated with raising children (e.g., education and marriage), loss of income associated with retirement, and age-related health issues.

Supplementary Income Provided by the Wife

Present economic conditions sometimes require the young wife to work until the first child is born. Typically, she quits the labour force until the children are in school. She may then return to work to help meet family costs, and to assure that the children have adequate schooling and the family standard of living, to which she and her family aspire, is acquired or maintained.

Conflicting Loyalties and Burdens of Guilt

During the establishment of a marriage, the young wife may be torn between her loyalty to her husband and her devotion to her parents, and she is apt to feel guilty about neglecting one or the other. When the young mother becomes engrossed in childcare procedures that are new and demanding, she may feel guilty and her husband may resent her neglect of him. All children disobey their parents from time to time and have subsequent feelings of guilt, while their parents undergo periods of anxiety, insecurity, and doubt about their parental competence. The father may feel guilty about neglecting his family while he pursues his career. Shifting loyalties throughout the family life cycle inevitably bring some feelings of guilt to various family members.

Types of Family Problems/Crises in Different Stages of Life

Married Couple Stage

(a) *Infidelity*: A majority of people enter marriages expecting and committed to sexual fidelity. Extramarital affairs have varying effects on both husbands and wives, their intimate relationship, and ultimately their families. Some marriages are never the same afterward. Guilt, anger, jealousy, distrust, loss of respect, and the destruction of love and intimacy are common. Why do adults become involved in extramarital affairs even though they say don't believe in them? There are a variety of reasons, such as emotional need, unresolved marital problems, ambivalence about marriage, seeking pleasure and excitement, permissive values, ulterior motives, and the need to build one's ego.

(b) *In-law problems*: Difficulties with relatives decline usually throughout the family life cycle. Early in marriage, both the husband and wife are getting used to their roles as members of each other's families. They must leave their own parents and give their first loyalty to their mates. Thus, in-law problems tend to loom larger early in marriage than they ever will again in the family history.

(c) *Divorce*: Divorce is one of the most stressful experiences that one can have in adulthood. It is a crisis event that forces the family to make many short and long-range adjustments. Divorce is defined as the undoing of a marriage, a process of unmarrying people who have been married. It is an official recognition that their marriage is a failure and therefore has more cause for being terminated rather than continuing. The effects of divorce vary from family to family. Both personal and general losses are involved. Each party blames the other and there is general yearning, frustration, and a sense of emptiness. Certain consequences of divorce are common, such as separation, distress, sadness, loneliness, and economic problems. Some major causes of divorce are:

— Feeble mindedness, dementia praecox.
— Poverty, economic troubles, or economical disparity between husband and wife.
— Neglect of the wife by the husband or vice versa.
— Alcohol or drug abuse.
— Sexual incompatibility.
— Adultery, infidelity, bigamy.
— Troublesome relatives or in-laws.
— Personality problems.
— Conflicting ambitions, values and needs of the couple.
— Extreme cruelty.
— Desertion.
— Conviction for crime.

(d) *Spouse abuse*: Spouse abusers may be ordinary citizens in other aspects of their lives. They typically have poor self-images, which they hide by being outwardly violent. Those who are excessive jealous, or are alcohol or drug addict, commonly are abusers. Because they are insecure individuals who do not feel good about themselves, they typically choose a partner who is passive and compliant, whom they can bully, and whom they can blame for all of their own personal problems. Abusers reportedly have lower levels of marital satisfaction, and have significant problems with communication, anger control, and in maintaining their employment status.

(e) *Wife abuse*: In a family, wife abuse is the most prevalent form of family violence. Violence against wives can be viewed as a logical extension of a patriarchal family system in which the husband as the dominant ruler or head, uses whatever means necessary to obtain obedience and control. Most abuse and violence towards wives does not take the form of beating, but rather it involves throwing the things, shoving, pushing, grabbing, slapping or hitting. These events appear to be more common at selected times, such as during a wife's pregnancy or when the husband is drunk, although, the exact extent of abuses is an unanswered question. Precipitating factors of wife/spouse abuse are:

(i) Personality factors.

(ii) Violence in the family of origin increases both a woman's vulnerability and a man's propensity to abuse his wife or children. Men who have experienced violent childhoods are more likely to grow up and assault their wives than are individuals who have not experienced childhood violence.

(iii) Wife abuse is also associated with the employment status of the husband.

(iv) Wife abuse is related to the employment status of wives. Women who stay at home and do not work outside the home as paid workers, and do not contribute to family income, are at greater risk of being abused.

(v) Women's risk of victimization increases if their occupational and educational status is inconsistent with that of their husband's.

(vi) Men who drink often are likely to abuse their wives.

(vii) Power imbalanced relationships are associated with spousal abuse, especially when the imbalance threatens the male's power.

(f) *Sexual abuse*: Sexual abuse, including marital rape, appears to be a relatively common form of violence sustained by wives and female children. The forcing of sexual intercourse on a wife by her husband technically is marital rape, although legally not recognized yet. Many wives may blame themselves or learn to accept the forced sexual intercourse. All age groups and social classes are affected by sexual abuse. Moreover, teasing, molestation, and indecent representation or exposure are forms of sexual abuse. Poverty, illiteracy, unemployment, ignorance, and certain beliefs and superstitions are some causes of sexual abuse.

(g) *Childlessness*: Couple's hope of having their own children is complicated by a problem that appears to be affecting a growing segment of the population: infertility on the part of the husband, the wife, or both. Usually, inability to conceive a child is attributed to barrenness on the part of wives. Other causes are:
- A low sperm count in males.
- Exposure to sexually transmitted diseases.
- Long-term usage of oral contraceptives.
- Ovulatory disorders that arise from hormonal imbalances.

(h) *Conflict in marriage*: Conflict in marriage is not only inevitable, but it is normal and is to be expected. Conflict, however, can have either positive or negative consequences for the development of the marital relationship, depending upon how it is managed and resolved, and if it leads to family problems or crises. Conflict usually involves some degree of hostility, anger, or other negative feelings. Conflict might be viewed as synonymous with the words 'argument' or 'quarrel', and may involve an attempt of partners to psychologically or physically hurt one another. Power and control of marriage partners over each other also leads to conflict. Strife can arise over a number of issues and at any time. Most frequently cited issues of conflict in marriages are:
- Money management.
- Discipline of children.
- Household jobs and duties (one or both the partners).
- In-laws relationships.
- Being away from home too much (one or both the partners).
- Personalities and habits (smoking, drinking, snoring, so on).
- Time spent together as a couple.
- Condition of house and furniture.
- Plans for the future.

— Sexual relationship and general demonstrations of affection.

Conflict can yield either productive or destructive outcomes, depending on how it is managed. Productive conflict involves a rational approach, issue confrontation, willingness to compromise, empathy, and effective communication and problem-solving skills. Destructive conflict, on the other hand, involves uncontrollable emotionality, issue avoidance, tough bargaining, insensitivity to the other's point of view, and physical or verbal violence.

Childbearing and Rearing Stage

(a) *Role conflicts*: Role conflict occurs when the demands of one role interfere with doing what needs to be done in another role.

(i) *Feeling neglectful:* Employed parents sometimes find it difficult to stay at home to care for a sick child or to always be available for school or community-related activities because of rigid and demanding work schedules. This situation creates possible conflict.

(ii) *Realizing the expectations of others:* Another role conflict for employed couples is dealing with disparities between how they choose to plan and organize their lives as family members and parents vs. how neighbors, relatives, and people at work expect them to behave. Demands imposed by others often conflict with what the couple thinks is best for their family.

(iii) *Fighting internalized norms:* Discontinuities between what the couple was socialized to believe about family life and how they are managing currently their family responsibilities can also cause role conflicts.

(iv) *Making time for kin and friends:* Couples can feel conflicted about their inability to maintain close contact with relatives and friends due to heavy workloads and family responsibilities.

(b) *Role overload*: Role overload is feeling like there is too much to do and never enough time to accomplish everything that needs to be done. Role overload is experienced frequently when couples start a family. Dual-earner families with young children are burdened particularly by role overload. It is not unusual for couples to feel exhausted when they get home, and guilty about being so tired when their families need them – dinner must be prepared, dishes must be washed, children fed and bathed, and so on.

(c) *Illness*: Sickness is no stranger to most families at sometime or other. Families with young children and with aging members go through bouts of sickness more often than childless couples or those who do not have aged family members. Illness can occur at any time to any family, but it happens more often at some stages of the family life cycle than at others.

(d) *Transition to parenthood*: The birth of the first child is a crisis, in that it calls for reorganization of the family. Couples may want children, but be dismayed or unprepared to discover what they are like. Results from studies of hundreds of couples over the years indicate that parenthood is a critical experience and that marital satisfaction drops sharply with the birth of the first child. It is parenthood, even more than marriage, that demands maturity in both husband and wife. As the child matures and begins schooling, parents experience the highest level of stress.

(e) *Child marriage*: The practice of child marriage is another example of child abuse. In rural areas, child marriages are still common. Child brides, wherever they exist, frequently suffer ill-treatment from their in-laws.

(f) *Sibling violence*: Battering a sibling is a form of violence that is granted a high degree of tolerance. Physical violence among siblings often goes beyond beating up and including the use of knives and guns. It may result in suicide of the victim, imprisonment or institutionalization of the perpetrator, or running away of the victim. Violence of any kind brings down the family's status.

(g) *Hospitalization*: People are hospitalized due to accidents, illness, or bad injuries. It is a very stressful time for the family members who have to cope with uncertain outcomes. During such time, the patient and family members must live through a continuing period of acute crises. Further, costs associated with hospitalizations can result in an economic crisis in the family.

Schooling Stage

(a) *Child abuse*: In the family, children are beaten or otherwise punished for misdeeds. Parents are allowed to use whatever means they wish - no matter how cruel or inhumane to punish their children for alleged misbehavior. Parents are granted these rights because children are defined as the property of their parents. Child abuse may include not only physical assaults that result in injury, but also malnourishment, abandonment, neglect, and emotional and/or sexual abuse. Moreover, children can be abused also by their siblings or by classmates. The main causes of child abuse are:

— Lack of social and emotional maturity of parents.
— Broken homes or divorced parents.
— Poverty.
— Workloads in large families.
— Children with physical or mental defects.
— Authoritarian parents who demand unquestioned discipline.
— Personality problems in parents that predispose them to violence or irrational behavior, or parents who have an abnormally low level of tolerance for stress and frustration.
— Parental lack of information or education relating to (i) normal patterns of child growth and development,

(ii) the normal problems of childbearing, and/or (iii) realistic expectations regarding childbehavior.

- Economic and other life stresses, including illness, death in the family, unemployment, divorce, marital conflict, poverty etc.
- Not wanting a child who is born; stress associated with a child who is born prematurely, or one with physical or mental defects.
- Lack of a supportive network of family, relatives, or friends.
- Parents who were abused themselves as children or were a sibling of a child who was abused.
- A child who is unusually active, hostile, aggressive, and/or ill-tempered, slow to learn, learning-disabled or otherwise difficult to get along with, is more likely than others to be abused.
- Teenage pregnancy and parenting is also associated with child abuse.
- Alcoholism/drug abuse and related psychological problems in one or both parents increase the potential for child abuse.

Adolescence/Young Adult Stage

(a) *Sexual abuse*: When sexual exploitation occurs within the family, it is likely to be repeated over a period of time. Sexual abuse of the child ends when the abuser decides that it is no longer in his or her best interest to continue it. Abuse can cease when the child grows up and leaves the home, or when someone intervenes. This includes cases of incest, where a parent, cousin, brother, or any other male member in the family fondles the child's genital area or engages in sexual intercourse with the child. The family faces its primacy crisis when the sexual abuse comes to the attention of other family members or persons outside the family. After the abuse has been disclosed, the family suffers a suppression phase, during which time parents, siblings, and sometimes even the victim, deny or minimize the sexual abuse that occurred.

(b) *Adolescent-parent conflict*: Adolescent-parent conflict is widely recognized as a corollary of a teenagers' struggle for economy. The pressures felt and exerted by young adults for lives of their own conflict with parental concern about their grown children's choice of mates (leading to in-law problems), of careers and of different lifestyles may lead to family crisis.

(c) *Alcoholism*: Alcohol abuse is a generic term that includes both alcoholism and problem drinking (functional disability as a result of alcohol consumption). Both alcoholism and problem drinking create problems in and for the family. Alcohol is a major factor in marital disruption, domestic violence, and child abuse. Alcoholism is a chronic illness – psychic or somatic – which manifests itself as a disorder of behavior. It is characterized by the repeated drinking of alcoholic beverages to an extent that exceeds customary dietary use or compliance with the social customs of the community, and that consumption interferes with the drinker's health or his social or economic functioning. Many special categories of alcoholics have been identified, including alcohol addicts, who cannot control their drinking and has led to recognizable physical or mental sequels. An alcoholic is anyone whose drinking interferes frequently or continuously with any of his important life adjustments and interpersonal relationships. The cause of alcoholism can be due to an inadequate or insecure personality, culture, or inherited susceptibility.

(d) *Illegitimacy*: Illegitimate children suffer from this stigma; they invariably suffer mental torture, besides physical injury. A child born to a lawfully wedded couple at any time after the date of the marriage is presumed to be legitimate. However, in practice, people have not abandoned the traditional law on the subject. Therefore, children who are illegitimate often suffer abuse and cruelty. Lower caste or lower class illegitimacy is of less concern to the society than is illegitimacy in other social strata. Lineage and family honour are much less a focus of attention in the lower social strata. There is usually no property to inherit and thus none to protect by making certain that the proper families are united. The families of the young man and woman lose less rank if an illegitimate child is born. Moreover, lower strata families control their young less strictly than do the upper. One consequence is that the illegitimate birth rate is higher towards the lower social strata.

(e) *Runaway*: If a child runs away, the family status in society is lowered. The family will always be referred to as an improper family. A child may choose to leave the home due to such issues as negative parental attitudes towards the child, or ill-treatment of the wife by her husband or any family member.

(f) *Drug abuse*: Drugs hinder a person's ability to develop intimate relationships by altering one's sensations, mood, consciousness, and thinking process. An addicted individual functions with a distorted picture of the world. Various causes of drug abuse are as follows:
   (i) Curiosity is the primary reason; many young people turn to drugs to test their tranquilizing and hallucinatory effects.
   (ii) Peer influence, sense of adventure, escape from feelings of inferiority, relief from boredom, and easing of stress, tension, anxieties, frustration, or depression are the other reasons for induction into drug abuse.
   (iii) Some use drugs to free themselves from their inhibitions, or because of guilt, shame, or disappointment in life.

(g) *Suicide*: Suicide is a tragedy for the individual as well as for the family. It leaves hurt, disagree, remorse, and bitterness.

Because of stigma attached to suicide, family members often feel shame in addition to their grief. They feel that somehow they must be responsible for not having prevented one of their own from reaching such a point of desolation. There are a multitude of reasons that teenagers and young adults consider suicide, including family problems; failure in school or in significant friendship or love relationships; escape from overwhelming feelings of pain, loneliness, hopelessness, or disappointment; use of drugs and alcohol; to get attention; as an act of aggression; and loss of significant persons in their life.

(h) *Homicide*: Homicide is most often an outgrowth of quarrels and violence among family members or friends. The quarrels get out of hand resulting in one family member killing another in the privacy of their own homes.

(i) *Stepparents*: A positive, accepting, and loving relationship between stepparents and stepchildren is often very difficult to develop. One hears rarely of a case in which a stepchild has been amicably absorbed in the newly created family. In worst case scenarios, stepmothers have been reported to brutally torture the children. Problems arise when a stepparent comes into the home and tries to establish his or her role in the family. The stepparent cannot replace the missing parent, nor should he or she try to be the missing parent. Some possible areas of early conflict include: (i) the attitudes and behaviors of the stepparent are likely to differ from the missing parent and create anxiety, anger, fear, or other emotions within the children; (ii) the children may view the stepparent negatively, no matter what the stepparent does or does not do within the family unit (e.g., "No one can take the place of my mother/father", "I don't have to do what you say because you're not my real parent", "My mother/father never did it that way"; and (iii) failure on the part of the real parent to deal with expected problems in an open and consistent manner while involving all family members in conflict resolution. Unlike in their first marriages, the parents have no opportunity to establish a wholesome, intimate relationship before the parenting role is assumed. In general, the home climate is better when stepparent is the father.

(j) *Disgrace*: A disgraced family is one in which all or some of members feel dishonored, humiliated, ashamed, discredited, or degraded. Behaviors that generally bring disgrace to a person and to his family are drunkenness, infidelity, drug addiction, abortion, embezzlement, failure in school, failure to pay one's debts, divorce, and occupational failure (including the employment in an occupation of low status). Disgrace is generally associated with illegitimacy, intoxication, veneral diseases, crime, mental illness, suicide, imprisonment, etc.

(k) *Economic distress*: Many families have to face the crisis of economic distress due to employment instability or underemployment; declining income due to demotion, cutbacks or retirement; or the inability to earn an adequate income because of the lack of education and skills, disability or health problems. Economic distress has profound effects on individual and family functioning.

The effect of unemployment on individuals and families partly depends on the duration of unemployment, whether it involves permanent job displacement, or a temporary layoff, whether there are other comparable or replacement jobs readily available, and whether there is more than one wage earner in the family. Young couples and single mothers with a number of children, especially with young children, are the most affected by unemployment. They have minimal skills and resources so they have to turn to others for help.

Middle-Aged Parenthood Stage

(a) *Empty nest*: In this period, the 'in-house' parenting years begin to draw to a close. It is not easy for parents to face the first break in their family. Nor is it any easier for them to deal with their emotions as the younger children, too, leave home. Parents want their children to be happy adults with rich, full lives of the own, but even so, they usually have mixed feelings about the steps that need to take place for a child to become an adult. When husband and wife began their married life, they could look forward to a long period of being useful and important. Through the years, there was always someone whose life and well-being depended on them. Now, they must get used to being less needed. A mother, after being extremely busy much of her adult life, may find her life empty or meaningless. She might begin looking for things to occupy her time. Both parents may need to shift paradigms from depicting their principle purpose in life as primary caregivers to their children to different, yet-to-be-defined roles (e.g., developing one's gifts and talents or wishes – painting, writing, reading, traveling, working outside of the home, volunteering one's time to needy causes). The parents still maintain some of their parental responsibilities. For example, married children may need their parent's help in meeting a financial or emotional crisis. Also, the middle-aged couple may be called upon to care of one or more of their own aged parents.

(b) *Widowhood*: Many marital partners eventually face the death of a spouse. This is not an easy adjustment. If the death is sudden or unexpected, the adoptability is even tougher than if there is an extended period of declining health prior to death. Widows suffer from the lack of preparation for dealing with bereavement and for adjusting to society as a single person. Widows or widowers miss their spouses as companions and partners in activities. Social participation is a problem because so many activities are couple-oriented. The primary problems faced by widows are: loneliness, decision-making, financial management, and role changes. The problems faced by widowers are: loneliness, acceptance of loss, going to places/doing things alone, and housework. Apart from these, both widows and widowers face troubles like illness, single-parenting, managing retirement life, and economic problems.

Aged Period of Family Life

(a) *Problems during old age*: During the last years of life, most old people are dependent on someone. Some old people need financial help. Some need physical care; some need help in decisions; and all need love and attention. It is their grown children who must meet these needs as best they can. When a man no longer goes to work, both he and his wife have many adjustments to make. The wife has to adjust to having her husband around the house in the daytime. When the working spouses retire, they have to look for things to occupy themselves. A man or woman may be feel isolated and alone after many years of married life. Old friends die one by one, as do siblings. For many old people, the hardest job is adjusting to loneliness.

(b) *Retirement*: Upon retirement, income typically declines, and the couple begins to draw on their savings. No one knows how long he or she will live, which makes budgeting extremely important as well as difficult. Unfortunately, many people experience a lowered standard of living upon retirement. The equity provided by home ownership is often a big part of the couple's total wealth. Medical expenses usually increase during this period, which can deplete savings accounts.

(c) *Battered elderly*: Battered elderly are in a depended position, relying on caretakers for basic survival needs. It is generally assumed that elderly family members are provided for by loving and caring family members. Like children, however, elderly parents can be a source of emotional and financial strain. While some abuse comes in the form of neglect, other abuse is manifested with more physical means, such as restraining the aged parent in bed or in a chair, excessive use of medications to keep the parent more manageable (or sedated), or battering with fists or objects to enforce particular behavior. Other problems faced during this stage include illness related to old age, bereavement, and sometime institutionalization when family members find it difficult or impossible to take care of the individual at home.

Any Stage of the Life Cycle

(a) *Bereavement*: Bereavement in a family results from the death of a member. Even though somebody else may soon assume the deceased person's role, the personal loss of the member to the family remains forever. Bereavement may be the loss of mate, parent, child, sibling or other close relatives or associates. Its effects vary with the age of the bereaved, his emotional involvement with the family, and the degree of emancipation of the bereaved person. The degree of loss felt by the bereaved varies from individual to individual. If the deceased is the head of the family and a wage-earning member, all the family members feel his loss intensely, especially if there is no other member who can take up this role. The bereavement is deeper for a young man's death, than for one who dies at ripe old age. When bereavement and mourning became chronic in a family, the bereaved became psychologically affected. In such circumstances they need special care and attention.

There are various circumstances of death. These include:

- Uncertain death (a person is missing with whereabouts unknown).
- Certain death, either at a known or unknown time.

— Untimely death; this may include premature death, unexpected death and calamitous death, accidents, involuntary manslaughter, homicide and suicide.

(b) *Single parents*: Single-parent families are created in a variety of ways through births to never-married mothers, separation, divorce, and widowhood. Single-parent families, regardless of how they are created, are overwhelming female headed.

Single-parent mothers: Single-parent mothers usually live alone with their children. The problems of single-parent mothers are twofold: economic and social, both of which impose severe hardships on many such mothers. They are most likely to fall at or below poverty level income, because of the following reasons:

— They have a lower earning potential than do men because of their concentration in lower paying occupations. Women are also paid less than men for some types of work.

— Maintaining responsibility for the care and support of their families means that single-parent mothers cannot take time off to go back to college or receive extra training to enhance their job-related skills.

— Many single-parent mothers experience loneliness and social isolation following the loss of a spouse to divorce or death. The stress and strain they experience present serious adjustment difficulties.

Single-parent fathers: Very few single-parent households are headed by fathers. Most of the problems of single-parent fathers are related to the social aspects of their status, rather than to the economic. They tend to experience the same kinds of social stresses that single-parent mothers do. Adjustment to the single-parent situation is more difficult for the widowed father than for the divorced. Single-parent fathers are likely to experience a lack of role clarity in their childcare and home management roles. The economic situation of single fathers is far superior to that of such mothers, but worse than families headed by a husband-wife couple.

(c) *Economic distress*: Many families have to face the crisis of economic distress due to job instability or uncertainty; declining income due to demotion, cutbacks or retirement; or the inability to earn an adequate income because of the lack of education and skills, disability or health problems. Economic distress has profound effects on individual and family functioning. Effects of the crisis on the family depend upon the type of crisis and how long it is expected to last.

(d) *Disaster*: Disasters are considered as a mass rather than an individual phenomenon. There are many kinds, including fires, earthquakes, cave in of mines, railroad accidents, etc. Each kind has its particular aspects and they are unexpected and sudden.

(e) *Desertion*: Desertion consists of irresponsible, but willful, departure from the family, followed by failure to uphold family responsibilities. Usually, an individual leaves one's spouse for another woman or man. It is one of the most common reasons for broken homes. In many cases of desertion, the whereabouts of the deserting person is not known. Deserters are generally men. Women rarely leave the family, especially if they have children. Desertion is a symbol of deeper difficulties, which make further cohabitation in the family setting seem undesirable to the deserter. The deserter may set up a new family somewhere else and feel guilty about leaving the original home for many years. Occasionally, desertion is associated with some crime or an act of shame caused by the deserter.

Family Problems: Effects, Coping Strategies, and Possible Prevention

(a) *Conflict in marriage*: Some common conflict management styles in marriage are:
Avoidance, typified by

— brooding or sulking behavior;
— avoiding an issue by keeping the concern to yourself; and
— joking around and teasing; trying to make the situation seem not so serious.

Destructive engagement includes:

— Insulting and blaming the spouse for being at fault in the disagreement.
— Becoming physical with the partner by pushing, grabbing or shoving.
— Threatening to hit or throw something at the life partner.
— Hitting or trying to hit the partner but not with anything.
— Hitting or trying to hit the partner with something hard.
— Being untruthful to the partner in words or through actions.
— Arguing heatedly or yelling at the partner.
— Threatening to do something the partner would not like.
— Throwing something or smashing something.
— Refusing to relinquish one's point of view by taking a strong position and stubbornly sticking to it.
— Vacating the premises.
— Begging and pleading with the partner.

Constructive engagement involves:

— Actively seeking new way to settle the disagreement, ones that had not been tried before.
— Trying to see the partner's point of view, acknowledging that view, and communicating understanding.
— Seeking an outsider, who both partners trust, to act as a mediator in helping to settle the conflict.
— Discussing the issues calmly and rationally.
— Following each partner's rules of 'fairness'.

- Seeking to resolve the disagreement by compromising or doing something for each other that is mutually satisfying.
- Promising to change in order to ameliorate the partner's concern.
- Communicating feelings by letting the partner know what bothersome.

(b) *Divorce*: The effects of divorce vary from family to family. Children are affected the worst by divorce. The child is often in the middle between the two fighting sides. In order to avoid divorce, the following measures can be adopted:

(i) *Family life education:* The realities of marriage are not understood by many couples when they enter married life. Unrealistic expectations on the part of both parties can create conflict. The couple may be unaware of the multiple role demands, role sequences, and challenges that people encounter in marriage. They may lack an adequate understanding of the basic principles of human sexuality and family planning, so much that they find it difficult to communicate to their partners the pleasures and problems they might be experiencing in the important domains of the marriage relationship. In all these cases, family life education can help educate couples about the challenges and changes that are encountered in married life and possibly prevent separation or divorce.

(ii) *Premarital counseling:* Counseling is available through a family counselor, minister, or trained professionals. Premarital counseling helps the couple to understand the marital relationship and requirements, and perform premarital developmental tasks. The goal of premarital counseling is not to tell the couple whether or not they should get married. Rather, it is a useful way of diagnosing potential problem areas before they come up later in the relationship.

(iii) *Marriage enrichment program:* Marriage enrichment workshops are organized by marriage counselors and family life educators, and are appropriate for couples at any stage of marriage. They combine education with group discussion to assist couples in improving marital communication, relationships, and problem solving. The central purpose of such programs is to proactively address issues before they become unmanageable conflicts.

(iv) *Separation:* A trial separation is another alternative before divorce. The objective of separation is for individuals to determine how it feels to be living on a day-to-day basis without one's spouse; it is designed to interrupt old interactional patterns through the creation of an environment that may be conducive to change. It is characterized by ambivalent feelings between the spouses and towards the marriage. The anticipated result is that spouses will move closer together or farther apart.

(v) *Marriage and family therapy:* The above methods are all primary prevention initiatives. Marriage and family therapy is a method of secondary prevention, which is available to those couples who are in trouble and want to work on solving or resolving those problems. It implies something is wrong in the couple's relationship and needs to be fixed if the partners are to realize their goals and move back on the path to a successful relationship. It offers hope for those couples who have serious problems and who are heading for the divorce court.

(c) *Alcoholism*: Alcoholism creates a family crisis because the disease affects the whole family. Like the alcoholic, family members also go through various stages as they attempt to cope with the crisis. In the initial stages of alcoholism, the husband's drinking may be sporadic, alternating between periods of sobriety and intoxication. During this stage, the amount of stress in the family depends upon the frequency of the drinking bouts. The family members are constantly adapting and readapting first to an intoxicated husband/father and then to a sober one.

When drinking becomes heavy enough and frequent, the wife attempts to get the husband to cut down before it leads to trouble. The husband may make promises to cut down but these promises are rarely kept for very long. The wife experiences great disappointment and strain because of a succession of broken promises. She begins to move from logical discussion to nagging. When these efforts do not work, the wife may turn to emotional pleading and threats.

Wives use a variety of strategies to help the alcoholic. When nagging, pleading, or threats do not work, some try an opposite strategy: act normal or natural, like nothing is wrong. Another strategy is to take over all household responsibilities and create a 'perfect' home in the hope that an extremely pleasant, burden-free atmosphere will reduce the husband's need to drink. Wives also try other strategies; e.g., they select non-drinking companions or visitors for social occasions; money is hidden or restricted so that little or none is available for alcohol; and liquor is poured out or bottles smashed. An attempt is also made to keep the husband busy with household chores or a variety of hobbies and free-time activities, so there remains no time for drinking. Some wives even start drinking along with their husbands to show them what it is like living with an alcoholic. Others resort to it at home so they will not go out to drink.

If wives get professional help, they may begin to realize that alcoholism is a disease that the alcoholic cannot control and that he needs help. The most important role wives can play is to get help, and through professional assistance, discover what type of treatment is available that the husband might be motivated to seek or accept.

(d) *Infidelity*: In order to possibly prevent infidelity, certain measures need to be taken, such as:

- The lines of communication must be open in the marriage relationship. One must share feelings, disappointments and expectations, as well as positive reactions. Solve small problems as they arise by learning to discuss them rationally, calmly, and sympathetically. Try to take the other's point of view.
- Strive to fulfill one another's physical, social, emotional, and intellectual needs through the relationship. Find out what are the needs of the partner; take them seriously and strive to meet those needs.
- Learn to be loving and affectionate, frequently expressing warmth and physical affection.
- Strive for variety and imagination in lovemaking.
- Resolve to make the sexual relationship a mutually satisfying experience by being concerned about one another's preferences, desires, and by giving as well as receiving pleasure.
- Show respect, appreciation, approval, and acceptance of one's spouse.
- Commit to sexual fidelity and live by that commitment.
- Avoid heterosexual situations that are conducive to involvements. Keep business associations on a professional basis.
- When one finds himself or herself physically attracted to another person, and not to the spouse, tell the mate and discuss the situation. Be honest and try not to hide anything.

(e) *Economic distress*: Economic distress has a significant effect on the individuals involved. Income loss and economic strain are negatively associated with marital quality and family satisfaction, related to financial conflicts, the psychological instability of family members, marital tensions and hostility, and the lack of warmth and support. Financial stress results in lower satisfaction with life and with marriage. In order to cope with the emotional distress, certain measures need to be considered, as follows:

— A more positive approach is to cut expenditures whenever possible and to postpone major expenditures, like buying a new car or starting orthodontic treatments.
— Selling property or possessions is sometimes necessary.
— Taking a second job, in addition to one's primary job, may help ease the financial burden. Another alternative would be employment of a wife who is not working presently.

(f) *Runaway and imprisonment*: Family counseling centers play an important role in the prevention and/or treatment of all social evils or malpractices. Family members can seek advice at these centers as the need arises, perhaps avoiding loosing a child to the streets (i.e., running away) or imprisonment. In the case of runaway children, they may be caught and admitted to a juvenile home or sent to jail. There, they may be provided with primary education and counseling.

(g) *Childlessness*: Childless couples face pressures to have children. One source of pressure is from the negative attitudes that various people have towards those who are childless. Wives are stigmatized to some extent because they do not have children. Other persons try to make them feel that they are abnormal, selfish, immoral, irresponsible, immature, unhappy, unfulfilled or non-feminine. Adoption and artificial insemination can improve family relationships, providing a childless couple with children.

(h) *Child abuse*: Prevention is the best course to follow. Family life and parenthood educational programmes for parents or couples in schools, churches, or community organizations may help by supplying information about the stresses and responsibilities which parenthood entails and about realistic expectations of children's behavior and development at different stages.

(i) *Desertion*: Though desertion causes severe problems, it is doubtful that an extremely punitive attitude does much good in these cases to improve the circumstances of either the marital relationship or the disjointed family unit, unless accompanied by therapy to improve attitudes and adjustments of the man or woman involved.

(j) *Loss of a child*: Its effect varies with the age of the bereaved, his or her emotional involvement with the family, the manner of death, the relationships of the bereaved, and the degree of emancipation associated with the death (e.g., if the child was suffering during a disease process). The pain and loss felt within family members may become chronic and individual members may become psychologically affected. In such circumstances, they need special care and attention. Parents experience despondency, concentration difficulties, time confusion, loss of appetite or inability to sleep, and a host of other feelings. They often blame themselves. Most families survive the loss of a child, although a small percentage of spouses divorce as a result.

(k) *Retirement*: Both spouses must adjust to retirement and to certain feelings that may accompany their retirements, including loneliness, isolation, uselessness, depression, loss of self-worth, etc. The couple's finances should have been managed in the years preceding the retirement by proper savings. Retirement may force some to rely on supplementary income, seek re-employment, and cut down the expenditures.

(l) *Suicide*: To reduce rates of suicide means to remodel the culture and thereby reduce tension, anxiety, and frustration for the individual. On the other hand, it is undoubtedly possible to rescue many people from their temporary suicidal state and restore them to normal functioning in the society.

(m) *Widowhood*: They can often solve both the loneliness and dependency problem of widowhood by marriage, employment, cordial relationship with the relatives, and rearing children in an ideal way.

(n) *Hospitalization of a child*: The hospitalized individual's fear can be reduced by one parent staying with the child, even sleeping overnight, and daily visits from other family members and friends. Providing occasional separations that are pleasant ahead of time can make an impending hospital visit less stressful. Children who are used to being left with grandparents or sitters, and/or who have stayed overnight at friend's houses are less likely to be upset by hospitalization.

(o) *Drug abuse*: To prevent and fight the challenge of drug use, three types of prevention exist, namely, primary, secondary and tertiary.

(i) *Primary prevention* involves organizing the community, education activities through specific target agencies to strengthen family life, deeper interpersonal relationships that inculcate positive human values so that young people do not resort to drug use.

(ii) *Secondary prevention* contains early diagnosis and treatment; it also includes the provision of counseling services to young people who have started experimenting with the use of drugs.

(iii) *Tertiary prevention* includes the establishment of linkages with treatment and rehabilitation centers so that those who are drug dependent can be provided with long-term support and can be helped to change their lifestyle. Parents can help by giving unconditional emotional and physical support to their child during these difficult times.

(p) *Sexual abuse*: The incidents can be prevented, or even reduced, but not completely stopped. Some methods that might help lower the occurrence of sexual abuse include:
- Moral and sex education should be made compulsory in schools and colleges.
- Pornographic literature and blue films should be banned.
- Sexual predators should be treated using psychological or medical techniques.
- Separate tribunals/courts should be constituted specifically for cases of sexual abuse. Penalties should be severe to discourage those who might be contemplating such an act.
- Awareness on sexual abuse could be created through mass media.
- School officials could learn about signs and symptoms of childhood sexual abuse for identification purposes. Further, specific action in reporting such cases should be outlined.

Conclusion

Problems within a family unit affect all members. Families with problems have certain needs, require specific coping skills, and therefore, may be considered 'high risk' families. When couples have strained relationships, children feel the effects, even when parents try to hide the conflict. In the same way, chronic illness, disability in a family member, unemployment, divorce, death, or any number of other family problems disturb the whole family system, potentially affecting both the physical and mental health of all family members. With the importance of the family that is seeped in Indian tradition, it is extremely important to apply the principles of family study in India to identify and help solve emerging family problems, to examine large effects, and to predict outcomes. Further, the application of these principles will expose the interconnectedness among the various aspects of family problems, and thus a holistic understanding of the family problems will be possible. Moreover, knowledge can be linked with action, providing a holistic approach to family intervention.

References

Bigner, J.J. (1994). *Individual and Family Development*, New Jersey: Prentice Hall, pp: 1, 5, 6, 7, 83 and 86.

Bird, G. and Melville, K. (1994). *Families and Intimate Relationships*, New York: McGraw-Hill, pp: 162, 172-174, 191-196, 223, 248-250 and 363-368.

Boss, P. (1998). *Family Stress Management*, New Delhi: Sage Publications, p: 49.

Brown, D.S. et. al., (2000). *Handbook of Counselling Psychology*, New York: Wiley and Sons, pp: 224, 802 and 361.

Dattatray Shankar, Kaushik (2001). When Parents Divorce, *New Woman*, India, pp: 106-09.

Devi, L. (1998). *Encyclopedia of Child and Family Welfare*, New Delhi: Anmol Publications, pp: 224-247 and 234.

Duvall, E. (1977). *Marriage and Family Development*, Philadelphia: J.B. Lippincott.

Eekelaar, J.M. (1978). *Family Violence*, Toronto: Sanford, N., Katz Bettenworks, pp: 283-284.

Menon, M.C. (2001). Marriage: The Oldest Institution, *Women's Era*, May (Second), Vol. 28, No. 659, New Delhi: Delhi Press Patra Prakashan Ltd., pp: 83-85.

Mira, S., (2001). Indian Supermom, *New Woman*, May, Dattatray Shankar Kaushik, India, pp: 131.

Rajan, Bhosle, M., (2001). Sibling Rivalry, *New Woman*, May, Dattatray Shankar Kaushik, India, pp: 123-125.

Shanbhag, R. (2001). Why husbands do not like their wife's relatives? *Women's Era*, January (First), Vol. 28, No. 650, New Delhi: Delhi Press Patra Prakashan Ltd., pp: 103-105.

Sharma, N. (2001). The Challenging Role of Women and Its Impact on the Family, *Women's Era*, January (First), Vol. 28, No. 650, pp: 20-24.

Shweta, (2001). 21st Century Marriages and the Challenges, *Women's Era*, January (First), Vol. 28, No. 659, New Delhi: Delhi Press Patra Prakashan Ltd., pp: 36-38.

Singh, M. (2001). Husband Having an Affair, *Women's Era*, January (First), Vol. 28, No. 650, New Delhi: Delhi Press Patra Prakashan Ltd., pp: 92-94.

Subramaniyam, C. (2001). Divorce in Haste, Repent at Leisure!, *Women's Era*, November (Second), Vol. 28, No. 671, Delhi Press Patra Prakashan Ltd., New Delhi, pp: 92-94.

9

Family Welfare Laws

Creating Awareness for Family Well-Being

Binayak Patnaik

This chapter examines different aspects of family law, including marriage, divorce, maintenance, succession, adoption, and guardianship of Hindus, Muslims, and Christians in India. The objective is to increase awareness of and understanding about these laws in order to create and facilitate more healthy family environments. In India, one of the main causes of family violence and destructive family relationships is ignorance, especially among women, regarding their rights in marriage, maintenance, adoption, guardianship, and property. These laws exist for the protection of all citizens, including women and children. The author also discusses welfare legislation concerning women and children and suggests practical steps, which can be taken to solve the problems that beset them and their children.

India is a country where people from different cultures and religious traditions, including Hindus, Muslims, Christians, Parsis and Jews, live together. Each community has its own set of laws. On the wake of the welfare state concept in the latter half of the 20th century, several pieces of social legislation came into force affecting the lives of women and children with respect to marriage and divorce, adoption and maintenance, succession, health and nutrition, domestic violence, and gender discrimination. However, most women and children in India do not know about or understand these laws, which are intended to protect them from injustices both within and beyond the family system. Learned helplessness syndrome also keeps women and children at the mercy of the male members of the family throughout their lives. Ignorance and learned helplessness have created long-term dependency and subjugation on the part of the children and women in the family, even though laws to protect them have been in place for decades.

This chapter presents a concise and up-to-date account of the entire gamut of family law affecting the lives of Hindus, Muslims, and Christians – particularly with regard to welfare legislation and its impact on women, children, and the elderly.

The basic objectives of this chapter are:

- To make each member of the family literate about the social legislation that regulates his/her day-to-day life.
- To emphasize that everyone has to know the laws because "ignorance of law is not an excuse".
- To stress the fact that knowing the law can prevent various problems of family and social life.
- To argue that it is against the principle of natural justice to punish the people by a law which they are not aware of.
- To bring uniformity in diversified personal laws and thereby bring unity and integrity among the people of India.

Marriage and Divorce Laws

Marriage Laws of Hindus

Hindu Marriage Act, 1955

The marriages laws of Hindus are based on the Hindu Marriage Act, 1955. The basic objective of this Act was to revise and reform all the piecemeal concepts on Hindu marriage which had hitherto been in existence. This Act is applicable to all Hindus in the whole of India except the state of Jammu & Kashmir and also to those who are domiciled in the territories to which this Act extends but are outside the said territories. The word 'Hindu' means Hindus of any sect or caste. It also includes Buddhists, Jains, Sikhs or any convert or reconvert to Hinduism. This Act is not applicable to the members of Scheduled Castes (SCs) or Scheduled Tribes (STs) within the meaning of Clause 25 of Article 366 of the Constitution of India. For the proof of Hindu marriage, registration of the same like entering the marriage particulars in Hindu Marriage Register is not compulsory. For a Hindu marriage the following are valid conditions:

- Both the boy and the girl must be Hindu.
- Neither the man nor the woman must be having the spouse living at the time of marriage.
- Bigamy, i.e., second marriage is an offence. Even if the real wife consents, the second marriage will not be valid.
- Both the boy and the girl should be mentally sound for giving valid consent to marriage.
- The boy should be at least 21 years of age and the girl should be at least 18 years of age at the time of marriage.
- Marriage must be solemnized according to the custom 'Saptabadi', i.e., seven steps before the sacred fire. The marriage becomes complete and binding when the seventh step is taken.
- The boy and the girl must not be within the degree of prohibited relationship unless the custom permits.
- The parties to the marriage are of 'sapinds' of each other unless the custom permits.

The institution of marriage, according to the Hindu philosophy, is a 'sacrament' (*sanskar*) but not a 'contract'. It is sacred and sacrosanct, permanent and eternal. However, this situation has changed somewhat today, in that the law now permits widow marriage as well as divorce. Still, the marriage among Hindus is considered sacramental. Therefore, jurists refer to all Hindu marriages as the semblance of sacrament and contract.

Hindu Widows Remarriage Act, 1856

This Act is intended to render remarriage of Hindu widows valid to legalize the legitimacy of the children.

Divorce Laws of Hindus

Section 13 of the Hindu Marriage Act, 1955 provides for divorce after solemnization of marriage by the husband or the wife. The dissolution of marriage will take place by a decree of divorce on the following grounds:

- Sexual intercourse with any other person other than his or her spouse.
- Treatment with cruelty.
- Desertion for a continuous period of two years or more.
- Conversion to another religion.
- Unsound mind which is incurable or mental disorder to such an extent that it becomes difficult to live together.
- Suffering from incurable form of leprosy.
- Renouncement of the world by entering into any religious order.
- Has not been heard of being alive for a period of seven years or more by those persons who would naturally have heard of it.

In addition to the above, a wife may also present for divorce on the following grounds:

- Prior to the commencement of this Act, if the husband has another wife and she is living at the time of presentation of petition.
- The husband has been guilty of rape, sodomy or bestiality consequent upon the solemnization of marriage.
- Co-habitation between husband and wife has not been resumed for one year or upwards after the passing of the

decree or order against the husband to award maintenance to the wife.

- The wife repudiated her marriage after she attained the age of 18 years whose marriage was solemnized before she attained the age of 15 years.

According to Section 13(b) of the Act, divorce is also possible by mutual consent between husband and wife. Moreover, according to Section 15 of the Act, it shall be lawful for either party to marry again when a marriage has been dissolved by a decree of divorce. There are also other marital rights and remedies under the Hindu Marriage Act, namely, judicial separation, restitution of conjugal rights and nullity of marriage (void and voidable marriages).

Marriage Laws of Muslims

Muslims consider their marriage as a 'contract' but not a 'sacrament'. However, at the time of solemnization of marriage, certain verses are recited from the 'Quran' (Koran) – the holy book of Muslims. However, according to C.J. Mohammad Sulaiman, marriage is not only a civil contract but also a religious sacrament. The holy Quran regulates the laws of Muslim marriage. The two major groups of Muslims – the Shias and the Sunnis – are governed by Ithena Ashari School and Hanafi School, respectively. The following conditions regulate the Muslim marriage:

- The age of marriage is on attainment of majority. Majority is attained on puberty. Puberty in either sex is presumed to have been attained on completion of fifteen years. In case of Shia female the age of puberty begins with menstruation.
- Both the boy and the girl should be mentally sound.
- The consent of the guardian is necessary if the parties to the marriage are minor or of unsound mind.
- There must be a proposal of marriage made by or on behalf of one of the parties and there must be acceptance by or on behalf of the other party at one meeting in the

presence of two male or one male and two female witnesses. The Shia law does not require any witness. This is called 'Nikah'.

- Both the bride and bridegroom as well as witnesses have to sign on the register which is called 'Nikhanama'.
- In the deed of the marriage all conditions of marriage, such as the amount of dowry, mode of payment, custody of children, etc., are laid down.
- For a valid Muslim marriage, neither writing nor any religious ceremony is essential.
- Muslim marriage is a polygamous marriage limited to four wives. If a Sunni Muslim takes five or more wives his marriage is not void but irregular. The Shia Muslims can go for a 'Muta' (temporary) marriage crossing the limit of four wives with a woman who is a Muslim, Christian, Jew or a fire worshipper. A Shia female can go for a 'Muta' marriage with only a Muslim.
- Both boy and girl should not be related to each other within the degrees of prohibited relationship by blood, foster age, and affinity.

Idda or Iddat

A marriage performed by a Sunni male with a woman during the period of *Idda* or *Iddat* is irregular. In case of a Shia male, it is void (*Idda* means a period prescribed by Muslim law after dissolution of marriage during which a woman is not permitted to remarry). Muslim law prohibits polyandry. A married woman cannot contract a second marriage during subsistence of the first marriage.

Divorce Laws of Muslims

The Dissolution of Muslim Marriage Act, 1939 outlines the concept of 'divorce' which extends to the whole of India except the state of Jammu & Kashmir. This Act allows a Muslim wife to seek judicial divorce on the following grounds:

- Whereabouts of the husband are not known continuously for four years.
- Husband's failure or neglect to provide maintenance to the wife for a period of two years or more.
- Husband is sentenced to imprisonment for a period of seven years or more. No decree can be passed on this ground until the sentence becomes final.
- Failure of husband to perform marital obligations for a period of three years or more without any reasonable cause.
- Impotency of a husband at the time of marriage, which continues until the suit is filed.
- Insanity of the husband for at least two years
- If husband is suffering from leprosy or any other virulent veneral disease.
- If the wife is a minor (i.e., she has not attained puberty and below 15 years) at the time of marriage and she has repudiated the marriage before attaining the age of 18 years provided the marriage has not been consummated.
- The husband treats his wife with cruelty, which includes:
  - Habitual assault making the life miserable.
  - Association with women of evil repute or leads an infamous life.
  - Attempts to force her to lead an immoral life.
  - Disposes her property or prevents her from exercising her legal right over the property.
  - Obstructs her to observe her religious profession or practice.
  - The husband has more than one wife and he does not treat her equitably according to injunctions of 'Quran'.
  - False charge of adultery is the ground that the old Muslim law recognizes by which one can divorce the husband.
  - Change of religion or renunciation.

  - — Any other ground which is recognized as valid for the dissolution of marriage under Muslim law. These grounds could cover 'Laan', 'Ila' and 'Zihar'.
- The husband can divorce the wife by uttering the word 'Talaq', thrice. This facility is not given to the wife.

Marriage Laws of Christians

In India, a Christian marriage is a contract. A Minister of Religion, who is licensed under the Christian Marriage Act of 1872, usually solemnizes it. The Marriage Registrar can also solemnize it. Marriage in Christianity is considered not only a contract but also a sacrament. The jurists consider it as a voluntary union for life. However, there can also be dissolution of marriage on certain grounds, including irretrievable breakdown of the marriage.

Christian Marriage Act, 1872

The major provisions of the Act are as under:

— Bigamy is not allowed and bigamous marriage is a void marriage.

— Minimum age of marriage for girls is 18 years and for boys 21 years.

— If either party to the marriage is an idiot or lunatic at the time of marriage, a decree of nullity can be obtained.

— This provision is not applicable to idiocy and lunacy after marriage.

— A marriage, which is forbidden by the personal law of the parties, is not valid, which includes prohibited degrees of consanguinity or affinity.

— Minister of Religion, Marriage Registrars and persons licensed to solemnize marriage can solemnize marriage.

— Registration of marriage is compulsory.

Divorce Laws of Christians

The Indian Divorce Act applies only to Christian marriage. Husband may dissolve a marriage on the ground of adultery by wife. A woman can get divorce on the basis of the following grounds when the husband has:

- changed the relation and has married again,
- been found guilty of incestuous adultery,
- bigamy with adultery,
- married with another woman with adultery,
- treated her with cruelty,
- adultery coupled with desertion without reasonable cause for a period of two years, and
- committed rape or sodomy.

Common Marriage Laws for Hindus, Muslims, and Christians

According to Special Marriage Act, 1954, all married couples, irrespective of religion, must undertake registration of their marriages after the marriage. However, this Act extends to the whole of India except the state of Jammu & Kashmir. The unique feature of this Act is that a marriage solemnized in any other form under any law between any two persons may be registered under this Act. On registration such a marriage for all purposes is treated as performed. The conditions, which are to be fulfilled for registration of marriage under this Act, are as follows:

- The parties have been married and have since been living together as husband and wife.
- Neither party has more than one spouse living.
- Neither party is a lunatic or an idiot.
- The male has completed the age of 21 years and the female of 18 years.
- The parties are not within the prohibited degree of relationship (unless a custom permits).
- The parties have been residing within the district of the marriage registration office for not less than 30 days immediately preceding the date on which the application for registration is made.

- An elaborate procedure is followed for the validity of marriage and a certificate is entered in the marriage certificate book duly signed by the parties to the marriage and three witnesses. The certificate is the conclusive evidence of the fact that the marriage is solemnized and all formalities are over.

Common Divorce Laws for Hindus, Muslims, and Christians

Under Special Marriage Act, 1954, a petition for divorce may be presented to the District Court either by the husband or by the wife on the following grounds:

- Voluntary sexual intercourse with any person other than his or her spouse after solemnization of marriage.
- Desertion for a continuous period of not less than two years immediately preceding the presentation of petition.
- Undergoing a sentence of imprisonment for seven years or more for an offence according to the Indian Penal Code.
- Treatment with cruelty after solemnization of marriage.
- Incurably of unsound mind or suffering from mental disorder to such an extent that one cannot reasonably be expected to live.
- Suffering from venereal disease in a communicable form.
- Suffering from leprosy, which is infectious and incurable and not contacted from other party.
- Unheard of for a period of seven years or more.
- Further, a wife may present a petition for divorce on the following grounds:
    - That her husband has been found guilty of rape, sodomy, and bestiality since the solemnization of the marriage.
    - That co-habitation between the parties has not been resumed for one year or more since the passing of the decree of maintenance or judicial separation.
    - That there has been no restitution of conjugal rights between the parties to the marriage for a period of one year or more after passing the decree for restitution.

- Finally both the parties may file a divorce petition to the district court by mutual consent.

Maintenance Laws

Hindus

The Hindu Adoption and Maintenance Act, 1956 discusses control maintenance of wife by the husband. According to Section 18 of the Act, a Hindu wife, whether married before or after the commencement of the Act, shall be entitled to be maintained by her husband during her lifetime. She shall be entitled to claim maintenance even if she is living separately on the following grounds:

- If husband is guilty of desertion.
- He has treated her with cruelty.
- He is suffering from virulent form of leprosy.
- He has any other wife living.
- He keeps a concubine.
- He has ceased to be a Hindu.
- There is any other cause justifying her living separately.

Furthermore, a Hindu wife, whether married before or after the commencement of the Act of 1956, shall be entitled to be maintained by her father-in-law after the death of her husband if she is unable to maintain herself out of her own earning or the earnings of her son or daughter or their estate; earnings from her husband or her parents.

A Hindu wife shall not be entitled to separate residence or maintenance from her husband if she is unchaste or ceases to be a Hindu.

The other provisions of the 1956 Act are:

- The legitimate as well as illegitimate minor children have a right to get maintenance from their parents (Section 20 of the Act).
- The old and infirm parents have a right to get maintenance from their children (sons and daughters).

- Only those persons are entitled to ask for maintenance who are unable to maintain themselves out of their property (Section 20 of the Act).
- The heirs of a deceased Hindu are bound to maintain the dependants of the deceased (Section 22 of the Act).

The quantum of maintenance depends upon the discretion of the court depending upon the condition.

Muslims

Under Muslim law also, a wife is entitled to maintenance from her husband. It arises out of her status. For the maintenance of divorced Muslim women, the Muslim Women (Protection of Rights on Divorce) Act, 1986 has made various provisions as follows:

- A divorced Muslim woman is entitled to fair and reasonable maintenance within the period of 'Iddat' from her former husband. 'Iddat' is period
    - during which a divorced woman is not permitted to remarry;
    - three menstrual cycles after the divorce;
    - if the woman is not subject to menstruation, then, three months after the divorce; and
    - if the woman is pregnant, then, up to the delivery of the child.
- After 'Iddat' period she is entitled to get maintenance from her parents/own children/those relatives of the woman who would be entitled to inherit or the State Wakf Board.
- A divorced woman is entitled to get the following things from her husband:
    - A sum equal to dower 'Mahr' at the time of marriage.
    - Maintenance of children till they are of two years of age.
    - Mother is entitled to be a custodian of her child until he is seven years old and a girl until she attains puberty.

- All gifts given to her by anyone at the time of marriage.
- When a woman demands divorce from her husband, then, it is known as 'Khula' and in this case wife is not entitled to 'Mahr'.

It is advocated by the jurists that Section 3 of the Muslim Women Act, 1986 contemplates fair and reasonable provision and maintenance for the wife by the husband for the 'Iddat' period and beyond this period as well.

Christians

A Christian wife enjoys similar rights of maintenance as a Hindu wife. Section 36 of the Indian Divorce Act provides for alimony. Alimony means an allowance for support made by one spouse to the other, usually by husband to wife, before and after divorce. Section 37 of the Act provides for permanent alimony to the wife, while maintaining her fortune, and considering the ability of the husband to provide support for her whole life.

Adoption Laws

Adoption is the admission of a stranger by birth to the privileges of a child by a legally recognized form of affiliation. The law of adoption enables a childless person to make somebody else's child his own. The objectives of adoption are twofold:
(1) for performance of funeral rights, and
(2) for preservation of the continuance of one's lineage.

Hindus

The Hindu are guided by the Hindu Adoptions and Maintenance Act, 1956. This Act extends to the whole of India except the state of Jammu & Kashmir.

Essential requirements of a valid adoption

A male/female Hindu must have the following capacities to take a child in adoption:

- Should have a sound mind.
- Should not be minor (below the legal age).
- Must have consent of spouse is necessary if alive.
- Consent of the spouse is not necessary when
    - he/she has completely renounced the world,
    - he/she is not a Hindu, and
    - he/she has an unsound mind.

Provision for widows, divorcees, and unmarried Ḥindu men/women who are over 21 years of age

- The adopted child should be treated like a biological child.
- For adoption, no fees are required.
- One can adopt one boy and one girl at the most.
- The adopted child should be Hindu and should not be over 15 years of age and should not be married.
- If the adopted child is of the opposite sex then the age difference between the child and the parents should be at least 21 years.

Provisions for the people, who are capable of giving a child in adoption

- Father, mother, or guardian should have the capacity to give a child in adoption.
- The mother can give the child in adoption if the father is dead or has renounced the world or is of unsound mind.
- The stepmother or stepfather has no capacity to give the child in adoption.
- If a widow is remarried, she cannot give a son in adoption by her former husband.
- The guardian has the capacity to give the child in adoption on the following conditions:
    - Both the parents of the child are dead.
    - Both the parents have renounced the world.
    - Both the parents have unsound mind.
    - Parents of the child are not known.

- The ceremony of giving and taking the child in adoption must be performed.
- Registration of adoption is not obligatory though the parties are free to enter into a registered deed.
- An adopted child shall be deemed to be the child of his/her mother for all purposes in effect from the date of adoption.

Muslims

Muslim law does not recognize adoption. Prior to the Shariat Act, 1937, some Muslims recognized adoption by custom. According to the Oudh Act, 1869, a Muslim 'Talukadar' was permitted to adopt. To a great extent, the custom of adoption is abrogated. If there is no declaration under the Shariat Act, it is open to a person to prove the custom of adoption and practise the same. In Jammu & Kashmir, adoption is recognized under custom.

Succession/Inheritance Laws

Legislation dealing with succession is appropriately considered as a social legislation. Any agreement or provision of documents changing the same cannot override the law of succession being the law of the land. An inheritance cannot remain in abeyance in anticipation of the birth of a preferable heir who was not conceived at the time of death of the owner. The right of succession must be vested in the person who is the nearest heir at the time of the death of the owner.

Hindus

The Hindu Succession Act, 1956 outlines the legal provisions of succession for Hindus. These are as follows:

- The Act seeks to provide a uniform law of succession to all Hindus.
- Blood relationship nurtured under love and affection, forms its base and all blood relations are heirs.
- No one is disqualified from succeeding because of any disease, defect, or deformity.

- Women stand at par with men in regard to heirship.
- The limited estate of a woman is abolished.
- Unrestricted testamentary power is given to the 'Mitakshara' coparcener in respect of his undivided interest. (Note: Mitakshara is the name of the school, which is applicable to the whole of India except Bengal. The Dayabhaga School prevails in Bengal. Coparcener means joint heir to an undivided property).
- The distribution of property of a person under succession law goes to class I heirs (sons, daughters, wife, etc.), and then to class II heirs (father, brothers, sisters, etc.), then to agnates, then to cognates, and finally to the government.
- Agnates and cognates are blood relations not covered under the class I and II heir categories, and where agnates are preferred to the cognates.
- Daughters do not have the right to seek a partition of property on which there is a dwelling house. They will get a share equal to that of a brother, if the later chooses for partition of property.

Muslims

Among Muslims, laws governing succession/inheritance are as under:

- When a Muslim dies intestate (without a valid will), his property would devolve on his heirs according to the law of the concerned school to which he belonged at the time of death.
- Unlike Hindu law, Muslim law does not recognize any joint family property or right by birth.
- The right of heirs comes into existence for the first time only on the death of the propositus.
- Though the succession never remains in suspension, the actual distribution of property takes place only after expenses towards debts, legacies, funeral, etc., of the deceased have been discharged.

- Muslim law does not recognize the principle of representation. If an heir presumptive dies in the lifetime of the propositus, the heirs of such an heir presumptive have no right to claim his/her share in the property of the propositus. However, the principle of representation is recognized in Shia law.
- The cardinal principle of Muslim law of succession is that the nearer in degree excludes the more removed in each class of heirs.
- In Sunni law, there are classes of heirs as follows:
  - *Sharers:* father, true grandfather, mother, true grandmother, husband, wife, daughter, etc.
  - *Residuaries:* son, son's son (howsoever low), full brother, full sister, consanguine brother, consanguine sister, etc.
  - *Distant kindred:* daughter's children, son's daughter's children, etc.
- Shias divide heirs into two groups as under:
  - Sharers and the descendants of the sharers, howsoever low.
  - The residuaries and the descendants of the residuaries, howsoever low.
- There is no ban to inheritance in case of physical or mental defects and unchastely.
- Slavery, infidelity or conversion to another religion, homicide and illegitimacy are the categories that are considered disabled for the purpose of inheriting property.
- Both male and female members inherit the property according to the rule of a double share to the male.

Christians

The Indian Succession Act, 1925 came into existence consolidating several pieces of legislation, which were in practice previously.

- This Act deals with intestate succession and is applicable to Europeans, Anglo-Indians, Jews, Armenians, Indian

Christians, and to persons marrying under the Special Marriage Act, 1872.

- It is also applicable to Parsee intestate.
- In this Act there is no discrimination based on sex among the heirs, for example, sons and daughters of an intestate.
- There is also no distinction between full blood relatives and persons related by half blood.
- The relations by adoption are not recognized in the Act.
- Christian widows get one-third of their husband's property and the remaining two-third goes to the children.
- Widows inherit half of her husband's property if she does not have children while the remaining share goes to the distant kin.

According to the Indian Succession Act, 1925, every woman, irrespective of her religion, has a right to:

- acquire and hold property for herself in her own name,
- use her property or earnings in whichever way she wants,
- buy or sell property the same way as a man has, and
- has a share in the property of her parents.

Guardianship Laws

A guardian is a person who takes care of a minor or his property, or both. It is for the welfare of the minors that the concept of guardianship came into existence.

Hindus and Muslims

The general laws relating to guardianship are dealt with under the Guardian and Wards Act, 1890, which is applicable to Hindus as well as Muslims. Its major provisions are:

- According to the Indian Majority Act, 1875, the age of majority is 21 for those whose guardian is appointed by the court.
- The law recognizes four types of guardians, namely, natural guardian, testamentary guardian, *de facto* guardian and guardian appointed or declared by the court.

- For all purposes a guardian takes care of the person as well as property of the minor.
- A guardian stands in the position of a trustee, and the ward in the position of a beneficiary.
- He is the custodian of the ward who looks after the health and education and other matters as the law requires.
- He also looks after the property as a man of ordinary prudence.
- When a guardian is appointed by will or court, his position as 'will' and the 'court' restricts a guardian.
- Guardianship may be terminated by death, removal, discharge, or cessation of the authority of the guardian.

Hindus

The Hindus are guided and controlled by two Acts, viz., the Guardians and Wards Act, 1890, and the Hindu Minority and Guardianship Act, 1956. In case of conflict, the later Act shall prevail over the former.

Hindu Minority and Guardianship Act, 1956

Important provisions under this Act are:

- Guardians may be a natural guardian, testamentary guardian (guardianship by will), guardians appointed by the court, or *de facto* guardian.
- Minor means a person who has not yet reached the age of 18 years.
- Guardian is a person having the care of the person/minor or of his property, or both person and property.
- The guardian is entitled to represent the minor in all litigations and may refer the matter to arbitration.
- He has the right to be reimbursed out of minor's property for reasonable expenses.
- Fathers, mothers, and husbands are natural guardians.
- A Hindu father and mother or Hindu widow are/is entitled to appoint a testamentary guardian (guardian by 'will') and the later acquires the right of a guardian after

the death of the formers. If the minor is a girl, the right of such a guardian shall cease on the marriage of the minor.

- The testamentary guardian has all the rights of natural guardian, subject to the provisions incorporated in the 'will'.
- A guardian or more than one guardian can be appointed or declared by the District Court.
- *De facto* guardians are guardians in fact because of their sympathy and affection.

Muslims

The Koran, the Ahadis and other authorities of Muslim law emphasize the guardianship on a minor's property, and the guardianship of the person is only on inference. There is no codified Muslim law for guardianship like Hindu law. In the provisions of the Guardians and Wards Act, 1890, the judicial decisions as well as other authoritative sources of Muslim law guide and control the guardianship of Muslims.

- The father is the recognized and natural guardian; and after the death of the father the executor is the grandfather (for Shias).
- The mother is not a natural guardian, even of her minor illegitimate children.
- The mother has the right of custody of her children with respect to the ages specified in each school, irrespective of the legitimacy of the child.
- Among Sunnis, the father has full power of making a testamentary appointment of guardian.
- On the failure of natural and testamentary guardian, the District Court may appoint or declare any person as guardians, as per the provisions of the Act of 1890.
- *De facto* guardian, as recognized in Muslim law, is an individual who is placed in charge of the minor and his property. Though he can transfer movable property for the welfare of the minor, he has no right to transfer immovable property.

- The following persons are entitled to be the guardian of the property of a minor:
  - Father
  - The executors appointed by the father's will
  - The father's father
  - The executor appointed by the will of the father's father

  In the absence of the aforesaid guardians, the court may appoint a guardian according to the provisions of the Guardian and Wards Act, 1890.

Welfare Legislations for Women in India

Constitutional Provisions

The Constitution of India contains a number of provisions for the welfare of women. These are:

- Article 14 lays down the general principles of equality before law.
- Article 15 prohibits any discrimination on the grounds of religion, race, caste, sex or place of birth. Further, it permits special provisions for women as well as children.
- Article 39 specially requires the state to direct its policy for the uplift of women.
- Article 51A (e) imposes a fundamental duty on every citizen to renounce practices that are derogatory to the dignity of women.

Laws Relating to Reproductive Health of Women

The decline in the number of females in India is an indicator of the discrimination against females from their birth. The reasons for this discrepancy include preference for male children, and the negative attitude of people towards girls, which results in female infanticide and prenatal sex selection. The female feticide is more disturbing. Besides early marriage, early pregnancy and childbearing, and lack of information about human sexuality, negative attitudes towards women and girls pose grave risks to the reproductive health of Indian females.

To avoid these problems, the Indian government formulated the following laws:

The Prenatal Diagnostic Techniques (PNDT) (Regulation and Prevention of Misuse) Act, 1994

It extends to the whole of India except the state of Jammu & Kashmir. It prohibits

- misuse of prenatal diagnostic techniques for determination of sex of fetus, leading to female feticide, and
- advertisement of prenatal diagnostic techniques for detection or determination of sex.
- It permits and regulates the use of prenatal diagnostic techniques for the purpose of detection of specific genetic abnormalities or disorders.
- It can also be applied to pregnant woman under following conditions:
  - Above 35 years old.
  - Has suffered two or more spontaneous abortions.
  - Has been exposed to potentially teratogens, such as drugs, radiation, infectious agents, or chemicals.
  - Has family history of mental retardation or physical deformities, such as spastically or any other genetic diseases.

Medical Termination of Pregnancy Act, 1971

This Act extends to the whole India, except the state of Jammu & Kashmir. As per this Act, a registered medical practitioner can terminate pregnancies on the following grounds:

- Continuing the pregnancy involves a risk to the mother's life.
- Continuing the pregnancy would cause grave damage to the physical or mental health of the mother.
- The pregnancy has been caused by rape.
- Any pregnancy that occurs as a result of failure of any device or method used by any married couple for the purpose of limiting the number of children.

- Chances are high for the fetus being seriously handicapped due to physical and mental abnormalities.
- With the consent of parents or guardian, the pregnancy can be terminated if the woman has not attained the age of 18 years.

Pregnancy can be terminated only on the advice of a doctor where its length

- does not exceed 12 weeks, and
- exceeds 12 weeks, but does not exceed 20 weeks. However, this second option requires the agreement of not less than two registered medical practitioners.

Pregnancy cannot be terminated if it exceeds 20 weeks. A midwife or nurse does not have the right to terminate the pregnancy.

Places for MTP may include:

- Hospitals established or maintained or recognized by the government.
- A place that is approved for the purpose of this Act by the government.

Protective Laws for Women

Women in India experience unacceptable levels of violence in the family, within the community, at the workplace, in public places, and the custodial institutions. It is a manifestation of the historically unequal power relations between men and women, which has led to domination over and discrimination against women by men. Almost 76 per cent of women in the country have suffered from some form of sexual abuse. In India, rape takes place in every 54 minutes.

Dowry Prohibition Act, 1961

The dowry given at the time of marriage is the bride's personal property and is called the 'Streedhan' (wife's wealth from parental property). No one else has any right over it. It is essential to make a list of all gifts received at the time of the wedding. The bride should keep one and another list should be kept with groom. Offences under this law are:

- Giving and taking dowry.
- Helping in giving or taking dowry.
- Harassing a woman physically and mentally for dowry.
- Forcing woman to commit suicide for the dowry.
- Compelling a woman after her marriage to bring money or other property.

Punishment for taking and giving dowry include:

- Five years' imprisonment.
- Fine up to Rs. 15,000.
- Imprisonment for at least six months or a fine is imposed for asking for the dowry.
- Even for an advertisement regarding dowry, there is punishment both by imprisonment and fine.

The Commission of Sati (Prevention) Act, 1987

- 'Sati' means burning or burying alive of any widow with the body of her deceased husband.
- Punishment for glorification of 'Sati' shall be imprisonment for not less than one year, which may extend up to seven years with fine of Rs. 5,000, which may extend to Rs. 30,000.
- Punishment for an attempted 'Sati' is both imprisonment and fine.
- Punishment for abetment of 'Sati' shall be punishable with death or imprisonment for life and fine.

Domestic Violence Bill, 2002

This Act provides that any conduct of relatives of the victim, which subjects her to habitual assaults or makes her life miserable or injures, or harms, or forces her to lead an immoral life, constitutes domestic violence.

The Suppression of Immoral Traffic (in Women and Girls) Act, 1956

According to this Act, it is an offense to:

- to keep a brothel,

- to sell a girl for the purpose of prostitution,
- to sell, procure, or induce a person for the purpose of prostitution,
- to solicit for prostitution in a public place, and
- to live on the earnings of the prostitute.

Indecent Representation of Women (Prohibition) Act, 1986

Indecent representation of women through advertisements, movie posters, and paintings is illegal. The maximum punishment is five years of imprisonment with a fine from Rs. 20,000 to Rs. 1 lakh.

Apart from the above-mentioned legislations, women have also been protected through the Indian Penal Code under its various sections. For example, it is a criminal offense:

- When a man tries to outrage the modesty of a woman by assault or criminal force.
- If a man teases a woman or behaves with her in an undignified manner by insulting her modesty by uttering any words, sounds, or makes a gesture or exhibition intruding on her privacy.
- To take away an adult person anywhere by force or enticement for any reason.
- To abduct a girl forcibly for the purpose of marriage.
- To keep a person forcibly under control.

Likewise, the following acts amount to rape if a man has sexual intercourse with a woman:

- without her consent,
- against her will,
- when her consent is taken by fear of death or hurt, and
- when her consent is taken by pretending to be her husband when he is not actually so.

Laws for Working Women

Factories Act, 1948

The important provisions of this Act are:

- The working hours of women are restricted to between the hours of 6.00 a.m. to 7.00 p.m.
- Women must get one day off per week.
- They are not made to clean or oil any moving machine.
- They must have separate toilets and washrooms with doors.
- If a factory has more than 30 women workers, the employers must provide a crèche for the workers children.
- Women are not made to work more than 48 hours in a week.
- They are not made to work five hours at a stretch.

Maternity Benefit Act, 1961

The major provisions of this Act are:

- Every woman worker will be eligible for maternity benefits for a maximum period of 12 weeks – six weeks before the delivery and six weeks after the delivery. During her actual absence, she is entitled to maternity benefits at the rate of an average daily wage.
- The Act prohibits the employment of woman during six weeks immediately following the day of delivery or miscarriage, and provides safeguards to the health of pregnant woman against arduous work over a specified period.
- Women workers, who have a miscarriage or MTP (medical termination of pregnancy), are entitled to get six weeks' leave with full pay. This leave can be availed only once in the entire service.
- A woman is entitled to additional periods of leave with wages up to maximum of one month if she falls sick due to pregnancy, delivery or miscarriage, MTP, or due to tubectomy operation because of delivering a premature child.
- A woman, who has undergone a tubectomy operation, is entitled to take work leave for a period of two weeks immediately after such an event with wages.

- A woman cannot be dismissed and discharged if she remains absent from work during pregnancy.
- She is given two nursing breaks in addition to normal breaks after giving birth to the child until the baby is 15 months old.

The Equal Remuneration Act, 1976

According to this Act,

- a woman should be paid wages equal to a man for the same kind of work; and
- no employer can discriminate against women in wages, recruitment, promotion, training and transfer.

National Commission for Women

The objectives of National Commission for women are to:

- present the problems and progress of women to Central Government, and
- monitor the socio-economic development of the women.

Welfare Legislations for Children in India

Children are always considered as the nation's supremely important asset. How children are nurtured today will ultimately benefit the country as they grow into adulthood to serve the nation tomorrow. Thus, to protect the interests of the children, every country has created laws and the Indian State, too, in accordance with Article (15(3) of the Constitution, has, made the following special provisions for the protection and development of children:

- According to Article 24, no child under the age of 14 years shall be employed in any factory or mine or engaged in any other hazardous employment.
- According to Article 39(f), the state shall, in particular, direct its policy towards the development of children in a healthy manner and protect them against exploitation and moral turpitude.

- According to Article 15, there should be free and compulsory education up to the age of 14 (according to the decision of the Supreme Court in the case of *Uni Krishnan* v. *State of Andhra Pradesh*, the right to education up to the age of 14 is fundamental).

Besides, the government has also enacted several Acts for the benefit of children. These are described as under:

Child Labor (Prohibition and Regulation) Act, 1986

This Act prohibits the employment of children below the age of 14.

- Child labor is prohibited in certain processes like transport of passengers, goods or mail by railway, work in a catering establishment at railways, ports, etc., which are listed in Schedule 'A' of the Act of 1986.
- The penalty for violation of the Act ranges from three months to one year of imprisonment with a fine of Rs. 10,000 to Rs. 20,000.
- Any person knowing of child labor can lodge a complaint.

Juvenile Justice Act, 1986

This Act is enacted for the protection, treatment, development and rehabilitation of neglected or delinquent juvenile by way of establishing Juvenile Welfare Boards, Juvenile Courts, Juvenile Homes, Observation Homes, and After Care Institutions. According to the Act, a juvenile is a person who is below the age of 16 years.

The Child Marriage Restraint Act, 1926 (Amended, 1928)

According to the amended Act, the marriage of girls below the age of 18 years to boys below the age of 21 years is invalid.

The Hindu Adoption and Maintenance Act, 1956

The important features of this Act are:

- A child who is to be adopted must not have completed the age of 15 years. But customs of the country are also recognized.
- For adoption, there is no distinction between legitimate or illegitimate children for the purpose of succession.
- According to court decisions, adoption is considered as one of the best alternatives to institutional care for the rehabilitation of the destitute, orphans, and abandoned children.
- For the purpose of maintenance, no distinction is made between legitimate and illegitimate children.
- There is no difference in respect of the rights between the children born in wedlock and out of wedlock.

The Hindus Minority and Guardianship Act, 1956

This Act directs that in deciding guardianship, the court must take the welfare of the child as paramount in this consideration. If the welfare of the child is involved, the mother may be appointed guardian in the place of father.

Hindu Succession Act, 1956

According to this Act, a posthumous child has a right to inherit property of the intestate.

In addition to the above-mentioned welfare legislations for children, Section 82 of the Indian Penal Code, 1860 contemplates that no child can be guilty of a crime in India under the age of seven years. According to Section 83, nothing is an offence that is done by a child above seven years of age and under age 12, who has not attained a sufficient understanding in order to judge the nature and consequence of his conduct. The parents are asked to pay fines, but not the child or young person.

Health and Nutrition

The National Policy of Children stresses the need to provide adequate services for children before and after birth and through out growth to insure their full physical, mental, and social development. For this purpose,

- the Infanticide Act is promulgated in order to lower the infant mortality rate;
- the Integrated Child Development Scheme (ICDS) is envisaged as one of the longest child development programmes; and
- laws like Pre-Natal Diagnostic Techniques (PNDT) (Regulation and Prevention of Misuse) Act, 1994, and the Medical Termination of Pregnancy Act, 1971, not only protect the interest of women, but also of the children.

The Family Courts Act, 1984

This Act has been enacted to provide for the establishment of family courts to promote conciliation in and secure speedy settlement of disputes relating to family affairs and other relative matters such as marriage and divorce, restitution of conjugal rights, matrimonial relief, judicial separation, maintenance, guardianship, property, etc.

Summary

To summarize, the following points need to be kept in mind:

- In respect of marriage laws, Hindus and Christians abide by monogamy while Muslims are polygamous.
- Under Hindu law, apostasy from Hinduism by either husband or wife does not affect a Hindu marriage. In Muslim law, a husband's apostasy from Islam results in automatic dissolution of Muslim marriage. Under Christian law, apostasy by either of the spouses has no effect on Christian marriage except where the apostate husband has married again, in which case the wife would be entitled to sue for divorce.
- Under Hindu and Christian laws, divorce is effected only on certain grounds as specified in those laws. A wife married under Muslim law can be divorced by the husband

by the utterance of the word 'Talaq' thrice, but the said facility is not given to a Muslim woman.

- In Hindu and Christian laws, a divorced wife is allowed post-divorce permanent maintenance. Under traditional Muslim law, a divorced wife is not entitled to any maintenance, except during the period of 'Iddat'. However, the courts have allowed payment of maintenance to wives by husbands beyond the 'Iddat' period by interpreting Section 125(1)(a) of Code of Criminal Procedure, 1973.
- Hindu law recognizes adoption, while Muslim law does not recognize the same, except in a few customary practices. Now-a-days, adoption is recognized throughout the world not as a support to childless couple, or as a means to go to heaven, but as a method of providing shelter to orphans and the destitute.
- Regarding succession of property, the Hindu law recognizes the wife, son and daughter as class I heirs, and there is no discrimination between son and daughter. However, such gender discrimination is found in the partition of the dwelling house. In Christian law, Christian widows get one-third of the husband's property and the remaining the two-third goes to the children. In Muslim law, both males and females inherit the property, with a double share going to the male.
- Hindu law recognizes a father as the natural guardian and after him the mother. The Muslim law recognizes only the father as the natural guardian, and the mother is entitled only to custody of her minor child up to a certain age, but she is not the natural guardian.
- The influence of religion on the personal laws has been noticed explicitly and implicitly.
- The gender bias, related to having discrimination against woman, is observed through personal laws.
- The role of judiciary, law, and constitutional mandates to protect the interests of women and children is quite significant.

- Conspicuous attention is not given to protect the interests of old people either by law or the judiciary.

Suggestions

Thus, only understanding and creating awareness regarding all family laws is not sufficient; rather, there are suggestions for improving the scope of these family laws. They are as follows:

- It is the need of the hour to dissociate religion from personal laws.
- The gender inequality issue witnessed through discrimination against women through the personal laws of each community should be removed.
- The institution of marriage should be permanent, sacred, and sacramental besides being a contract.
- Registration of marriage should be mandatory for all purposes.
- The system of monogamy is considered as the most acceptable form of marriage, which ought to be practiced by all communities.
- The divorce by either spouse should be done on sufficient grounds, by mutual consent, and through the court, and not on a whimsy or unilaterally.
- On the eve of either divorce or judicial separation, provision of maintenance should be a permanent phenomenon either by the husband or the wife, based on economic situation of the spouse. Besides women, children and old people should also be provided maintenance. Further, a married daughter should provide maintenance to her parents in case of necessity.
- All personal laws should recognize adoption more in a spirit of giving shelter to orphans and the destitute, than in a spirit of expecting support at an old age and going to heaven.
- There should be no gender discrimination in adoption; the interest of the child should be paramount.

- There should be a uniform scheme of succession for all intestates, irrespective of sex. The provision of two different schemes for male and female intestate is discriminatory, which should be deleted from law.
- In all personal laws, there should be the classification of heirs; and daughters should be given a share, which is equal to that of a son.
- The daughters of an intestate should be given not only the right of residence but also an absolute share in the dwelling house. The female heirs who become the owners of the property should be given the right to effect partition of the dwelling house. The distinction on the ground of marital status of the daughters should be deleted.
- Fathers as well as mothers should be treated as natural guardians in all personal laws. The other type of guardians should be clearly expressed in the respective personal laws. The welfare of the child should be taken as utmost important.
- A Uniform Civil Code for all communities (Hindus, Muslims, Christians, etc.) is the need of the hour in order to dissolve the variegated differences in personal laws. As a first step to formulate a uniform Civil Code, each personal law should be restructured in the light of the aforesaid suggestions. Then, as a second step, there should be a Uniform Civil Code, which should be operative vis-à-vis personal laws. At the last stage, there should be a Uniform Civil Code, which should be mandatory for all communities in India.
- Article 44 of the Indian Constitution can facilitate the formulation as well as implementation of a Uniform Civil Code.
- The Special Marriage Act, 1954 is an example for fulfilling the message of Article 44.
- The family courts, which are established under the Family Courts Act, 1984, should settle the disputes speedily, and without strict adherence to the rigidity of formalism.

Welfare Legislations for Women, Children, and Geriatrics

It is high time that all the pieces of welfare legislation for women be amalgamated into one code, namely, "Welfare Code for Women". Similarly, piecemeal legislation to protect the interest of the children should be codified into a single code known as "Welfare Code for Children". As there is no specific legislation to safeguard the interests of geriatrics, it is a timely endeavor to develop law protecting and serving them.

Conclusion

To conclude, a conscientious approach needs to be developed to deal with the problems of the family, besides adherence to the various pieces of legislations on family matters. Problems can be examined and solved through family counseling, and parent and child legal education on various family matters. Merely having family laws are not sufficient to empower family members. Rather, if these laws can really be translated in an action level, lots of our family problems can well be resolved. This is the message of the present hour.

References

Dhagamwar, Vasudha (1994). Fulfilling the right to primary education: India's supreme court opens a door. *Future.* Vol. 31-32, pp. 24-29.

Dhagamwar, Vasudha (1989). *Towards the Uniform Civil Code.* Bombay: N.M. Tripathi Private Ltd., p. 166.

Diwan, Paras and Diwan Peeyushi (2000). *Family Law.* Faridabad (Haryana): Allahabad Law Agency, p. 536.

Diwan, Paras and Diwan Peeyushi (2001). *Modern Hindu Law.* Faridabad (Haryana): Allahabad Law Agency, p. 509.

Gangrade, K.D. (1978). *Social Legislation in India.* Delhi: Concept Publishing Company, p. 288.

Goswami, V.G. (1999). *Labour and Industrial Laws.* 17th ed. Allahabad: Central Law Agency.

Government of India, Ministry of Information and Broadcasting (1994). *A Bold New Era.*

Government of India, Ministry of Welfare, UNICEF (1999). Enhancing the Role of the Family as an Agency for Social and Economic Development Unit of Family Studies (1994). Mumbai: Tata Institute for Social Sciences.

Hindu Law (2001). Bare Act, Faridabad (Haryana): Allahabad Law Agency.

The Indian Christian Marriage Act, (1872). Bare Act, Allahabad: Allahabad Law Agency.

Jaysree, L. (1994). Personal Law and Woman, *Supreme Court Journal*, Vol. 1, pp. 7-11.

Juneja, Prakash C.C. (1983). Child in domestic service: A need for protective legislation. *Indian Socio-legal Journal*, Vol. XI (1 and 2), pp. 32-41.

Mahmood, Tahir (ed.) (1975). *Family Law and Social Change*. Bombay: N.M. Tripathi Private Ltd., p. 172.

Misra, Srikanta (1990). An introduction to the personal law. *Supreme Court Journal*, Vol. 2, pp. 11-16.

Misra, Preeti (2001). Gender justice: Some issues. *All India Reporter*, pp. 149-153.

Musharraf, Ali (1983). Child labour and socio-economic problems in India. *Indian Socio-legal Journal*. Vol. XI (1 and 2), pp. 32-41.

National Institute of Public Cooperation and Child Development (1990). *Statistics on Child in India*.

Reddy, G.B. (2000). *Women and Law*. 4th ed. Hyderabad: Gogia Law Publications.

Singh, D.P. (2001). Issues and initiations in women empowerment. *Social Welfare*, 48(6), pp. 22-27.

Singhal, Bhagwati Prasad (1998). Uniform civil code: Framing is imperative, *All India Reporter*, pp. 164-169.

Sinha, R.K. (1995). *The Muslim Law*. Allahabad: Central Law Agency.

Websites

www.censusinindia.net\results\resultsmain.html:Census of India (2001).

www.expressindia.com: Women's Representation Bill (1999).

www.hindustantimes.com: Domestic Violence against Women (2002).

10

Developing Resiliency in Contemporary Indian Families

Aparajita Chowdhury and David K. Carson

The past few decades have witnessed numerous influences on and changes within the Indian family system. The uncertainty and rapidly shifting climate of modern social, political, and economic life in India has rendered families vulnerable to a host of challenges and difficulties. More than ever before, families need to become better equipped to handle internal stresses and problems and confront external threats and demands. Although no single approach to helping Indian families stay strong and healthy is inclusive enough to capture the diversity of families today, a resiliency framework may serve as a valuable conceptual map for orienting a wide range of human services, as well as education and prevention programs. This chapter outlines the advantages of a resiliency approach to understanding modern Indian families and then focuses on creative ways to strengthen families. Future directions for education and prevention efforts are discussed while keeping in mind the tremendous socio-cultural, religious, and economic diversity of families today.

Overview

> "Success in family life comes not from avoiding difficulties or problems, but rather facing them squarely and coping with them effectively."

The development of families in all societies is the result of many mindful choices that take place within the family's relationship system (Howard, 1978). The process of family learning is influenced by the behaviors that individuals use to form and refine their relationships. Healthy family development requires the use of proactive and reflective skills that enable family members to arrive at a sense of importance within the group. An abundance of research indicates that children and adults, who are a part of healthy families, perform better in their respective roles and have more positive views of life than people from dysfunction family environments (Stinnett, 1980; Stinnett and DeFrain, 1985; Swick, 1987). Less healthy families tend to allow their actions to follow a mindless course. Their relationships often lack planning, reflect inadequate communication, and appear to lack social meaning (L'Abate, 1998). In some cases these actions are symbolic of major problems within one or more family members. In other cases it may be symptomatic of major stressors (or trauma) the family is experiencing. Whatever the predicament, the family functioning is impeded when families are not coping well with immediate and/or past major life events (Schwartzman, 1985).

Central to a progressive and growing family, then, is the emergence of productive human relationships. In order for these relationships to develop, a family learning system needs to be given importance, and necessary steps should be taken to enhance this learning system. A family resiliency paradigm is extremely useful in understanding how normal family functioning can be maintained in spite of tremendous challenges to the survival and well-being of the family. Resiliency refers to coping and adaptational processes that help the family operate as a '*functional unit*' (Walsh, 1998). In modern

India the family has been neglected as the primary resource that fosters resilience in children, adolescents, and adults. A family resilience framework can serve as a valuable conceptual map for developing a wide range of human services in Indian society.

Challenges to Contemporary Indian Families

Indian families have the most vital task of the nation's well-being – that of caring for their members, promoting individual growth and development, and meeting their needs for food, housing, fuel, and other requirements essential to their health and safety. The family's ability to function as social unit in which children and adults are properly socialized and justly treated is paramount to the future of Indian society (Carson and Chowdhury, 2000). Family resources, composition, structure, dynamics, and stage of the family life cycle influence this process. However, in the past few decades, Indian families (rural and urban, rich and poor) have experienced many changes. The range and variety of problems that Indian families face are vast and complex. Moreover, all families at one time or other face everyday problems because they are linked to the natural stages in the life cycle and daily living experiences. In general, a disruption in family harmony may contribute to abuse against individual family members, especially children and women. Today's Indian family is in a fluid, transitional state and is experiencing ambiguities in family roles, relationships, responsibilities, and models for emulation. The emotional support structure is weakening and external entities (e.g., schools, religious institutions) are taking part of the socializing roles earlier played by the families. Such a scenario has far-reaching implications for the emotional and psychological well-being of individuals, as seen for example in the increase in mental and emotional disturbances among children and adults. In extreme situations, individual pathology and relationship difficulties are resulting in higher incidences of family disintegration. According to Murthy (1999), these radical changes in the Indian family system have a number of implications, including:

- Relative increase in some of the mental health problems (suicide, drug dependence, stress-related disorders, child mental health problems).
- Lesser availability of the family level care and caregivers, necessitating the organization of alternative care provisions.
- Those families who continue to care for the ill persons will require organized support in the form of visiting help and networking of the families.
- Families will require financial and other supports (insurance, aid, preferential housing, etc.).
- Professionals have to actively work with families as partners.

In sum, improvement in the general health and well-being of families in modern India requires a long-range understanding of social and economic problems affecting families. External conditions will continue to exert pressure on family role performances, responsibilities, and dynamics. Hence, families need to become better informed about how they can more effectively handle internal problems and confront external demands and changes. In essence, families need to have a "new deal" that ensures their economic security and functional resiliency. In turn, as families are strengthened, so is the economy, social fabric, and national security.

Strength and Weakness Perspectives of the Modern Indian Family

In every society families can be characterized as having strengths and weaknesses (limitations). Contemporary Indian families are often described as an ideal homogenous unit with strong coping mechanisms and capacities. However, both the strengths and limitations of Indian families must be understood so that families may be better equipped to face adversities and challenges.

Strengths

Some of the major strengths of Indian families today can be summarized as follows:

1. *Women in the family:* In modern India a woman is the center of the Indian family – the emotional and spiritual head. She plays an intermediate role between elder and younger members of the family, and she is constantly balancing various roles and responsibilities of everyday life in the family. Whether she is a housewife or employed outside the family, the major part of running the household lies on her shoulders. At the same time, she is physically as well as socially vulnerable to sexual attacks and patriarchal oppression. She is able to survive under such difficult conditions only because of her deep faith, her courage, her love for family, and indomitable will. As an old Indian saying goes, "Without a woman, the home is an abode of ghosts".
2. *Family values and traditions:* Preserving family values across the generations is another strength of the Indian family. Generally, family members take pride in their family values and traditions and fight to protect them as far as possible. Family values are an essential part of the family's identity and overall resiliency. In Indian philosophy, the family is not merely a concept, but an emotional experience. In nurturing the family, an emphasis is placed on the heart as much as the head. Happy marriages are believed to be the foundation of strong families. However, marriage is not so much a union of two individuals but two families. Not only, respecting parents, teachers, and elders, love for the young and kindness for the poor and needy is also taught invariably to the children and adolescents in the family. The concept that the "entire world is one family" is the sole of Indian family values. Even in the 21st century, families are realizing the importance of preserving traditional family values and trying to revive and transmit them to the next

generation even if they are outside India as NRI, as well as in all cosmopolitan cities inside the country.

3. *The sovereignty of the family:* The Indian family, whether joint or nuclear, derives its strength from its intense devotion to certain fundamental values, including the following:
   - The family system, referred to as the joint family, derives its strength from its intense devotion to its religious, moral, and ethical values built around a cluster of sovereign truths that are unalterable. There are certain salient features, which characterize this joint family system and which give it substance and durability. It is a corporate and corporal body with the key element of 'mutual aid' among its members.
   - Mutual aid is inspired by spontaneous love for kith and kin rather than any economic calculations applicable to a secular corporate body.
   - The family members are jealous of the prestige and hollowed name of their family and look down upon deviants.
   - The individual's own self-regard is strongly identified with the reputation, status, and honor of his family.
   - There is no dualism between self and others.
   - The family has sovereignty in the exercise of its obligations and rights, and thus maintains its monopoly in matters of marriage, mutual aid, succession, and bringing up children.
   - No family in India exists as a unitary family because no matter in what type of family individuals are born, they are bound to develop multidimensional, dependent interpersonal relationships with other in their social orbit.
   - This family system considers males and females as two radically different but complementary opposite kinds of creatures, neither of which is perfectly complete without the other. Marriage makes a kind of

corporate unity of them, but not a partnership. A woman as a wife has power and influence, but she is quite different from those of her husband.

4. *Family as a complete system of social security:* Indian families are seen as providing support and comfort to members with a large population size, have several built-in systems that act as buffers against problem situations, and cushion the effect of anxiety through such activities as:
   — caring and rearing children until they are adult or in some cases even after their marriages;
   — providing a heaven-like environment for the aged, destitute, and orphans (complete social security); and
   — social support for employed women, destitute women, and widow.
5. *Practice of monogamy:* It is due to the social practice of monogamy that Indian families maintain emotional and psychological stability. Moreover, all family members are quite clear about their roles and responsibilities in relationship to one another. To some extent, the practice of monogamy helps resource-limited families to be more stable, secure, mature, and resilient against all oppositions in life. In spite of some material deprivation, families in India are considered as the best nurturing center for the children, where parents are always there for the children to feel secure and receive nurturance and assistance. When these children grow up and became parents themselves, they tend to adopt the same practices with their young ones.
6. *Diverse marriage system:* India is a multicultural, multilingual, and multireligious country. However, marriage among all Indians is considered a sacrament and not civil contract. Moreover, the elaborate marriage functions and celebrations help the couple remember and realize the sanctity of marriage. In fact, religious rites and rituals for almost every event in a human being's life – be they fortunate or unfortunate – are conducted with intense

fervor. Hence, in Hindu families, the performing of the ubiquitous puja or prayers at an auspicious event such as marriage is a necessity. Essentially, a prayer celebration is an offering of obeisance to the ancestors, as well as to the family gods, asking them to bless the boy and the girl who are to be married with a long and happy wedded life. The couple gets married in such an elaborate, pious, and religious manner that they are expected to live together for years to come, despite their differences and difficulties. These marriages in India are unions between two families, and the process of getting married requires the involvement of both the families in such a manner that if anything goes wrong anywhere between the couple, members of both the families are also affected. Moreover, the couple is mentally prepared through the whole process of marriage ceremonies to live together even after death (as Hindus believe in life after death or rebirth). Hence, divorces in Hindu marriages are rare.

Weaknesses

The deep roots of Indian marriages and the family system have been linked to a Banyan tree, which expands by sending down new roots (individual families) into the ground from its branches. Even today, given the rapid and sometimes radical changes within Indian families, the family is still the greatest strength of Indian society. However, in an age of rapid social and economic change and the dominance of electronic media and computers, the Indian family is exposed to the waves of ideas and values sweeping across distant societies beyond national boundaries. Belief structures are undergoing a metamorphosis deprived of true happiness because of modern ways of life, which prescribes selfishness as its prime motive. Many Indian families are gradually losing their close ties, as can be seen in disrespect towards elders, neglect of children, and distrust between husbands and wives. Other weaknesses in modern Indian families may be described as follows:

1. *Home for idlers*: It is a common phenomenon in rural (and even in some urban) families that only one or two members will be earning while others will be mostly non-earning members who do not want to earn their livelihood nor share even in household chores. When a person can eat comfortably without exerting himself, he is unlikely to indulge in any strenuous activity. Moreover, although the earning member will often earn enough, at times his or her income will fall short of providing a comfortable life for everyone in the family. Idlers, on the other hand, find plenty of time to gossip and pollute the psychological and emotional environment of the family.
2. *Individual growth and development are affected*: Families generally provide very little opportunity for individual autonomy or independence. The Indian family milieu is not overly conducive for the growth of individual autonomy because individuals are bound by the minutest rules and regulations framed by certain heads of the family (e.g., often patriarchal, but also those in the mother-in-law role) who look upon men and women as children even after they attain adulthood. Whatever the age or status the individual may have, this person has to act and function in accordance with the wish and desire of the head of the family only. Personal privacy and independence have no place in families, thus increasing tension and conflicts among the family members.
3. *Property litigation*: Especially in case of agricultural families, property litigation leads to partition or fragmentation of landholdings, which is harmful not only to agricultural progress, but also the economic well-being of families. Moreover, household property litigation frequently disrupts personal relationships in the family. In recent years, family laws have given equal share to the daughters in the father's property. However, this often fails to create better status and understanding among the

family members since the attitudes of males in the family often do not change.

4. *Changes in gender status and roles*: India is traditionally a male-dominated society. The gradual move towards greater rights and educational/vocational opportunities for women, as well as the awareness that women are equally as competent and confident to carry out all types of activities, has created a situation that not all males can easily accept. These changes are contributing to increased marital conflicts and widespread family difficulties.
5. *Impact of new social legislations*: The family in India has been influenced by the new social legislations consisting of the Civil Marriage Act (1872), Hindu Marriage Act (1955), and Hindu Succession Act (1956). The Civil Marriage Act enabled boys and girls to marry against the wishes of their parents. The Hindu Marriage Act enables women to seek divorce under certain conditions. The Hindu Succession Act gives the right of equal inheritance to women. Some would argue that the laws have posed a threat to the solidarity of the Indian family, including relationships between brothers and sisters, parents and children, and husbands and wives. However, others would argue that it is not the laws themselves that are the problem (in fact, they are needed and justified) but the failure of those in positions of influence to more adequately prepare families for these changes and support them in these new legislative decisions – the idea that some members of the family cannot be free until all are free.
6. *Lack of preparation for family life*: Today's Indian families have neither the qualities of traditional joint families nor of modern nuclear families. Most young couples are starting families with no preparation or guidance from any sector of society. Moreover, with population explosion, a greater emphasis on competition and individualism, and a faster paced lifestyle, young couples are feeling increasingly stressed and overwhelmed. Hence, there is a

tremendous need for marriage preparation and life skill training to meet the demands of modern social and vocational life.

7. *Gender discrimination*: Gender discrimination remains one of the greatest threats to the security and well-being of family life in India today. Sons and daughters are treated differently even in highly educated families. Maximum importance and benefits are given by parents (and society at large) to sons with regard to education, socio-economic status, and even employment. Despite this many girls and young women continue to excel in all spheres of life. However, it is often difficult for some family members to accept the 'can-do' attitude and behavior of girls. Prejudice and discrimination are a common backlash of female accomplishment both within and beyond the family system.

Despite the challenges to contemporary Indian family life, it is important to remember that in many ways the Indian family continues to be strong and vibrant. Family attachments remain the most notable feature of Indian society. Compromise and mutual adjustment are the key features of the Indian family system, as is an emphasis on balancing individual and family interests, and inculcating social virtues. For hundreds of millions of people the family in India is the 'safe haven' in a rapidly changing and increasingly dangerous world. Yet, there is no denying that the modern Indian family is struggling for a new identity. The challenge for professionals is to encourage families (and society-at-large) to promote traditional family values and virtues while at the same time help families develop new traits and competencies needed to face a future filled with change and uncertainty.

Resilience and Its Application within Families

"The art of bouncing back is not born, but learned.".

Resilience has to do with an individual's or family's capacity to withstand or rebound from life's challenges. It involves "...key processes over time that foster the ability to 'struggle well,' surmount obstacles, and go on to live and love fully" (Walsh, 2003: 1). Such a perspective emphasizes seeing troubled families as challenged by life's adversities rather than as pathological or damaged beyond repair. According to Walsh (2003), crises can be a wake-up call, which heightens the family's attention to what really matters; e.g., an opportunity for reappraising priorities, and discovering and developing new insights and abilities. Resilient families take realistic, concrete steps to solve problems; seize opportunities; share a range of feelings genuinely, transparently, and respectfully; accept and appreciate individual differences; build on successes and learn from failures; take a proactive stance in preventing future problems and preparing for future challenges; avoid blaming; envision new possibilities; and engage in collaborative and creative brainstorming. They also practice and begin to master the concepts of fairness, reciprocity, and negotiation. In sum, family resiliency is a relationally based concept that runs contrary to the common Western cultural notion of the 'rugged individual'. Resiliency embodies the idea that life's challenges are much more manageable and solvable when people work together rather than alone.

Resiliency is a valuable concept in understanding and treating individual survivors of trauma and adversity. Families that learn how to cope with challenges and meet the needs of its members are most flexible and adaptable to life's stresses and crises. Family resiliency includes characteristics, dimensions, and properties, which help families to be resistant to disruption in the face of change and adaptive in the face of crisis situation (McCubbin et. al., 1993). Healthy families solve problems with cooperation, creative brainstorming, and openness to others (Curran, 1983; Stinnett and DeFrain, 1985). Members learn values and skills at home that give them the power to shape their lives through successful coping. Less unhealthy families are more likely to succumb to adversities and pressures, thus increasing the likelihood of broken relationships and individual difficulties and psychopathology. A family's goals, values, problem-solving skills, and support networks impact its adaptation to long-term stress and crisis.

The overwhelming pressures on family life today are contributing to a high rate of family turmoil and disintegration. It is imperative that professionals understand family dynamics and develop creative ways to strengthen them. Promoting successful adaptation can be done by establishing preventive interventions for families 'at-risk' and contributing to our knowledge base of both functional and dysfunctional family processes. Rather than pathologizing families today, it is much more effective to employ a strength-based approach to intervention and prevention efforts (Walsh, 2003). The strength-based approach enables family members (and those professionals working with them) to look for and tap the creative potential of all families, and to encourage an active process of self-growth and discovery. As families increase their capacity to rebound from immediate crisis and to manage persistent stress, they also gain vital resources to deal more effectively with future challenges. The concept of family resiliency offers a flexible view that can encompass many complex variables, similarities and differences, and continuity and change over time. Thus, in building family resilience, every intervention is in effect a preventive measure.

The need to enhance family resiliency has never been more urgent, as families of today are affected by the uncertainties of rapid economic change and social upheaval. As family diversity in India increases, no single model of keeping the families healthy can be proposed. However, the Indian family has largely been neglected as a target of intervention. To date the approach of human service workers has been to salvage individual 'survivors' without assisting families and exploring their potential for growth and change. However, it is important to foster a compassionate understanding of parental life challenges, encourage reconciliation in families, and search for unrecognized strengths in the network of family relationships. In sum, the growing body of systems-based research on healthy family processes can serve as a useful basis for identifying family strengths and vulnerabilities. These efforts can only serve to inform interventions geared towards building and reinforcing core process elements in effective family functioning.

Theoretical Approaches to Understanding Family Resilience

Various perspectives on family resiliency have been proposed. The *developmental perspective,* proposed by Garmezy (1987) and Garmezy and Rutter (1983), includes a detailed analysis of factors (or mechanisms) within and beyond the family that help family members (and the family as a whole) to adapt successfully to a host of challenges over time. Garmezy (1987) and Garmezy and Rutter (1983) emphasize risk and protective factors (or mechanisms) involved in the process of coping and adaptation, particularly in families experiencing continual stress. At each stage of family development there are ebbs and flows in the family's ability to maintain balance (homeostasis), or in a sense, stay resilient. Three models have been proposed through which protective process can mediate the relationship between stress and competence within individuals and the family system:

- In the immunity model, protective factors are thought to serve as reserves against a decline in functioning under stress.
- In the compensatory model, personal attributes and environmental resources are thought to counteract the negative effects of stressors. For example, with aging, the decline in some aspects of mental functioning can be offset by gains in wisdom and perspective accrued through life experiences.

- In the challenge model, stressors can become potential facilitators of competence, provided that the level of stress is not overwhelming. A crisis can provide opportunities for families to develop new assets and become stronger.

Family processes, such as effective communication and problem-solving skills, can increase the family's immunity to stress, thus reducing the harm of crises and traumatic life experiences. For example, in the case of a mother's lengthy hospitalization, more resilient families will be able to compensate for the mother's loss of functioning. Family members can reallocate responsibilities to ensure that the children's needs are met. The father may need to alter his work schedule and take on more of the nurturing role of the mother along with other instrumental duties. Older children can help out more with household chores and caring for younger siblings. In India, even the neighbors play a very important role at the time of a family crisis. As family members receive outside help and support, their internal bonds and ways of coping can be strengthened, with each member acquiring new areas of competence. Thus, resilience is fostered in families through a chain of direct and indirect influences that ameliorate the effects of a stressful event. On the other hand, problems within the family are compounded by ineffective family coping efforts.

The *family systems perspective* of family resilience, developed by Walsh (1998), includes several key principles. Includes are the following precepts:

- Individual hardiness is best understood and fostered in the context of the family and larger social world, as a mutual interaction of individual, family, and environmental process.
- Crisis events and persistent stresses affect the entire family and all its members, posing risks not only for individual dysfunction, but also for relational conflict and family breakdown.
- Family processes mediate the impact of stress on all members and their relationships.

- Protective processes foster resilience by buffering stress and promoting recovery.
- Family processes can influence the course of many crisis events.
- All families have the potential for resilience; it can be maximized the potential by encouraging their best efforts and strengthening key processes.

According to Walsh (1998), crises and challenges are part of the human condition. The concept of family resilience affirms the potential for survival and growth in all families and offers a valuable framework for strength-oriented approaches to intervention and prevention practices. Just as families face diverse challenges, there are many pathways to family resilience. Understanding key processes in families can help family members mobilize untapped resources and to help them cope more effectively with both daily stressors and strains as well as major life events. Rutter (1987) outlines a number of general principles by which resiliency in families can be initiated and enhanced. These include:

1. Decrease risk factors:
    - Anticipating and preparing for threatening circumstances.
    - Reducing exposure or overload of stress.
    - Providing information; altering catastrophic beliefs.
2. Reducing negative chain reactions that heighten risk for sustained impact and further crisis within families:
    - Buffering stress effects (cushioning the impact) and overcoming obstacles.
    - Altering maladaptive coping strategies.
    - Withstanding after shocks, prolonged strains; rebounding from setbacks.
3. Strengthening protective family processes and reducing vulnerabilities among family members:
    - Enhancing family strengths; increasing opportunities and abilities for success.

- Mobilizing and shoring up resources toward recovery and mastery.
- Rebuilding, reorganizing, and reorienting in aftermath.
- Anticipating, preparing for both likely and unforeseen new challenges.

4. Bolstering family and individual esteem and efficacy through successful problem mastery:
   - Gaining competence, confidence and connectedness through collaborative efforts.
   - Managing challenge processes over time for sustained competence under stress.

In sum, on the basis of these useful principles, families can better assess their crisis situations and identify ways to reduce risk factors, the rendering challenges less threatening and more manageable.

Building Family Strengths and Resiliency

> "Resiliency is the power of the human spirit to embrace challenge, guided by wisdom and experience."

Family strengths are "made, not born". Learning new skills, adopting positive attitudes, accepting the situation as and when it occurs, and trying time and again, can make a difference in the lives of individuals, families, and communities. Discussed as follows are practical suggestions for building strengths and resiliency within families as they to face modern day challenges both large and small.

Identifying Family Strengths and Utilizing Its Resources

Most of us have more inner resources than we think. No family is strong in every respect or free from certain weaknesses or lacunas (blind spots in awareness). It is also not realistic to expect that all family members will be equally committed to better family living. However, every family possesses strengths and resources along with weaknesses and limitations. Family resiliency can be fostered through identifying each family member's assets and potentials, and nurturing their positive qualities, intentions, efforts, and achievements. At the same time, negative traits and behaviors can be modified and sometimes reduced through effective family interventions. According to Pollak (1953), identification of family strengths are keys to family adaptation such as altruism, a balance of independence, positive outlook, flexibility, compromise, and the ability to foster growth of members and supportive relationships. Further, untapped family resources can be identified and efforts taken to maximum existing family strengths. Young members within Indian families are given lesser preference over the aged, despite brilliance in work and other activities, because of hierarchical family structure. However, if 'youth power' can be tapped and utilized properly, many difficulties faced by today's Indian families can be reduced if not prevented. Hence, productive use of each and every family member in any educational or prevention effort is vital.

Adopting Positive Family-Oriented Goals

Every family needs to be encouraged to develop positive thinking and effective approaches to adapting to each stage of the family life cycle. Moreover, families can be helped to create goals, which may provide them with some direction, purpose, and fulfillment. The goals may be both material (e.g., someday have a new place of residence) and non-material (e.g., parents getting more involved in each child's formal education). All individuals in the immediate and extended family can participate in the creation of these family goals, as well as the practical means to achieve.

Inculcating Family Values and Religious Faith

Promoting family values and standards within families (i.e., of the family's own design and establishment) can help create stronger bonds among family members. Indian families, which tend to be very traditional, will tend to feel rather comfortable in revisiting their roots and deciding to follow or re-establish age-old family values and religious practices. In addition, other family values (e.g., commitment, connectedness, respect, open communication, honesty, etc.) can be encouraged through various family-oriented activities, rituals, and ceremonies. Faith and religious practices engaged in as a family can help provide stability and meaning to people's lives, especially in times of hardship and adversity. Religious faith can give family members an assurance that "things will work out in the end, despite unfavorable odds".

Understanding Family Crisis Situations and Making Sense of Them

It is essential for all the family members to understand and make some sense of a crisis or threat. Resilience is fostered when families gain a sense of coherence and render their crisis experience as more comprehensible, manageable, and meaningful. On the other hand, if secrets are kept and each family member is not made a part of the solution, the family's ability to cope and adapt will be seriously compromised.

Normalizing Family Stresses and Crises

There is a tendency among individuals and families to blame themselves for their problems and feel unique and alone in the world in the midst of their difficulties. Normalizing family distress has to do with not pathologizing the family or its problems as outsiders, but also helping them realize or remember that countless other families have undergone similar life experiences. Many family problems can be reduced and even neutralized through the very knowledge that other families have had analogous experiences and come out the other side not only having coped with the crisis or trauma, but made even stronger than they were before it occurred.

Parent Education and Family Support

Parent education and family support during crises are central to building and maintaining resiliency. Part of this involves helping parents understand the developmental needs of their children and adolescents, and develop an attitude of greater compassion and understanding. Mobilizing community resources in support of families (school, neighborhood, religious) is another way of helping them become stronger.

Applying Humor in Communication and Family Activities

According to Herman Hesse, "humor is a third kingdom where the spirit becomes tough and elastic". Humor has been defined as the ability to perceive relationships between people, objects, or ideas in congruous ways. Good-natured humor allows people to laugh with each other and not take themselves so seriously. According to Berg and Beckern (1995), humor is a way of establishing connections, defusing conflict, coping with pain and anxiety, and bringing others fun and enjoyment. The application and creation of humor have been credited with many adaptive functions (Ziv, 1984), including the following:

- Social functions for enhancement of interpersonal relations and group cohesiveness.
- Physiological functions that include arousal reduction or relaxation produced by laughter.
- Defensive functions include the avoidance or alleviation of fears and anxiety.
- Cognitive functions ascribed to humor center on the process of "pleasure in mastery", referring to enjoyment derived from successfully meeting the intellectual challenge involved in understanding or creating humor (McGhee, 1974).

Further, a "good sense of humor" is often associated with adjustment in terms of maturity, health, or effective coping (Martin and Lefcourt, 1983). It is also positively related to competence – a primary characteristic of adjustment referring to the capacity for effective functioning in the environment (McGhee, 1974). Thus, the value of humor is great but generalized and underutilized in Indian family life. Humor not only reduces stress, but also facilitates better communication among family members. It can well be applied within families as an outlet for negative emotions, sharing of feelings, and increasing understanding among family members. Humor further reduces the drudgery of household work and increases the competencies of the individual family members for better overall quality of life. Researchers have also found that strong correlation exists between humor and cognitive development and functioning. Hence, use of humor in daily family life may help children to think, judge, and act more rationally, as well as to develop their creativity and imagination (Amabile, 1989). A healthy sense and use of humor is never used to humiliate or bring disgrace or disrespect to anyone, but rather to lift one's soul.

Developing Social Competencies of Family Members

Bolstering the development of social skills, decision-making, and problem-solving abilities has been proposed as an effective strategy for building coping skills and preventing mental health problems among individuals in any stage of family life. These capacities can be encouraged through various family activities (e.g., psychodrama, role play) as well as through direct teaching and modeling.

Facilitating Effective Coping Skills

Stress reactions and coping abilities are directly related to various areas of development, psychological adjustment, and physical well-being (Lazarus and Folkman, 1984). These abilities, of course, are important to family resiliency (Walsh, 1998). Although resiliency is dependent to some extent on health and constitutional factors (Wolin and Wolin, 1993), including temperament (Carson and Bittner, 1994), much of what is involved in individual coping and family adaptation can be learned or acquired. Such behaviors and ways of thinking include reality-based optimism, effective communication and conflict management skills (as well as creative problem solving), acceptance of and appreciation for each family member's uniqueness, increased community involvement and elicitation of support, and cultivating a deeper sense of both individual and shared spirituality.

Developing Creativity among Family Members

According to Anna Freud, "creative minds have always been known to survive any kind of bad training". Creativity entails sound judgment as much as the ability to both see and, when necessary, "break out of the box". Creativity is believed to be a central component of healthy family functioning (Carson, 1999). Other writers have stressed the importance of creativity to individual mental health. For example, Freud (1964) viewed creativity as a key component of the defense mechanism of sublimation. According to Gestalt theorists, creativity involves trying out new behaviors that may seem strange or unconventional, but can be a positive step towards integration and change (Yontef, 1995). Cognitive psychology has emphasized the role of divergent thinking (paramount to any creative endeavor) in positive behavioral change and emotional relief (Corey, 1991; Freeman and Reinecke, 1995). One study by Carson et. al., (1994) showed that creative thinking was associated with better coping in the school environment, as well as fewer problematic responses to stress and behavioral difficulties among children. However, neither creative thinking abilities nor creative behaviors are generally recognized or valued by most Indian parents in today's society. However, encouraging creativity in individuals and families may be a crucial step towards enhancing resiliency.

Activities for Building Family Strengths and Resiliency

As we said earlier, family strengths are "made, not born". Families can learn new skills and adopt positive attitudes that will strengthen their relationships both within and beyond the family system. These efforts can be conducted by a variety of educators and social service professionals in Indian communities – both large and small. Some simple ways that the various components of family resiliency can be facilitated are discussed as follows:

Commitment

Commitment in families can be encouraged through conducting regular family meetings, planning a vacation or undertaking cooperative family ventures such as gardening, music, dance, crafts, art, games, etc.

Connectedness

Connectedness within and between families can be achieved through involvement in neighborhood projects geared towards helping and serving those in need.

Coherence

Coherence can be facilitated through recalling family successes and hopes, helping and encouraging families to face and work through problems rather than giving up, and acknowledging efforts of family members as much as individual achievement.

Cohesion

Cohesion might be increased through developing a family photo album, and organizing small religious functions as a family such as "Satyanarayan Puja" or other commonly performed rituals and ceremonies in different parts of India. It can also be increased by developing a family motto, emblem, or banner; setting parent-child as well as spouses "fun days or nights out"; and discussing changing boundaries and rules for privacy in the home if necessary.

Time Together

Family members should be encouraged to spend some time with each other (both immediate and extended family members). This can include daily routines such as meals or puja time, evening walks, or various types of play.

Communication

One of the most important ingredients in building family strengths is having clear, consistent, and honest communication among family members. This kind of communication is severely lacking in many Indian families, where everything tends to be taken as a "matter of fact". Poor communication among family members often leads to conflicts and misunderstandings. Effective communication involves acknowledging and accepting the feelings of others, active and reflective listening, paraphrasing what one thinks another has said in order to reduce confusion, and trying to solve problems as they come up rather than denying they exist or dealing with them all at once. Most important of all is creating a 'sensitivity' among family members to express, react and respond to each other in an open and caring manner.

Developing and Preserving a Strong Marriage

The health of the marriage directly influences the strength of the family. In many corners of the world, including India, it is common for couples to neglect their partner and the well-being of their marriage during the childrearing years. Indian couples can benefit from marriage education and enrichment activities. They can learn to balance the needs and demands of their children with those of their marriage and partner, while at the same time, acquire new problem-solving and conflict management skills.

Balancing Work and Family and Developing a Healthy Family Lifestyle

Developing healthy habits such as proper rest, good nutrition, adequate exercise, and balancing time and energy between work and family are all parts of becoming a more resilient family.

Flexibility, Adaptability, Mastery, Active Initiative, and Perseverance

These characteristics involve an openness to change, a willingness to take needed and calculated risks in meeting new challenges, and a belief in mastering the possible while accepting what cannot be changed.

Shared Spirituality and the Cultivation of a Healthy Morality

A shared sense of spirituality is a vital part of family resiliency. India is a land of great religious plurality. Reading and telling stories from the Koran, the Bhagwat Gita, Bible, or other holy books, as well as participation in daily prayers and rituals, can help family members bond and experience a greater purpose together. Spirituality and religious practice can also help provide strength in facing the trials and tribulations of life. Moreover, since the concept of forgiveness is central to most, if not all, major world religions, forgiveness should be modeled, taught, and nurtured in families. Forgiveness involves avoiding bringing up old issues that should be put to rest (i.e., not nursing of old wounds), learning from our mistakes, and letting things go in order to gain peace of mind and a deepening love for one another as family members. Finally, a healthy kind of morality can be developed in families which stress the importance of justice and kindness, self-responsibility and initiative, an informed conscience, and the use of sound judgment and decision-making based on one's own experience and that of others from whom one has learned. Moral reasoning and behavior also tends to be augmented in families, which value honesty, fairness, compassion, and the importance of serving and helping others, both publically and privately.

Rituals

Rituals do not have to be spiritual or religious in nature to be significant. Historically, rituals have been a major component of Indian family life. It is through rituals associated with child-birth, childrearing, marriage, and even death that families can continue to bond and meet one another's needs. These rituals must continue to be respected and supported by communities and society at large.

Involvement with Friends and Community

Resilient families are those that stay in close touch with extended family members, friends, neighbors, and community citizens. Support provided by other individuals and families might be a tremendous help in times of normal life transitions and major life crises or trauma.

In addition, families in India can be supported through encouraging individual talents, accepting differences, and teaching siblings to resolve conflicts. Families can also "make room" for friends and relatives who have little or no support or sense of belonging. Entire communities can gradually acquire values associated with forgiveness and healing rather than punishment or estrangement of families experiencing difficulties or who have members with handicapping conditions.

Importance of a Family Resilience Approach to Family Life Education

Family resilience cannot be captured in a snapshot at a single moment in time. More than an immediate crisis response or short-term adjustment, resilience involves many interactive processes over time – from a family's approach to threatening situation, through its ability to manage disruptive transactions, to varied strategies for coping with emerging stresses in the immediate and long-term. When considering the role and significance of a family resilience approach to family life education, professionals must consider a variety of interactive processes over different periods of family life. Moreover, families are empowered not by dwelling on what is wrong with them, but on that which is strong already and can be built upon. India is a nation of stark contrasts and unlimited diversity, and no two families are alike. Hence, coping styles and behaviors will be unique to each family and situation. However, a resilience-based paradigm, while not downplaying or overlooking family problems and pathology, encourages each family's potential for renewal and growth. This perspective stresses the importance of the family's need (and capacity) to draw from the wisdom and knowledge of its particular culture and traditions as it faces the future.

In closing, we would like to summarize four substantive *family intervention objectives* that family life educators and social service professionals should carefully consider. These are:

1. To promote positive parent, child and family functioning through identifying family needs, aspirations, problems, and personal projects.
2. To enhance successful efforts geared towards meeting needs, and to use existing family functioning styles (strengths and capabilities) as a basis for promoting the family's ability to mobilize resources.
3. To place a major emphasis on strengthening the family's social network, as well as promote the utilization of untapped but potential sources of informal aid and assistance.
4. To enhance the family's ability to become more self-sustaining with respect to meeting its needs, as well as to employ helping behaviors that augment the family's acquisition and use of competencies and skills necessary to mobilize and secure resources.

Other considerations in the enhancement of family resilience include:

- Positive effects of growing up within a stronger and healthier family.
- Consequences and potential positive benefits of sibling caretaking.
- Role of grandparents as 'resistance resources'.
- Contribution of family demographic variables to the development of resilience.
- Impact of family life education programming – both formal and informal.

In sum, family resilience "...does not mean bouncing back unscathed, but rather struggling well, effectively working through and learning from adversity, and attempting to integrate the experience into the fabric of their lives" (Walsh, 2003: 14). According to Werner and Smith (1982), resilience should be encouraged through cooperation with each family's natural design, rather than wholesale intervention and control by outsiders. On this issue we wholeheartedly agree. Those who work with families must do so courageously, yet with a spirit of service and humility. This is because it is usually families themselves that know what they need and how they want to change. Our job is to offer them a little help and encouragement along the way.

References

Amabile, T. (1989). *Growing Up Creative*. New York: Crown.

Arcus, M.E., Schvaneveldt, J.D. and Moss, J.J. (1993). *Handbook of Family Life Education: The Practice of Family Life Education*. Newbury Park, CA: Sage Publications.

Batson, M.C. (1994). *Peripheral Vision*. New York: Harper Collins.

Bharat, S. (1997). Family socialization of Indian children. *Trends in Social Science Research,* 4(1), pp. 201-216.

Carson, D.K. (1999). The importance of creativity in family therapy: A preliminary consideration. *The Family Journal: Counseling and Therapy for Couples and Family,* 7(4), pp. 326-334.

Carson, D.K. and Bittner, M.T. (1994). Temperament and school-aged children's coping abilities and responses to stress. *Journal of Genetic Psychology,* 155 (3), pp. 289-302.

Carson, D.K., Bittner, M.T., Cameron, B.R., Brown, D.M. and Meyer, S.S. (1994). Creative thinking as a predictor of school-age children's stress responses and coping abilities. *Creativity Research Journal,* 7(2), pp. 145-158.

Carson, D.K. and Chowdhury, A. (2000). Family therapy in India: A new profession in an ancient land? *Contemporary Family Therapy,* 22(4), pp. 387-406.

Corey, G. (1991). *Theory and Practice of Counseling and Psychotherapy* (4th ed.). Pacific Grove, CA: Brooks/Cole.

Curran, D. (1983). *Traits of a Healthy Family.* Minneapolis: Winston Press.

Dunst, C., Trivette, C. and Deal, A. (1998). *Enabling and Empowering Families: Principles and Guidelines for Practice.* Cambridge, MA: Brookline Books.

Freeman, A. and Reinecke, M.A. (1995). Cognitive therapy. In A.S. Gurman and S.B. Messer (eds.), *Essential Psychotherapies: Theory and Practice* (pp. 182-225). New York: Guilford.

Freud, S. (1964). *An Outline of Psycho-Analysis.* London: Hogarth Press.

Garmezy, N. (1987). Stress, competence and development: Continuities in the study of schizophrenic adults and children vulnerable to psychopathology, and the search for stress-resistant children. *American Journal of Orthopsychiatry,* 57, pp. 159-174.

Garmezy, N. and Rutter, M. (1983). *Stress, Coping, and Development.* New York: McGraw-Hill.

Howard, J. (1978). *Families.* New York: Berkeley Brooks.

L'Abate, L. (1998). *Family Psychopathology: The Relational Roots of Dysfunctional Behavior.* New York: The Guilford Press.

L'Abate, L. (1990). *Building Family Competence.* Newbury Park, CA: Sage Publications.

Lazarus, R. and Folkman, S. (1984). *Stress, Appraisal, and Coping.* New York: Springer Publications.

Martin, R.A. and Lefcourt, H. (1983). Sense of humor as a moderator of the relation between stressors and moods. *Journal of Personality and Social Psychology,* 45, pp. 1313-1324.

McCubbin, H.I., Olson, D.H. and Zimmerman, S. (1985). Family dynamics: Strengthening through action-research. In R.N. Rapoport (ed.), *Children, Youth and Families* (pp. 126-165). Cambridge, MA: Cambridge University Press.

McCubbin, H., McCubbin, M. and Thompson, A. (1993). Resiliency in families: The role of family schema and appraisal in family adaptation to crisis. In T. Brubaker (ed.), *Family Relations: Challenges for the Future*. Newbury Park, CA: Sage Publications.

McGhee, P.E. (1974). Cognitive mastery and children's humor. *Psychological Bulletin, 81*, pp. 721-730.

Murthy, R.S. (1999). Socialization and mental health in India. In T.S. Saraswathi (ed.), *Culture, Socialization and Human Development: Theory, Research and Applications in India* (pp. 378-397). New Delhi, Sage India.

Pollak, O. (1953). Design of a model of healthy family relationships as a basis for evaluative research. *Social Services Review,* 31, pp. 369-376.

Rapoport, R.N. (1985). *Children, Youth, and Families: The Action-Research Relationship*. Cambridge, MA: Cambridge University Press.

Schwartzman, J. (1985). *Families and Other Systems*. New York: The Guilford Press.

Sethi, B.B., Thakur, V.R. and Gupta, S.C. (1965). Changing patterns of culture and psychiatry in India. *American Journal of Psychotherapy, 19*, pp. 46-54.

Stinnett, N. (1980). *Family Strengths: Positive Models for Family Life*. Lincoln, NE: University of Nebraska Press.

Stinnett, N. and DeFrain, J. (1985). *Secrets of Strong Families*. Boston: Little Brown.

Swick, K.J. (1987). *Perspectives on Understanding and Working with Families*. Champaign, IL: Stipes Pub. Co.

Swick, K.J. (1993). *Strengthening Parents and Families during the Early Childhood Years*. Illinois: Stipes Pub. Co.

Walsh, F. (2003). Family resilience: A framework for clinical practice. *Family Process, 42*(1), pp. 1-18.

Walsh, F. (1998). *Strengthening Family Resilience*. New York: The Guilford Press.

Walsh, F. (1998). Editorial: The resilience of the field of family therapy. *Journal of Marital and Family Therapy, 24*(3), pp. 269-271.

Werner, E.E. (1989). Vulnerability and resiliency: A longitudinal perspective. In Brambring et. al. (eds.), *Children at Risk:*

Assessment, Longitudinal Research, and Intervention. Berlin: Walter de Gruyter.

Werner, E.E. and Smith, R.S. (1982). *Vulnerable but Invincible: A Longitudinal Study of Resilient Children and Youth*. New York: Mc Graw Hill.

Wolin, S.J. and Wolin, S. (1993). *The Resilient Self*. New York: Villiard Books.

Yontef, G.M. (1995). Gestalt therapy. In A.S. Gurman and S.B. Messer (eds.). *Essential Psychotherapies: Theory and Practice* (pp. 261-303). New York: Guilford.

Ziv, A. (1984). *Personality and Sense of Humor*. New York: Springer.

11

Family Life Enrichment

Some Practical Considerations

Arundhati Rath

India is proud of its ancient heritage of a united and stable family system. Indian families have demonstrated a unique strength of keeping themselves together in spite of growing stress and strains from both internal and external changes. However, the fast changing trends in the social, cultural, economic, and psychological scenario pose a growing threat to the institution of family in India. Hence, there is an urgent need to strengthen families in India through equipping its members with right attitudes, beliefs, and understanding regarding the significance of family life. This process has been termed 'family life enrichment'. Family life enrichment aims at promoting quality life through responsible decision-making, and an improved understanding of family roles, responsibilities, dynamics, and relationships. The present chapter emphasizes the need for family life enrichment in India and discusses the various conceptual issues involved in it. It further explains the need for setting family goals and improving family interactions in order to enhance the quality of family life.

The family in India is often viewed as an ideal homogeneous unit with strong coping mechanisms. However, it is important to recognize that there may be problems in the family. Moreover, families in a large and culturally diverse country such as India have plurality of forms that vary with class, ethnicity, and individual choice. In the patriarchal structure of the family, roles, responsibilities, control, and distribution of resources are strictly determined by age, sex, and generation. Control over resources and assumption of superiority give the man the authority to make decisions about his dependents, which mainly include women and children. Thus, the family has historically not been a cradle for nurturing democratic values. In fact, the child gets socialized into an understanding of inequality by gender and age – all in name of familism. Women also ingest patriarchal values and, in turn, utilize their power and position over others such as younger women within the family and both men and women of lower castes and classes. Patriarchy in the family is also internalized by members of the community, which spreads throughout Indian society. Therefore, the need for a democratic family structure is a major challenge for everyone in the family and just for women.

Industrialization, together with technological development, has brought several new challenges to the Indian family. The family is no longer the unit of production as it was in the pre-industrial society. It now encounters the forces of a market economy. Migration has fundamental implications for both women and children. A woman suffers whether only the man migrates to a new area to find work, or if they migrate with him. The kinship network is stretched and sometimes broken, and one's traditional skills are no longer useful in the urban economy. Repetitive migration deprives the children of their basic services of education and health and of the schemes that may have been offered to them had they not migrated. Moreover, increased longevity has resulted in a greater proportion of the elderly population. However, in the new work structure, the status of the elderly as the repositories of experiential wisdom is diminishing. As they are considered non-productive, they are often perceived as a burden to their adult children. Hence, socio-economic changes have brought several challenges to the family with reference to finding a rightful place in its socio-economic environment.

Simultaneously, the value system and goals of family life have changed in recent times. There is little doubt that Indians today are having some success at eradicating several social evils, such as child marriage, 'sati' and the 'purdha' system. At the same time, rapid growth of science and technology, women's education, economic independence, and industrialization have given rise to migration of families from rural and tribal areas to urban areas. This movement has resulted in a serious disintegration of joint family system, and a growing number of nuclear families and intercaste marriages. Growing per capita income and technological advancements have made life more comfortable for significant numbers of people in India today. However, we cannot overlook the fact that the traditional value-based culture of India is slowly being replaced by a materialistic culture. Outcomes of such a trend include a loosening of emotional bonds among the family members, neglecting the old, less quality time spent with children, an increased divorce rate, and an overall lack of family coherence.

In sum, families of today are exposed to various forces, both internal and external, which are bringing about radical changes in family structure and function. These changes are threatening the integrity and very survival of the family. In order to make families a safe and healthy place for normal human development to occur, it is essential that contemporary Indian families be strengthened through a variety of enrichment activities.

Conceptualizing Family Life Enrichment

According to the United Nations (1989), "human rights could be generally defined as those rights which are inherent in our nature and without which we cannot live as human beings.

Human rights and fundamental freedoms allow us to fully develop and use our human qualities, our spiritual and other needs". This concept of human rights needs to be applied in any attempts to enrich family life. Denial of them creates conditions of exploitation, deprivation, and destitution of families and their individual members. Family responsibilities are as important as family rights to ensure family happiness and well-being. Family rights and responsibilities can serve as a foundation for the goals of family life enrichment even in such a diverse country as India.

Individual's Rights and Responsibilities within the Family

According to Desai (1994), every child has the right to be reared by his or her natural family. Parents have the primary responsibility to rear their children. Every adult has the right to marry and have a family; and every elderly person has the right to be cared for by his or her children at home. There are natural caring qualities in family relationships. These may be used and strengthened by promoting and protecting every individual's rights for status, worth, dignity, equality, non-discrimination, freedom, social security for family members, and protection from family abuse and violence. It is the responsibility of every family member, as well as the community and the state, to promote and protect these rights. These rights and responsibilities are further elaborated on as follows:

Every family member (male/female, boy/girl, man/woman) is equal in dignity and worth, irrespective of age and gender. Every family member, therefore, has the right to equal allocation of available family resources, and equal responsibility towards household work. More specifically:

- Every family member has an equal right to family housing. All the adult members should share the title to the house.
- Every family member has an equal right to physical care and development through food and health care.
- Every family member has an equal right to education and training, work and earning, and leisure time activities.

- Every family member has an equal responsibility to do household work.
- Every child has an equal right to inheritance of parental property, irrespective of gender and marital status.
- Both married partners (husband and wife) have the right to gender equality in marriage with respect to monogamy, role, power, status, parenting, guardianship and custody of children, title to matrimonial home and property, and dissolution of the marriage and division of matrimonial property.

In spite of these clear-cut rights and responsibilities, Indian families suffer greatly with regard to providing and creating a democratic atmosphere for its family members. A proper understanding and practice of individual and family rights may enable Indian citizens to create a more just and compassionate society.

Maintaining Family Mental and Relational Health

Health is defined by the World Health Organization (WHO) of the United Nations as the "state of complete physical, mental and social well-being and not merely the absence of disease and infirmity". The essential components of 'family health' include the following:

Love

Both children and adults crave affection from others. Children who receive genuine affection and know that adults truly care for them tend to see themselves as persons of worth and lovability. Children who are genuinely loved for who they are, without any conditions attached, develop strong positive self-concepts and have little need to try to obtain love and attention from others in unhealthy ways.

Security

Children must feel safe and protected. They need to see the world as reliable and non-threatening. Parental behavior which is unjust and inconsistent tends to make the child feel anxious. Parents should help children perceive themselves as having the inner resources to deal successfully with the world.

Acceptance

Family members should adopt an "I am OK – you are OK" approach to human relationships. Children who are genuinely accepted develop a sense of belongingness and security. Children who are not accepted are likely to feel rejected and undesirable.

Trust

Trust is developed after the physical and emotional needs of family members are met. If these needs are not satisfied, children are prone to develop mistrust and feel that the world is hostile and unpredictable.

Self-esteem

Children have strong needs to value themselves and their contributions. They need recognition, attention, and appreciation in order to have a positive self-concept and high self-esteem. When self-esteem needs are not addressed, children tend to develop feelings of inferiority, inadequacy, and helplessness.

Limits

Children need limits and boundaries, which help them become more autonomous and self-directed.

Freedom

Children should be given freedom within reasonable limits to explore, to be independent, to make decisions, and to learn. Lack of freedom tends to make children dependent on their parents and peers.

Understanding Family Functions

The family is the basic unit of a society. The strength and solidarity of a society is highly dependent on how the basic unit performs its functions. It is the responsibility of all members of a family to understand and fulfill important family functions. However, the parents generally shoulder a large portion of it. Failure on the part of parents to perform their duties can lead to social problems for generations to come. Many social problems among our children can be traced back to a failure of parents to perform their essential functions. The family maintains itself as an ongoing unit through:

- *Affection*: Affection is a product of family living. The family remains united through love.
- *Personal security and acceptance*: The family is the home base to which we belong. It is here that we received help and guidance and know that we will always be accepted. The family is the main source of mental and emotional health for its members.
- *Satisfaction and a sense of purpose*: The family provides us with a sense of satisfaction and accomplishment with regard to our work and efforts that may go unnoticed by society.
- *Continuity of companionship and association:* While we move from job to job and from town to town, friends and acquaintances are often forgotten, but the family provides continuing companionship to all members. Companionship provides a place for us to vent our feelings and share our disappointments over the years.
- *Establishing limits:* The family not only establish limits but also reinforces among its members a sense of what is right and wrong. Hence, the family is our valued teacher and clarifier.

Individual Family Members Role and Responsibilities within Family

A role refers to an expected behavior in any social interaction. A clear understanding of family roles is very important. Role confusion can lead to problems and sometimes crises. The issue of roles within the family is further complicated by changes that happen in and around the family system, i.e., the change from a joint to a nuclear family structure, greater participation of women in economic activities outside the home, and the influence of Western culture and religion on Indian society today. Happiness and prosperity in families are directly tied to the extent to which family members adhere to family rules, roles, and obligations. For example, some important characteristics of family roles today are briefly discussed as follows:

(a) Role definitions and boundaries are more likely to be sharply defined in large families than in small families.

(b) The marital role of man and woman as a couple provides for companionship, security, physical relationships, reproduction, and friendship.

(c) As family size increases, parental roles tend to dominate over marital roles.

(d) Parents are basically responsible for the guidance and rearing of children, but in the extended family, other members of the family may share this responsibility at different levels.

(e) Older children are often delegated parental responsibilities in large families.

(f) Parental roles are fulfilled more successfully if parents have a basic knowledge of the factors that contribute to the growth and development of children.

(g) Parents must also perform work roles to support and care for their families.

(h) The financial demands of a large family can force parents to spend an excessive amount of time in their work roles in order to support the family.

(i) Roles played by family members, and the time spent in each role, is based on which stage of the life cycle they are in, as well as by the family's cultural values. Family relationships can be affected by:
   - the communication channel between family members;
   - conflicting expectations, especially between parents and children;
   - personality type of the family members; and
   - needs of individual family members.

Enhancing Family Well-Being through the Meeting of Family Goals

Achievement of the following goals would strengthen the family unit and help to prevent exploitation, discontinuation, and destitution of families:

Developing Positive Attitudes towards Achieving Family Well-Being

All members of the family must develop a positive attitude to achieve the goal of a happier and healthier family life. A mother may positively face the problems and challenges she confronts during childrearing. There should be equal allocation of family resources and responsibilities among family members. Democratic decision-making and freedom of choices about family life must be allowed to all the family members, including children and women. Each member of the family must be involved in all family activities to feel special.

Education for Enrichment of Family Interactions and Relationships

Members of the family must develop positive communication patterns with each other. They must eat meals together often and share their whole day activities and experiences. Each family member must feel comfortable in discussing problems –

be they personal, or problems involving family members or others.

Enhancing Relationships between Family Members and the Community

Family life can be strengthened only when members have a meaningful association with people in the community. Family members need to be aware of community support systems and resources available – be they health, service, or educationally related.

Improving Family Dynamics to Enhance Quality of Life

Family dynamics are broadly comprised of family interactions, norms, and stages. Some major family dynamics are discussed as follows:

Family Interactions

Family interactions refer to the distinctive character of interpersonal relationships, which occur between members of the family. An interpersonal relationship is a relationship based on a personal interaction rather than on any legal or structural basis. Family interactions are manifested through varying types and levels of cohesion, communication, role performance, decision-making, and adaptability. The following case study may help illustrate family dynamics in action:

Ruby and Sekhar have been married 10 years ago. Both of them work hard and have a positive self-image. Although they are both from Bangalore, Sekhar works as an executive at Bharat Heavy Electrical Limited in Bhopal. Their in-house family consists of husband, wife, son, and Ruby's mother, Mrs. Shetty. Ruby's father is dead and her mother stays with her, as she is the only daughter. Both Ruby and her mother are caring and affectionate women. The major problems the family generally encounter include:

- Both Ruby and Sekhar feel a lack of privacy at home as Mrs. Shetty is always present and demands attention.

— Ruby does not express her feelings, and Shekhar is very unhappy and spends more time away from home - at the office, various clubs, and with friends. Frequently, he comes home late at night.
— Mrs. Shetty is very uncomfortable when Ruby and Sekhar go out. She complains of health issues that seem to be associated with being left alone in the home.

All of these concerns have had a negative impact on the relationship of Ruby and Sekhar. Ruby could not withstand the problem and thus developed severe manic depression and was admitted to a hospital. In this case, there was a lack of personal interaction between husband and wife due to the presence and interference of another person (Ruby's mother). The couple needed to have some personal and private 'space' to nurture their relationship; however, this time was not available or was not recognized as a high priority. Besides, family members needed to understand individual roles within the family structure, and come together as a unit in solving the problems that were affecting family inter-dynamics.

Family Cohesion

Family cohesion is defined as the emotional bonding that family members have towards one another. There are three levels of cohesion, ranging from disengaged (very low), separated (low to moderate), and connected (moderate to high). It is hypothesized that the central levels of cohesion (separated and connected) make for optimal family functioning. The extreme levels (disengaged and enmeshed) are generally seen as problematic (Olson, 1988), as too much or too little emotional bonding creates dysfunction within the family. Hence, learning to create a healthy balance in terms of intra-family connectedness is an important component in resilient family systems.

Family Communication

Family communication is all about the verbal and non-verbal behavior that occurs within the family and between the family and its social environment. Intra-family communication needs to be clear, consistent, and comfortable, so that proper understanding, interpretation, and adjustment are possible. Without good communication, it is very difficult to maintain a peaceful and well-balanced family atmosphere. The style, pattern, and nature of communication between family members have tremendous influence on children's communication styles. The family setting is the place where the children first learn to communicate with others.

Role Performance

Another important aspect of family dynamics is role performance on the part of the family members. Family members need to understand their respective roles within the family – roles that change during different stages of life and in different situations to make the family run smoothly for the general well-being of all. Further, each family member must be committed and develop competency in performing their respective roles. Adults have the responsibility to be clear and consistent in defining and allocating specific roles to children and adolescents.

Decision-Making

Family decision-making serves as the cornerstone of the family dynamics. In order to manage the family, the skills of making decisions have to be learned in the context of family. The head of the family is responsible for taking family decisions and making others learn the skill. Whether it is with regard to family finance, or education of children or health care of the elderly at home, making decision is important. Who will do this and how it will be taken, all the family members must be aware of it. It is everybody's responsibilities but is has to be made by one person or jointly has to be clear and open to all.

Family Adaptability

With changing family dynamics, due to both internal and external forces, the family needs to develop adaptability in terms of power structure, role relationships, and managing with family stresses. Flexibility on the part of the family is essential, so that adjustments can be activated and maintained.

Family Learning

There is more to learning about families than simply understanding their context form. Values, attitudes, and major living skills are acquired through involvement with the 'intimate others' such as parents, brothers/sisters or other family members. There are three main dimensions of family learning, involving ritual, time, and space usage. An understanding of how families use these dimensions of learning in developing bases for a positive and meaningful relationship is important for healthy family life.

Rituals

Ritualization of time, behavior, and other events are vital elements that help compose a framework for initiating and maintaining family life. It is through rituals such as feeding, bathing, and loving that families form the needed bonds to meet their needs, to support the development of each person's individuality and mutually meaningful interactions among the members.

Time Usage

Time usage permeates all aspects of the family's relationships. For example, parents and children need plenty of 'informal time' to learn about each other, and to understand the needs and requirements of others. The mentality that family life just happens naturally, and that parenting, childcare, and family relationships are a low priority is negatively influencing the way most Indian families function.

Space Usage

It is in the family context where we learn about space: what it is, how it is used, and the various refinements that can occur within it. It is in the family that we learn how to begin shaping our 'space' as individuals and relating that space to outside relationships with others.

Conclusion

In the post-independence era, Indian traditions and culture have undergone significant changes by altering the value system and family lifestyles. With the increased application of advanced science and technology, there has been a shift in family life dynamics from traditional mores to a distinctly materialistic pattern. Family life enrichment offers a means to maintain healthy functioning family systems that provide support, comfort, and security to members. Family life enrichment or education is a relatively new concept in India. It aims at promoting quality of life through responsible decision-making and improved understanding of human relationships and family roles. The term 'family life enrichment' has different meanings ranging from the narrow concept of education in family planning, to the broader notion of education for leading a healthy, purposeful, and constructive life. In a developing country like India, where poverty and ignorance are rampant and where the pressures and strains of life relate to mobilizing the basic resources necessary for mere existence, the concept of family life enrichment assumes different ramifications. A well-integrated package would help families adapt themselves to new changes and assume greater responsibility for the betterment of society.

References

Desai, M. (1994). Towards Family Life Enrichment. Enhancing the Role of Family as an Agency for Social and Economic Development. Mumbai: Tata Institute and Social Sciences.

Mane, Purnima Gandevia Katy, Y., (1993). *Mental Health in India: Issues and Concerns*, Mumbai: Tata Institute of Social Science.

Ministry of Welfare, Government of India, UNICEF, (1994). Enhancing the Role of the Family as an Agency for Social and Economic Development, Mumbai: Tata Institute of Social Sciences.

Olson, D.H. (1988). *Family Perspective in Child and Youth Services*, New York: The Haworth Press.

Piercy, P. Fred, Sprenkle Douglas, H. and Associates, (1986). *Family Therapy Sourcebook*, New York: The Guilford Press.

Rapoport, Robert, N. (1985). *Children, Youth, and Families, The Action-research Relationship*, New York: Cambridge University Press.

Sarada, D. (1999). *Family Life Education For Adolescent Girls*, New Delhi: Discovery Publishing House.

Srilaxmi, B., (2000). *Nutrition Science*, New Delhi: New Age International (P) Ltd.

Swick, K.J. (1993). *Strengthening Parents and Families during the Early Childhood Years*, Illinois: Stipes Publishing Company.

12

Family Life Education in India

Needs, Settings, and Training Opportunities

David K. Carson, Aparajita Chowdhury, and Cecyle K. Carson

This paper examines the need for Family Life Education (FLE) in India and its development as an essential and additional component of professional practice for those who work with couples, families, and youth. It also discusses numerous factors placing Indian families at risk today, and the common and more extreme difficulties experienced by married couples, families, and youth. The potential benefits of FLE to strengthening families and marital relationships are outlined. Targets of and settings for and its training are highlighted, and a brief outline of a training-the-trainer approach is provided.

India is the second largest nation on earth and also the world's largest democracy. Although it is a rapidly developing country, it is a land steeped in tradition. It is also unparalleled in terms of ethnic, cultural, economic, political, linguistic, and religious diversity. Despite the fast-paced socio-cultural and economic changes that are challenging marriage and family life, the family unit remains at the core of society. Indeed, contemporary Indians continue to hold marriage and family life in the highest possible regard and reverence (Mullati, 1995). Children and adolescents have a special place in the family and community (Madan, 1990), and interdependency, support, and nurturing across the generations are commonplace in the Indian family system (Simhadri, 1989). Parents and extended family members maintain their roles as the primary socializers of children in ways that are no longer evident in many parts of the world, and parents and adult children strive to retain close relationships even when they are separated by long distances (Baral and Bishoyee, 1999; Mishra, 1995).

On the reverse side, Indian families today are experiencing a complex array of problems and challenges. Some of these difficulties are ancient and deeply embedded in Indian society, and some of them have seemingly never before been encountered in this country's history (Baral and Bishoyee, 1999; Baral and Chowdhury, 1999; Desai and Bharat, 1989). The majority of the roughly 80 per cent of Indians, who live in villages and rural areas, remain poor and are generally lacking in social resource and supports. They continue to be isolated from the mainstream society. Urbanites are also facing a multitude of problems that are challenging traditional family structures and relationships, and putting marriages and families at risk. An overabundance of urban and rural dwellers continues to experience a plethora of difficulties, including poverty and disease; overcrowding; water and air pollution; migration of individuals and families from rural to urban areas due to a lack of viable employment and vocational opportunities; a gradual weakening of age-old traditions including transformations in religion, caste, and other social institutions; natural disasters that make transportation, communication, and modernization difficult; ethnic conflicts and ongoing political instability; increased crime, social violence, and terrorism; inadequate housing and sanitation; poor nutrition and health care; illiteracy and low quality (and sometimes non-existent) education for children; minimal enforcement of child labor laws; and especially in rural areas the continual promotion of early marriages and large families, which facilitates more than impedes the cycle of poverty. In addition, families in contemporary India are experiencing newer kinds of problems similar to those which have permeated most Western societies the past four decades or more. These include marital strain and dissolution, parent-child conflicts, various forms of family violence, substance abuse, juvenile delinquency, school dropout or low school attainment among the lower class, and excessive pressures in many middle and upper class families for adolescents and young adults to achieve academically (Agarwal, 1989; Chowdhury, 1999; Das, 1999; Madan, 1990; Nanda and Dash, 1996; Parikh and Krishna, 1992; Patnaik, 1999; Sarkar, 1988). The result of all of these changes and difficulties has been a gradual segmenting of Indian society into the very rich, a flattening of the middle class, and a rise in the percentage of people living in deplorable conditions with little hope of ever improving their lives. In short, the future and well-being of the Indian family is highly precarious. Families are in tremendous need of assistance, resources, and support.

As part of a comprehensive mental health promotion effort in India, Family Life Education (FLE) is an essential component in helping professionals and concerned citizens work with the populace in maintaining and restoring family strengths and traditions. However, FLE is a relatively new concept in India, and one that, with few exceptions, has not been implemented in current mental health, social welfare, or educational programs. Yet, the need for educating families about various aspects of parenting, child and adolescent development, and other facets of family life, has been emphasized by key Indian social scientists. For instance, the prominent psychologist Durganand Sinha (1988) noted that there was a general consensus in the mental health community in India that (echoing the words of Channabasavanna and Bhatti, 1982: 149), "a patient is only a symptom of a troubled family". More recently, Oommen (2000), Professor of Sociology at Jawaharlal Nehru University in New Delhi, indicated that today's Indian family is ripe for and in great need of family-based education and intervention.

This chapter examines the range of marital and family difficulties in light of the undercurrent of social and economic changes in India today, and how an FLE 'movement' might take root in the current mental health, social service, and educational system. It also discusses the potential benefits of FLE training and services in meeting the tremendous needs of married couples and families in India today. This discussion will include an integration of the authors' practical experiences and observations in India that are based on the research they have conducted on Indian couples and families, educational programming they have engaged in with couples and families, and the counseling they have done with those experiencing a wide range of difficulties. Before we begin our discussion, however, it is important that we share three key assumptions that in many ways set the stage for FLE in this vast and diverse society.

First, FLE (as with the notion of counseling or therapy) is generally an unknown, misunderstood, and sometimes devalued enterprise in India (Carson and Chowdhury, 2000). Any activity or movement, which implies that couples and families need education or training, especially in such a sacred area as marriage or childrearing, can easily be viewed in negative terms. This is partly because such practices connote a 'deficit' in marriage and family life or functioning that needs to be fixed or remedied. Second, it is likely that FLE in India will entail a much greater involvement of extended family members, as well as interdisciplinary integration of prevention practices, than in many Western countries, which emphasize both education about and treatment for existing problems and disorders. Finally, the training and practice of family life specialists in India, and the growth of FLE as a profession, is likely to follow a radically different pathway than it has in other countries around the globe, including the United States; for example, a widespread lay training component that involves a high level of volunteerism. Each of these issues will be discussed in greater depth as this chapter unfolds.

Changing Indian Family and the Need for Family Life Education

In rural areas, villages, and even in large cities today, family life in India continues to be deeply rooted in the community. In fact, for centuries, friends, neighbors, relatives, and community members have shared responsibility for children's lives and well-being. The family system remains a source of stability and support when problems arise and maintains the physical and psychological integrity of individual family members over time. Traditional Indian society has been based on the joint family system, which, while in transition, is still the norm. This is particularly the case in rural areas where mobility of family members is much more restricted. The family, as a social system, consists of well-defined rules, roles, and sentiments that bind people together. Members share feelings of solidarity (familism) and strive to uphold family dignity and status in the society. A high premium is placed on family unity and cohesiveness, which are necessary for family stability and survival. Any behavior that threatens this cooperative spirit and unity is discouraged both from within and without. Sharing and mutual dependence are common at all stages of the family life cycle, which contributes to a sense of safety and security in the family. Elaborate family practices and rituals foster feelings of belongingness and convey the message that family bonds are immutable, dependable, and life long (Bharat, 1997; Mullati, 1995). Yet, the family structure has not gone unchallenged in recent years.

There are numerous and fast-paced changes occurring in India, which are having far-reaching implications in family, social, cultural, economic, and political life. These include the widespread growth of education (especially women's education), the impact of the mass media and modern communications, Westernization (i.e., gradual adaptation of values and lifestyles of Western nations), industrialization and modernization, and economic liberalization. In an age of the electronic media, including televisions and computers in even remote areas, the Indian family is being exposed to ideas, ideals, and values that are sweeping across the entire nation (Baral and Bishoyee, 1999). Some Indian social scientists and family scholars have proposed that, once the conditions of equality are negotiated and obtained at all levels, mental and relational well-being will be an inevitable outcome for a large portion of the society, including the family (e.g., see Bharat, 1991; Belle, 1990; Sinha, 1984). However, in the modern age, these changes continue to be slow and are often met with resistance (Baral and Bishoyee, 1999; Mishra, 1995; Sinha, 1988).

Other everyday problems encountered by contemporary Indian families include the stresses and strains of rearing children, conflicts with in-laws, difficulties associated with various chronic illnesses, and developmental delays and disabilities of children or other family members. Sinha (1984, 1988) argues that the majority of urban and rural dwellers today prefer to live in small nuclear family units. At the same time, however, they want to maintain close relationships with their extended family and have them available during times of crisis. The gradual trend towards nucleation has created greater role strain, ambiguity, and conflict between family members (such as authority over children between mothers and their mother-in-laws), as well as confusing expectations for children. Moreover, unlike the scenario in the traditional joint family system, elderly persons today have few roles to play in childrearing and socialization. They are also less likely, especially in educated families, to live with their adult children and grandchildren. The result in many families is an absence of clear and consistent role models for children beyond their own parents. In addition, parents are becoming more restrictive of their children (partly due to safety reasons) in having free time to interact with peers, either at school or in the neighborhood. This situation not only limits children's social network but also tends to instill more feelings of fear and distrust in them. The mass media (especially the electronic media) also aggravates the situation by creating unrealistic aspirations in children and parents, including a "you can and should have it all" materialistic kind of mindset.

Additional influences on the family include increased exposure to Western thinking (e.g., European and American), which has brought about changes in attitudes towards conventional methods of disciplining, toilet training, feeding, and other childrearing practices (Mullati, 1995; Sinha, 1984, 1988). However, because traditional attitudes have not been completely abandoned, many parents alternate between permissive and strict (authoritarian) childrearing, thus creating anxiety and confusion in children. This ambivalence and ambiguity makes them more vulnerable to acquiring a variety of behavioral and emotional disorders (Bharat, 1997). Moreover, difficulties in marriage relationships, coupled with inadequate or conflictual co-parenting practices, are becoming more prevalent, in part because women are breaking out of traditional roles, becoming educated in greater numbers, and advocating for equal rights both at home and in the workplace (Baral, Das, and Dash, 1999; Mohanty, 1999). Given that so many women are employed outside the home today, some Indian researchers contend that children's needs are not being met nor their development facilitated (Desai and Bharat, 1989; Mullati, 1995). Research on female-headed households has shown that these women face numerous problems, including low income, a lack of social support, and discipline problems with their children (Pati and Patnaik, 1999). Some social scientists are convinced that the increase in single-parent families has contributed to a greater number of children and adolescents experiencing serious difficulties (Bharat, 1991; Das, 1999). Hence, increased role strain, marital difficulties, parent-child conflicts, feelings of guilt, and status confusion are commonly observed among working women (Chowdhury, 1995; Muni, 1995), despite the fact that there may be some economic and self-esteem related advantages in some of these families (Mohanty, 1999). Since more women in India are joining the labor force without proper support and assistance (often in the face of extended family and community opposition), the increase in family-related problems is perhaps not surprising (Das, 1999; Kapur, 1995).

Other Factors Placing Children and Families at Risk

Inadequate Teacher Training and Changes in School Functioning and Curriculum

Also contributing to child and adolescent difficulties (with repercussions to the family) is the school curriculum and environment that often does not meet children's needs, whether they are academic or personal. It is not uncommon for teachers to use strict and sometimes physical punishment to maintain order, and practices which today's Indian youth are not always in agreement. Perhaps, the most notable in educated families are the extreme pressures for children to achieve academically so that they can gain entrance into the better colleges and universities (often with little free time with peers or family play time). This pressure tends to increase the vulnerability of older children and adolescents to various personal and relational difficulties (Nanda and Dash, 1996). Further, Carson and his colleagues (1999), as well as Padhi and Dash (1994), have found strong evidence of a connection between positive parental attitudes and adolescent social and academic competence. Studies conducted among lower income families in India, have indicated that children who are the at most risk for school difficulties and failure are from multiply disadvantaged groups, including those commonly referred to as Scheduled Castes (SCs) and Scheduled Tribes (STs) (Chowdhury and Chowdhury, 1996; Gupta, 1987; Mishra and Mohanty, 1995; Padhi and Dash, 1994; Sahoo and Sia, 1988). Those SC and ST children, who are rejected by their higher class and caste peers, are particularly at risk for developing behavior problems, dropping out of school, and experiencing disorders such as anxiety and depression (Chowdhury and Choudhury, 1996; Ota, 1995; Sarkar, 1988). However, Chowdhury and Choudhury (1996) suggest that, if such children received the necessary resources and support to successfully navigate this transition, patterns of long-term poor achievement and school failure might be averted.

Families with Disabilities and Multiple Crises

Indian families with a disabled or chronically ill member experience all of the burdens associated with life-long care (Kapur, 1995). These families need social support and require special coping skills to manage. Further, families facing situations caused by demoralizing events, such as suicide, rape, family violence, unwed motherhood, 'bride burning' (caused by the dowry system), and loss of home or property due to exploitation, job loss, or natural disasters, run the risk of breakdown or disintegration (Davar, 1999; Desai and Bharat, 1989). Serious marital maladjustment in families is more likely to result in abuse, conjugal separation, juvenile delinquency, mental health problems, extended family disputes, and an unhealthy environment for children (Boral et. al., 1999; Das, 1999).

Mental Illness as Other Handicapping Conditions

Mental health problems in India are often associated with inter-relational or intra-family conflicts. These are typically everyday difficulties that in many cases could be prevented or resolved, but frequently tend to accumulate. Due to decreasing assistance or support systems within communities, more serious problems such as suicide, homicide, rape and sexual harassment are increasing (Davar, 1998, 1999; Kapur, 1995; Sharma and Chadd, 1990). In the last 50 years, philosophically at least, and to some limited extent pragmatically, medical and mental health efforts have gradually moved from the institutionalized care of the mentally ill to the promotion of mental health. Yet, relatively little is available to individuals and families in immediate distress. Furthermore, public attitudes towards couples and families in crisis, or person's with mental or emotional disorders, are often judgmental and compartmentalizing. For example, research not too many years ago conducted in Delhi indicated that educated laypersons generally viewed the mentally ill as aggressive, violent, and dangerous (Prabhu et. al., 1984). Optimism about the outcome of psychiatric treatment for these individuals was not high, and there was a lack of awareness about available facilities to treat the mentally ill. Another study (Boral et. al., 1980) revealed that relatives of the mentally ill preferred magic healers, ayurveds, and homeopaths to psychiatrists and psychotherapists. Moreover, a majority of participants believed that marriage would cure mental illness, even though (paradoxically) a majority did not want to forge marital alliances with a mentally ill person. Hence, treatment of personal and family difficulties is still at a rudimentary stage of development in India.

A survey of prevalence studies of child mental health problems (Sitholey and Chakraborthi, 1992) highlighted a number of issues relevant to intervention, education, and prevention. These investigators found that there were considerable differences in psychiatric disorders in the small number of general population studies that had included children. Disorders varied greatly across age, gender, social, and demographic status. When the extremely high or low reported prevalence rates were excluded (about 1 per cent of children under 18), the acceptable range of mental and emotional disorders ranged from 50 to 150 per 1,000 children and adolescents (approximately 5 to 15 per cent). Often these individuals had accompanying developmental delays and/or scholastic difficulties. Considering the pervasiveness of psychiatric disturbances among youth, inpatient and outpatient mental health care facilities are extremely sparse. Presently, there are only about 100 child guidance clinics in the entire country, and most of these are located in large cities such as Mumbai, Pune, Bangalore, Hyderabad, and Delhi. These clinics do provide services to children with mental retardation and emotional problems. Indeed, much of the emphasis on mental health treatment in India is geared towards children in accordance with the National Mental Health Program. However, while this program covers adults and children alike, whole family mental health coverage receives little attention and is downplayed in its importance, despite the abundance of research showing a string connection between conjoint marital and family functioning, and the social/academic competence and psychosocial well-being of youth.

In sum, mental health professionals in India are presented with numerous challenges in working with couples and families. Individual psychopathology is often associated with family problems and dynamics. When individuals are treated apart from the family (as is customary), therapy sometimes yields positive results (Sharma and Chadd, 1990). However, when someone who has had counseling or has undergone psychiatric treatment returns to the family, it is believed that this person more often than not regresses to earlier patterns of behavior and functioning. This is because even though the individual may have changed, the family system has not (Davar, 1998, 1999; Sethi and Manchanda, 1978). Until family units are transformed through education and sometimes therapy (Carson and Chowdhury, 2000), individual family members have little chance of maintaining any gains made.

Relation between Strong Families and Child/Adolescent Resiliency and Competence

As we have observed, there are seemingly countless millions of young people in modern India who are failing to acquire the competence and skills needed for success in adult life. The adolescent segment of India's population has been rapidly expanding since the early 1950s, and individuals between 10 and

21 years of age make up more than half (57 per cent) of India's population (Shukla, 1994). The number of rural adolescents is rising at unprecedented rates and now constitutes approximately 73 per cent of the total youth population. Indian society has generally been unsuccessful in providing the necessary assistance and guidance to today's children and youth, most notably (but not exclusively) among lower caste rural dwellers. Even in villages and small communities today youth are exhibiting a host of difficulties that include disobedience and even violence towards parents, school dropout, smoking, alcoholism and other drug use, petty crime, and various other manifestations of juvenile delinquency (Chowdhury and Choudhury, 1993; Shukla, 1994; Simhadri, 1989).

Despite these increasing problems and risks, however, many children and youth are thriving in their development, and it is from these children and their families that we have much to learn. Elsewhere, these individuals have been referred to as resilient (Garmezy, 1983; Rutter, 1987) or invulnerable (Anthony, 1987), and in an Indian context they are like "lotus in the mud" (Chowdhury and Choudhury, 1993). Even though these youth are growing up in resource-limited and often stressful environments (familial, social, cultural, economic), they generally find ways to cope well with stress and are socially and academically competent. Understanding the processes that contribute to their adaptation, particularly family dynamics and relationships and key community factors, will provide crucial clues for improving education, prevention, and intervention efforts.

Resilient children and adolescents are those who turn their disadvantages into advantages and emerge as successful and competent individuals in society. While constitutionally based individual characteristics and abilities certainly play a role in resiliency or invulnerability (e.g., health-related, temperamental), familial and extra-familial support systems, especially in an Indian context, are believed to be the most powerful influences (Acharaya, 1992; Choudhury, 1991; Chowdhury et. al.,

1996). Results from several empirical studies have suggested that highly competent Indian adolescents, regardless of whether they are socio-economically advantaged or disadvantaged, share a common set of characteristics, including an emotionally healthy family climate (Carson et. al., 1999, 2002; Choudhury, 1991, 1999; Hariharan, 1991; Padhi and Dash, 1994; Sahoo and Sia, 1988). Parents of adolescents in these families tend to have a positive attitude towards themselves, each other, and their adolescent, as well as high expectations of their adolescent with regard to behavior, education, and achievement. They are highly nurturing and consistently involved in their child's school and extra-curricular activities. Despite differences in living conditions, more competent youth generally have strong family, peer, and community supports (Chowdhury et. al., 1996; Chowdhury and Choudhury, 1997). Findings from other investigations (e.g., Sharma et. al., 1981) indicated that firm and consistent discipline, both at home and in school, promoted mature behavior patterns and cognitive and social competence in older school-aged children (see also Gore, 1983; Hariharan, Dash, and Acharaya, 1987; Nanda and Dash, 1996; Sahoo and Sia, 1988).

In summary, a substantial body of research has shown that the family plays a major role not only in augmenting successful coping in children and adolescents, but also in facilitating their learning and school performance (Carson et. al., 1999; Chowdhury, 1990; Chowdhury and Choudhury, 1993; Gupta, 1987; Hariharan, 1991; Nanda and Dash, 1996; Padhi and Dash, 1994; Sahoo and Sia, 1988; Sethi and Manchanda, 1978; Simhadri, 1989; Tiwari, 1990). Parents in particular, along with siblings, grandparents, and other relatives, thus serve as protective factors against stress and risk in the lives of youth. This is still normative in Indian families today, despite the growing tendency of youth towards independence, self-definition, and departure from some beliefs and practices of the past (Chowdhury and Muni, 1995). However, protective factors do not automatically result in positive outcomes. As

Rutter (1987) indicates, protection does not lie in the availability of potentially supportive resources, but in the use made of them. It is in this context that FLE can perhaps make a unique and long-lasting contribution in Indian society.

Targets of and Settings for FLE Training

Recipients of FLE Training

There is a currently a severe shortage of professionals who have received training and supervised experience in family life education theory and methods. Information about FLE is almost non-existent in traditional academic disciplines, such as psychiatry, psychology, sociology, social work, and education. The field of home science education, however, is one such exception, which is an applied academic field, built upon the discipline of science, arts, commerce, and management for the purpose of achieving the welfare of whole family in an ever-changing society. Its curriculum provide an opportunity to integrate the knowledge from very many fields many from sociology, psychology, social work, anthropology, education, biochemistry, etc., giving the subject a much needed practical applications with wholesome approach to family living in India. Thus, the academic program of home science education around the country can serve as pivotal place for training and dissemination of FLE information and materials. Home science as foundation education for FLE is already in existence throughout the country and with little inclusion of focused curriculum on FLE, can able to achieve effective result. Moreover, unlike home science program, FLE program can be started for both boys and girls or males/females for achieving its sole purpose of healthy and happy family life.

Rather than developing stand-alone FLE programs, it is our contention that, at this point in time, FLE training could most effectively be integrated into traditional academic programs mentioned previously. Indeed, these departments and programs already include some of the course work background essential to working with couples and families (e.g., human development, family studies, women and child welfare issues and practice). These programs are presently lacking certain basic theoretical issues, and at a minimum what an essential FLE curriculum should contain, may includes: (a) essential courses in family theory (including systems-oriented theories) and human development as taught from various Indian perspectives; (b) identification and assessment of couples and families in need of education and prevention efforts; (c) current FLE theories, models, and methodologies that are relevant and applicable to Indian families; (d) professional ethics and practice in working with couples and families; and (e) supervised practical experiences which provide trained professionals and students at the graduate level opportunities to enhance their skills in working with couples and families. Whether some kind of credential is tied to such training is a matter of debate. However, it would be well within the realm of possibility to offer a 3- or 4-month postgraduate certification as a 'Family Life Educator' to individuals who could take part in such a training experience.

A combined effort by psychiatrists (and other interested medical personnel), psychologists, sociologists, social workers, educators, and home scientists could involve the creation of different strategic centers around the country for FLE training. Involvement of those working in child and family welfare programs and services would also be vital to the success of this training effort. This is because government and non-governmental organizations (NGOs) run most of the child and family welfare programs in India. Although, presently, the training and competency of child welfare workers is exceedingly limited, provision of FLE training for these individuals is well within reach. Hence, these working professionals, as well as physicians, nurses, and other health specialists, academicians, and graduate students, are prime targets for FLE training. Promoting FLE as a legitimate and much-needed enterprise in

India may also have secondary benefits, in that it may provide additional employment opportunities for trainees.

Settings for FLE Training

One ideal setting for FLE training is in college and university academic departments, and colleges of medicine, where this type of training and course work can be integrated into existing programs and curricula. Those with previous training and experience in FLE, including faculty members and students associated with various home science programs around the country, could serve as trainers and facilitators. Further, while many students who complete a degree in medicine or a graduate program in the social sciences (e.g., psychology or sociology), social work, or education, will seek employment in larger towns and cities, some inevitably go back to area in which they grew up (i.e., their town or village) to live and work. Undergraduate and graduate students in training who need to meet practicum or internship requirements, could also spend time in or visit centers, hospitals, or agencies which regularly to provide psychiatric, medical, or family counseling services. Part of what they offer could be FLE-oriented.

Schools are also an excellent location for FLE training and services, and according to Kapur (1997), are the best places in India to develop mental health programs for children and adolescents. This is because community life in India often centers around the school and children's inter- and extra-curricular activities associated with school. Getting teachers, school administrators, and students to "buy in" to an FLE program by observing an effective program in action is often a turning point (Powell and Cassidy, 2001). Having timely and agreed-upon goals that are carried out in a cooperative manner are also essential. Since Indian parents (and other family members) are typically very concerned about the child well-being and educational success, they can become involved in (and recipients of) FLE efforts in a way that helps them feel empowered as well as, when necessary, save face in their community. Students too can benefit from a wide range learning experiences that include such topics as conflict resolution in families, relationship development and marriage preparation (e.g., so-called love marriages versus arranged marriages and everything on a continuum), effective parenting, and sexuality education.

As has been discussed, the large sector of professionals working with child and family welfare agencies that identify and work with families at-risk in both urban and rural areas would be prime recipients of FLE training. As in other countries of the world, which have discovered that "an ounce of prevention is worth a pound of cure," India's child welfare and social service contingent is in an ideal place to engage in. For example, early parent training and conduct marriage readiness and marital enrichment seminars and workshops on a large-scale basis can be started. In addition, training professionals associated with mental health treatment centers and training institutes in various aspects of family life is generally lacking in India. Some exceptions may include the 100 or so child guidance clinics positioned around the country. Other strategic centers for FLE training might include the National Institute of Mental Health and Neurosurgery (NIMHANS) in Bangalore, the Tata Institute of Social Sciences (TISS) in Mumbai, and a handful of other social science institutes (e.g., in Ranchi and Patna) and graduate training programs in counseling or clinical psychology (e.g., Chennai, Allahabad, Bhubaneswar). A mental health program in Amritsar (Vidyasagar) was one of the first in India to encourage families to stay with the patient during the entire treatment program. Bangalore and Vellore are two other cities which have programs where family members are actively involved in the active treatment of family members as well as follow-up (Verghese, 1988). However, these few institutes and training programs cannot even begin to provide the educational preparation, research, and services to meet the needs of India's vast population (Davar, 1998; Shanker and Menon, 1991).

The employment settings of parents can also be an opportune place in which to involve parents or parents-to-be in various aspects of parenting education, marriage preparation, and marital enrichment. Admittedly, since approximately 80 per cent of Indians live in rural areas, with many being self or sporadically employed, conducting FLE in work environments is a challenging task. These efforts may be better suited to those living and working in an urban milieu. Nevertheless, limited research from other countries of the world, including the United States, has shown that employee participation in regular FLE activities increases job satisfaction, commitment, productivity, social support, and longevity (Powell and Cassidy, 2001). Hence, there is much room for creativity when it comes to planning and implementing FLE programming for parents and others in work settings in an Indian context.

One can hardly travel anywhere in India, no matter how remote, without being reminded of the significance of religious philosophies and practice. Indeed, India is a country of intense religious activity and fervor. Religion permeates the lives of the vast majority of Indians – rich and poor, urban and rural – on a daily basis. Moreover, the concept of 'family' is central to virtually all of the major religions of India (Hinduism, Islam, Sikhism, Buddhism, and Christianity, as well as a variety of sects, castes and tribal religions, etc.), as is the idea of service to others. Thus, working in the context of these religious traditions to provide training and outreach in FLE could (at least in many cases) be a natural and readily accepted activity, but only if conducted in a way that was in harmony with the essential tenets and practices each particular group. For example, in cities as well as rural areas, FLE services could be provided through Primary Health Centers (PHCs), schools and *Anganwadi* centers where caring for women and children is a common undertaking. All the blocks of the country are covered by the government sponsored program like ICDS (Integrated Child Development Services). Besides, under local self-government system (Panchayat Raj) in rural areas, this type of training can be given at panchayat level for the benefits of the grassroots level people.

Finally, South Asia in general, and India in particular, has a large number of international development organizations and NGOs (non-governmental organizations) operating within its boundaries. Our observations have been that, aside from various aspects of family planning and community health (e.g., prenatal care, disease prevention, nutrition education), there are a wide range of opportunities in these agencies and organizations for FLE that are yet to be tapped. Specialists working in various programs are prime candidates for basic training in FLE. Activities and information that can be realistically integrated with their regular duties and responsibilities may receive the greatest reception, as opposed to expecting or requesting that these professionals conduct additional programs and training with those whom they are involved. However, our impression is that these agencies are ripe for FLE training and implementation, whatever form and approach is taken. Trained FLE in India can decide whether, and in what situations, they wish to adopt the role of expert, consultant, or facilitator, and with which group of professionals associated with particular NGOs and international development organizations. In sum, the success of any community mental health education and prevention program in India may depend on each community's sensitivity to mentally distressed children, adolescents, and adults, as well as married couples and families, in conflict (Sethi and Manchanda, 1978; Sinha, 1988). Thus, in order to meet the needs of a rapidly expanding society, mental health and social service agencies may need to be provided in large part by motivated para-professionals and citizens in cities, small towns, and rural areas (i.e., volunteerism). One untapped resource, for example, includes older adults and aging family members. Given the large percentage of retirees from government services in India and the fact that the mandatory retirement age is now

55, these individuals would be ideal candidates for counselor training. In our view, members of this age group not only have the time but also often have the need for a greater sense of purpose and involvement with others. As known and respected members (and often elders) of their community, their impact as designated lay counselors could be significant. In this regard, families would be both a contributor to and receiver of services provided by a strong and encompassing force of lay family counselors.

Training-the-Trainer Approach to Family Life Education

We are convinced that a 'training-the-trainer' model, which has proved successful in the United States and other countries, could be adopted for use in India. This approach to education and preparation of family counselors/therapists in India has recently been proposed by Carson and Chowdhury (2000). It could be used for FLE training and implementation as well. Exchanges between family life specialists in India and other countries, where psycho-education and family therapy are common and respected forms of mental health treatment, can serve as the impetus to program development and identification of FLE trainees, supervisors, and training sites. As mentioned in the article by Carson and Chowdhury (2000), sources of funding for these exchanges might come primarily from NGOs, including various external grant-funding organizations, agencies and programs (e.g., WHO, UNICEF, Fulbright Commission, World Bank). A general outline of such a training approach to FLE is outlined below:

Phase One

This phase includes: (1) identification of a 'metavisor' in India for the entire training program; (2) identification of FLE training sites in key areas (e.g., initially, three or four in one or more 'test states' or geographical areas; and (3) identification and training of an FLE supervisor or key trainer at each of these sites (i.e., training-the-trainers) over a two or three month period through grant-sponsored international exchanges, where participating agencies and institutions would send designated supervisors abroad for FLE training, and/or host visiting family life educators as initial trainers in India. Supervisors-in-training might include experienced mental health professionals, social workers and child welfare specialists, physicians/psychiatrists, and university faculty in fields such as home science, psychology, social work, sociology, and education who have had some prior training in, or at least familiarity with, some of the core content and process components of FLE.

Phase Two

In this phase identification of interested and committed FLE trainees, representing various disciplines, including, (a) post-graduate professionals in medicine, child/family welfare, social work, psychology, education, home science, etc.; (b) graduate students in appropriate academic disciplines (as indicated above); and (c) interested academic faculty in colleges and universities in the aforementioned (or related) disciplines, is made.

Phase Three

This phase comprises a three-month academic (content-based) training programme (including in-class experiential learning and role playing), which incorporates a minimum of one month of supervised internship experiences in FLE practice (at approved locations and sites, both urban and rural) with couples and families. Part of this practicum experience could include lay training of motivated community citizens (i.e., those who are concerned about families in their area/social milieu) in basic FLE knowledge, skills, and delivery. A community-based approach that includes some 'home visiting' activities would be used extensively in both the practicum/internship and lay training activities.

Training Processes and Procedures

FLE academic work in the classroom, as well as practicum/internship experiences, could be integrated with current academic programs in graduate schools of psychology, social work, home science, and even medicine. Training sessions for full-time working professionals could occur weekly (3-4 hours) in both professional (e.g., child/social welfare) and academic environments, as well as key locations in surrounding communities where trainees live and work. Trained supervisors would be responsible for coordinating and overseeing trainees' internship and lay training activities, both at designated learning (educational) sites and out in the community. Supervisors and trainees in particular geographical regions would meet once every month (total of three times) for one day of consultation. Each trainee's supervisor would provide ongoing feedback to that person with regard to strengths and needed areas of improvement. The supervisor, in conjunction with the metavisor, would provide the final evaluation of the trainee that would determine successful completion of the training program.

The training approach described above, of course, could be modified and even reconstructed based on the needs and desires of the trainers, the trainees, and those couples and families who would be participating in such home and community-based education and services. Given India's mushrooming population, designers of programs and training will also need to have creative and empowering ways of involving lay persons of all ages and at all stages of life.

Conclusion

Our observation has been that, while educated parents in India as a general rule may be more involved in their child's education than in countries such as the US, participation with their adolescents in both family and school-related activities that might enhance competence and self-esteem is still lacking in scores of families. Work, health, and transportation problems, and limited family income may contribute to this lack of parental involvement. Many parents in India are also reluctant to violate school/home boundaries, and teachers and school administrators sometimes discourage parental involvement in the adolescent's process of learning while in school, and at times school-related functions. Hence, competency promotion needs to be part of a nation-wide thrust in family life education. School and community leaders, agencies and organizations are in an ideal position to assist parents not only in becoming more effective in their parenting roles, but also in augmenting marital and family strengths and providing education and opportunities for family recreation and activities. As Chowdhury et. al. (1996: 46) conclude, ".....positive interpersonal/social support within families such as positive help, mutual support and cohesion, provides opportunities for the development of mastery and competence..." Hence, parental counseling and education need to be "...introduced to the parents regarding the childrearing styles and positive support rendered to their children". Joint experiences for parents and adolescents might include the enhancement of communication and decision-making skills, problem-solving and conflict resolution abilities, anger management, self-esteem, and goal-setting/career exploration. Augmenting family strengths will tend to enhance adolescent competence, perhaps even more so in countries like India where immediate and extended family members play a unique and powerful role in the lives of the next generation. FLE can positively and significantly influence the lives of couples and families who are struggling to balance traditional family structures and practices with the changing values, attitudes, and lifestyles that permeate contemporary Indian society.

References

Acharaya, S. (1992). Personality, Motivational, and Cognitive Competencies of Invulnerable Children. Unpublished Ph.D. Thesis, Utkal University, Orissa, India.

Agarwal, U.C. (1989). *Creativity and Adjustment of Adolescents.* New Delhi: DK Publishing.

Anthony, E. J. (1987). Risk, vulnerability, and resilience: An overview. In E.J. Anthony and B.J. Cohler (eds.), *The Invulnerable Child* (pp. 3-48). New York: Guilford Press.

Baral, J.K. and Chowdhury, A. (1999). *Family in Transition: Power and Development.* Delhi: Northern Book Centre.

Baral, J.K. and Bishoyee, A.P. (1999). Family in transition: Some theoretical and methodological questions. In J.K. Baral and A. Chowdhury (eds.), *Family in Transition: Power and Development* (pp. 1-15). New Delhi: Northern Book Centre.

Baral, J.K., Das, U. and Dash, S. (1999). Power equation in family. In J.K. Baral and A. Chowdhury (eds.), *Family in Transition: Power and Development* (pp. 57-82). New Delhi: Northern Book Centre.

Belle, D. (1990). Poverty and women's mental health. *American Psychologist*, 45(3), pp. 385-389.

Bharat, S. (1991). Research on families with problems in India: Utility, limitations and future directions. In: *Research on Families with Problems in India* (Unit of Family Studies, Editors). Bombay: Tata Institute of Social Sciences.

Bharat, S. (1997). Family socialization of the Indian child. *Trends in Social Science Research,* 4, 201-216.

Boral, G.C., Bagchi, R. and Nandi, D.N. (1980). An opinion survey about the causes and treatment of mental illness and the social acceptance of the mentally ill patients. *Indian Journal of Psychiatry, 22*(3), pp. 317-321.

Carson, D.K., Chowdhury, A., Perry, C.K. and Pati, C. (1999). Family characteristics and adolescent competence in India: Investigation of youth in southern Orissa. *Journal of Youth and Adolescence,* 28(2), pp. 211-233.

Carson, D.K. and Chowdhury, A. (2000). Family therapy in India: A new profession in an ancient land?" *Contemporary Family Therapy, 22*, pp. 387-406.

Carson, D.K., Chowdhury, A., Choudhury, R. and Carson, C.K. (2002). Competence and family support of vulnerable and invulnerable adolescents representing scheduled tribes and scheduled castes in India. *Journal of Comparative Family Studies,* 33(2), pp. 249-270.

Channabasavanna, S.M. and Bhatti, R.S. (1982). A study of interactional patterns and family typologies in families of mental patients. In A. Kiev and A. Venkoba Rao (eds.), *Readings in Transcultural Psychiatry* (pp. 149-161). Madras: Higginbotham.

Chowdhury, A. (1990). Development of social competence in children. *International Journal of Behavioral Sciences*, 10, pp. 55-69.

Chowdhury, A. (1995). Employed mothers and their families in India. *Early Child Development and Care,* 113, pp. 65-75.

Chowdhury, A. (1999). The status and perceptions of aged in Orissan families. In J.K. Baral and A. Chowdhury (eds.), *Family in Transition: Power and Development* (pp. 47-56). New Delhi: Northern Book Centre.

Chowdhury, A. and Baral, S. (1999). A study on vulnerable families. In J.K. Baral and A. Chowdhury (eds.), *Family in Transition: Power and Development* (pp. 131-138). New Delhi: Northern Book Centre.

Chowdhury, A. and Choudhury, R. (1993). Exploring research strategies for identifying invulnerable children: An Indian context. *Early Child Development and Care,* 93, pp. 87-100.

Chowdhury, A. and Choudhury, R. (1996). Peer socialization: A new direction towards socio-personal growth. *Trends in Social Science Research*, 3, pp. 105-112.

Chowdhury, A. and Choudhury, R. (1997). Peer social support: A protective factor for children in poverty. *Experiments in Education*, 25, pp. 163-171.

Chowdhury, A., and Muni, A. (1995). Role of parental support in children's need satisfaction and academic achievements. *Journal of Community Guidance and Research*, 12, pp. 135-144.

Chowdhury, A., Muni, A., Rath, A. and Pati, C. (1996). Assessing social support network among socio-culturally disadvantaged children in India. *Early Child Development and Care*, 121, pp. 37-47.

Choudhury, R. (1991). Invulnerable children: An exploratory attempt to identify and study them. Unpublished Ph.D Thesis, Utkal University, Orissa, India.

Choudhury, R. (1999). The changing family scenario in Orissa: Its impact on mental health. In J.K. Baral and A. Chowdhury (eds.), *Family in Transition: Power and Development* (pp. 21-30). New Delhi: Northern Book Center.

Das, R.C. (1999). Marriage in transition: A biosocial approach. In J.K. Baral and A. Chowdhury (eds.), *Family in Transition: Power and Development* (pp. 16-20). New Delhi: Northern Book Center.

Das, T. (1999). Employed women and problems of childcare. In J.K. Baral and A. Chowdhury (eds.), *Family in Transition: Power and Development* (pp. 139-147). New Delhi: Northern Book Center.

Desai, M. and Bharat, S. (1989). Research on families with problems in India: A seminar report. *The Indian Journal of Social Work*, 50(4), pp. 531-536.

Davar, B.V. (1999). *Mental Health of Indian Women: A Feminist Agenda.* New Delhi: Sage Pub.

Davar, B.V. (1998). Writing Phenomenologies of Mental Illness. Extending the Universe of Ordinary Discourse. Paper presented at the Annual Culture Studies Workshop, Centre for Studies in Social Sciences, Bhopal, India, January 15-20.

Garmezy, N. (1983). Stressors in childhood. In N. Garmezy and M. Rutter (eds.), *Stress, Coping, and Development in Children* (pp. 44-83). New York: McGraw-Hill.

Gore, M. (1989). Socialization of rural adolescent girls from an ecological perspective. Unpublished master's thesis, M.S. University Faculty of Home Science, University of Baroda, India.

Gupta, A.K. (1987). *Parental Influences on Adolescents.* New Delhi: Ariana Pub. House.

Hariharan, M. (1991). Invulnerable children: Some studies on disadvantaged children's competence and coping styles. Unpublished Doctoral (Ph.D.) Dissertation, Utkal University, India.

Hariharan, M., Dash, A.S. and Acharya, S. (1987). School, grade, sex, and academic achievement differences in peer rating. *Journal of Educational Psychology*, 45, pp. 32-36.

Kapur, M. (1995). *Mental Health of Indian Children.* New Delhi: Sage Pub.

Kapur, M. (1997). *Mental Health in Indian Schools.* New Delhi: Sage Publications.

Madan, G.R. (1990). *Social Welfare and Security.* New Delhi: Vivek Prakashan.

Mishra, G. (1995). Reflection on continuity and change in the Indian family system. *Trends in Social Science Research*, 2, pp. 27-30.

Mishra, P.K. and Mohanty, R.P. (1995). Some demographic characteristics of the scheduled caste population of Orissa. In R.N. Senapati,

P.K. Nayak, and P.K. Das (eds.), *Population Profile of Orissa* (pp. 129-144). Bhubaneswar, Orissa: Association for Population and Development (OAPD).

Mohanty, B. (1999). Dual-earner family: A journey to freedom and equality. In J.K. Baral and A. Chowdhury (eds.), *Family in Transition: Power and Development* (pp. 120-130). New Delhi: Northern Book Centre.

Mullati, L. (1995). Families in India: Beliefs and realities. *Journal of Comparative Family Studies, 26* (1), pp. 11-25.

Muni, A. (1995). Development of competency among advantaged and disadvantaged adolescents. Unpublished Ph.D. Thesis, Berhampur University, Orissa, India.

Nanda, G.K. and Dash, A.S. (1996). *Disadvantage, Schooling, Competence, and Invulnerability*. Bhubaneswar: Panchajanya, c/o URPL House.

Oommen, T.K. (2000). Family therapy: Challenging the system. *Hindu*, 26th March.

Ota, A.B. (1995). Changing demographic scenario of the scheduled tribes in Orissa. In R.N. Senapati, P.K. Nayak, and P.K. Das (eds.). *Population Profile of Orissa* (pp. 113-128). Bhubaneswar, Orissa: Association for Population and Development (OAPD).

Padhi, J. and Dash, A.S. (1994). The relation of parental attitudes to adolescent competence. *Psycho-Lingua*, 24, pp. 33-42.

Parikh, J.C. and Krishna, K.S. (1992). *Drug Addiction: A Psychosocial Study of Youth*. New Delhi: Friends Publications.

Pati, C. and Patnaik, S. (1999). Status and problems of single women. In J.K. Baral and A. Chowdhury (eds.), *Family in Transition: Power and Development* (pp. 166-172). New Delhi: Northern Book Center.

Patnaik, M.M. (1999). Family violence in traditional Oriya society. In J.K. Baral and A. Chowdhury (eds.), *Family in Transition: Power and Development* (pp. 148-156). New Delhi: Northern Book Center.

Powell, L.H. and Cassidy, D. (2001). *Family Life Education: An Introduction*. Mountain View, CA: Mayfield Publication Co.

Prabhu, G.G., Raghuram, A., Verma, N,. and Maridass, A.C. (1984). Public attitudes toward mental illness: A review. *National Institute of Mental Health and Neurosurgery Journal,* 2 (1), pp. 1-14.

Rutter, M. (1987). Psychosocial resilience and protective mechanisms. *American Journal of Orthopsychiatry*, 57, pp. 316-331.

Sahoo, F. and Sia, N. (1988). The socio-cultural antecedents of helplessness among rural adolescents. *Indian Journal of Community Guidance Services,* 5, pp. 34-47.

Sarkar, C. (1988). *Juvenile Delinquency in India*. Delhi: Daya Pub. House.

Sethi, B.B. and Manchanda, R. (1978). Family structure and psychiatric disorders. *Indian Journal of Psychiatry*, 20(3), pp. 283-288.

Shanker, R., and Menon, M.S. (1991). Family intervention programme in schizophrenia: The SCARF experience. In: *Research on Families with Problems in India*, (Unit of Family Studies, Editors). Bombay: Tata Institute of Social Sciences.

Sharma, S. and Chadd, R.K. (1990). *Mental Hospitals in India: Current Status and Role in Mental Health Care*. Delhi: Institute of Human Behaviour and Allied Sciences.

Sharma, P., Saraswathi, T.S. and Gir, S. (1981). Role of parents and teachers in promoting social competence in children. *Child Psychiatry Quarterly*, 14, pp. 134-137.

Shukla, M. (1994). India. In K. Hurrelmann (Ed.), *International Handbook of Adolescence* (pp. 191-206). Westport, CT: Greenwood Press.

Simhadri, Y.C. (1989). *Youth in the Contemporary World*. Delhi: Mittal Publications.

Sinha, D. (1984). Some recent changes in the Indian family and their implications for socialisation. *The Indian Journal of Social Work*, 45, pp. 271-286.

Sinha, D. (1988). The family scenario of a developing country and its implications for mental health: The case of India. In P.R. Dasen, J.W. Berry, and N. Sartorius (eds.), *Health and Cross-Cultural Psychology: Towards Applications* (pp. 48-70). Newbury Park, CA: Sage Publications.

Sitholey, N., and Chakraborthi, A. (1992). Child psychiatric research in India: Epidemiology, assessment and treatment. In S. Malhotra, A. Malhotra, and V.K. Varma (eds.), *Child Mental Health in India*. Delhi: Macmillan.

Tiwari, R. (1990). *Adolescents' Personality and Frustration*. New Delhi: D.K. Publishing.

Verghese, A. (1988). Family participation in mental health care: The Vellore experiment. *The Indian Journal of Psychiatry*, 30(2), pp. 117-121.

Index